DECISIVE BATTLES
FROM YORKTOWN TO OPERATION DESERT STORM

Decisive Battles

From Yorktown to Operation Desert Storm

Jonathon Riley

continuum

Continuum UK
The Tower Building
11 York Road
London SE1 7NX

Continuum US
80 Maiden Lane
Suite 704
New York, NY 10038

www.continuumbooks.com

First published 2010

British Library Cataloguing-in-Publication Data
A catalogue record for this book is available from the British Library.

ISBN 9781847252500

Typeset by Pindar NZ, Auckland, New Zealand
Printed and bound in the UK by the MPG Books Group

Contents

List of Maps

Foreword

A book on decisive battles in the history of military campaigns is not exactly a new idea; the genre was invented by Sir Edward Creasy with the publication of *The Fifteen Decisive Battles of the World* in 1851. Subsequently reprinted at least 15 times, this covered a series of battles from Marathon to Waterloo. In philosophical terms, Creasy's method was deeply influenced by the Whig view of history: that everything virtuous according to the standards of Victorian muscular Protestantism – everything that, in his words, 'helped to make us what we are' – resulted from some noble action on the battlefield which had preserved human progress from the assault of some barbaric – often Romish – enemy. One catches a whiff of this in Churchill's famous 'broad, sunlit uplands'. George Bush's obsession with bringing the benefits of American-style democracy to the oppressed of the world might be seen in the same vein. Unspeakingly, this view ascribes the attainment of a decisive result to the action of virtue against vice, interpreting, perhaps, the Augustinian view of *jus ad bellum* in terms of the inevitability and desirability of the advance of civilization as understood in nineteenth-century England.

Creasy's successful model has been followed by a whole string of works: Malleson's *Decisive Battles of India* (1883); Whitton's *Decisive Battles of Modern Times* (1922); Liddell Hart's *Decisive Wars of History* (1929); and J. F. C. Fuller's *Decisive Battles of the Western World and their Influence on History* (1945), last republished in 1970. More recently there has been John Colvin's *Decisive Battles*, written in 2004, although this ends in 1943. In addition, there has been a raft of titles associated with particular wars, such as Jo Mitchell's *Decisive Battles of the Civil War* (1985) and Nigel Cawthorne's *Decisive Battles of the Second World War* (2003).

In all these books, Creasy's idea is apparent: that war has a purpose, and the purpose is to make the world as we wish it to be; battles are therefore important, because in deciding wars, they improve matters. In common with John Keegan, Michael Howard, Alastair Horne and others, I have some difficulty with this view – perhaps because I am a general as well as an academic historian and have seen too many instances in which battles either decided nothing – they were simply bloodletting – or made matters worse. If, therefore, we are to say there is such a thing as a decisive battle, we need to be clear about what we mean by decisive, and whether in the postmodern period such a concept is any longer valid. I take a technical, rather than a moral, standpoint: I am far more interested in the exercise of generalship than in the supposed rights or wrongs of a cause; and I make no judgements on the decisions of those responsible for the conduct of battle at the time, since they did not have the benefit of hindsight and made those decisions based on very partial and incomplete information, most of which – if my experience is anything to go by – later turned out to be rubbish. 'Life,' as Søren Kierkegaard so truly said, 'can only be understood backwards; and yet it has to be lived forwards.'

Acknowledgements

Illustrations and photographs used in the book are all individually acknowledged where appropriate. In addition I would like to record my obligation to Steve Waites and Alex Lee at the Joint Services Staff College Graphics Office, who drew the maps; to the staffs at The Joint Services Staff College library, Prince Consort's Library, Royal United Services Institute, and the Liddell Hart Centre for Military Studies, King's College London.

What Is Decisive?

I. BATTLES AND CAMPAIGNS

Bernard Brodie characterized the Tet Offensive as the decisive engagement of the Vietnam War – not because the Americans won all the tactical battles, including Hue, but because the campaign persuaded them ultimately that they could not win the war. By implication, it is not battles that win wars but campaigns. A decisive battle, therefore, is one that, whatever its tactical outcome – win, lose or draw – leads to the achievement of one or more key objectives in a campaign and, in doing so, brings about strategic success. The Oxford Dictionary's definition of 'decisive' is useful in this context: 'Having the power or quality of deciding a question or controversy; putting an end to contest or controversy; final; conclusive.' Such a definition contains no moral judgements, and neither virtue nor vice have any effect on the outcome.

In modern parlance, the level at which campaigns and major operations are planned, sustained, sequenced and directed is described as the 'operational' level of war. It is the vital link, or gearing, between military strategic objectives and the tactical employment of forces in battles and engagements. 'It is,' says the British Army Doctrine Publication, *Operations*:

> . . . the responsibility of the operational level commander to determine the campaign plan required to achieve the desired military strategic end-state within the designated theatre of operations.

In stating this, the authors are drawing on the writings of Napoleon's contemporary Baron Jomini and of Soviet theorists such as Marshal Mikhail Tukhachevskii and A. A. Svechin, the last of whom tells us that 'tactics make the steps from which operational leaps are assembled; strategy points the path'. Explicit in the business of campaigning is the military defeat of an enemy; that is, the reduction of the effectiveness of one's enemy to the extent that he is unable to participate in combat, or at least cannot fulfil his intentions. This is a concept that earlier generals like Frederick the Great, Napoleon or Ulysses S. Grant would have understood completely. It encapsulates both the physical destruction of an enemy's ability to prosecute war, and the destruction of his will to fight – of which more later.

Put very simply, a campaign is a set of military operations planned and conducted to achieve a strategic objective within a given time and geographical area. In modern terms, it normally involves lines of operation for maritime, land and air forces. It may also include economic warfare and, in complex emergencies, the reconstruction of essential infrastructure, reform of the security sector and the establishment of governance. Thus, a campaign is set within the context of operational art: it is not just grand tactics, or strategy writ small.

II. GENERALSHIP AND THE DECISIVE ACT

Next, we must acknowledge the role of generalship in shaping and delivering the decisive battle. I do not propose to go into this in detail here, since I have recently done so in *Napoleon as a General*. Suffice to say that the General is the man in a military organization who must, through a combination of analytical process and intuitive judgement, define those matters that are likely to be decisive and, having done so, change the situation to advantage in order to *win*. As General Rupert Smith explains it, he must 'employ *force*, by *design*, to achieve required *objectives*'. Put yet another way, he must balance his ends, ways and means while preventing the other side from doing so. Most important in this equation are the ways: to employ means without ways will lead to disaster; and whereas the ends and the means may be given, it is the General who must decide or devise the ways. Sun Tzu says:

> In war, then, let your great object be victory, not lengthy campaigns. Thus it may be known that the leader of armies is the arbiter of the people's fate, the man on whom it depends whether the nation shall be in peace or peril . . .
>
> . . . the highest form of generalship is to baulk the enemy's plans; the next best is to prevent the junction of the enemy's forces; the next is to attack the enemy's army in the field; and the worst policy of all is to besiege walled towns and cities . . . the skilful leader subdues the enemy's troops without any fighting; he captures their cities without laying siege to them; he overthrows their kingdoms without lengthy operations in the field. With his forces intact he disputes the mastery of the empire . . .

Thus, the General must consider first the enemy, the object of his problem. Superior intelligence and the generation of superior tempo – that is, the rate or rhythm of activity relative to that of the enemy – will be foremost in the General's mind as he formulates his probable course of action. These he will test against the factors that may create decisive conditions. There are only three of these, and they bear equally on both sides. They can be summarized as time and space, resources, and the environment. Under resources must be included such things as the relative strength and capability of the forces, the morale and discipline of the troops, the quality of subordinate leadership or staff work and the availability of logistic support. The environment includes climate and weather and their effects, the prevalence of diseases, the density and attitude of the civilian population, and, in particular, the terrain, which is not important in itself, only in the way it may confer advantage.

In reaching his judgement of what is decisive, a General must exercise command like a sovereign his power: indivisibly, at every level. Napoleon remarked on this at an early stage in his career as a General, when faced with a division of command of the Army of Italy between himself and Kellermann. Writing to the Directory in Paris in May 1746, he said: 'I am certain that one bad General is better than two good ones.' This is because war in general, and battle in particular, remains as much art as science, and, as Clausewitz declared, as much a clash of wills as a clash of arms. 'Know your enemy, and know yourself,' says Sun Tzu, 'and you will never be defeated in a hundred battles.'

The General engaged in campaigning must therefore satisfy himself on a number of key questions at the outset of his planning, and these have not changed much since Napoleon's day, despite differences in circumstances. Which military conditions must be attained to achieve strategic and operational objectives? What sequence of actions is most likely to produce these conditions? How should military resources be applied to best accomplish that sequence of actions? Are the associated risks acceptable?

Risk is all about the likelihood of a course of action going well or badly and the impact, for good or ill, of that. The adverse consequences of risk are threats, and the benign consequences are opportunities; usually a General is presented with both of these. He will therefore take risks on campaign when he is obliged to do so in order to fulfil his mission, and if he can accept the consequences of failure. In weighing them, he must distinguish between strategic risks and operational risks. Adverse strategic risks may bring ruin because they bear on the national standing and the ability to influence events at home and abroad. Operational risks may incur threats to the campaign – through bad planning or execution – or present an unforeseen opportunity that can be exploited. But even the best General cannot exclude the possibility of risks arising during a campaign because of events outside his control – such as a change of government – or through the performance of his force, which can be better or worse than expected. In 1939, the German General Staff was unhappy with the operational risks in Hitler's invasion of Poland, and surprised that the campaign was so successful, so rapidly; but it failed to grasp the invasion's strategic risks and consequences: an excellent example, therefore, of catastrophic success.

When he considered the business of campaigning in his great work *On War*, Clausewitz hit on two vital ideas. First, the principle of culmination

– that is, the point at which one side starts winning and the other starts losing, either offensively or defensively. Secondly, the notion of the decisive act or operation which causes that culmination. War is seldom so straight-forward as to permit one single decisive act; usually what is decisive is a combination of several actions. But herein lies the very essence of general-ship at the operational level: determining those circumstances that are going to be decisive, and then bringing them to pass. Thus, sequencing events through a series of decisive points is a key part of planning, as is deciding on simultaneous actions and effects to overwhelm an enemy.

In order to achieve a decisive effect, the General must direct his atten-tion to the enemy's centre of gravity – that is, those characteristics, capabilities or localities from which a nation, an alliance, a military force or even a loose confederation like al-Qaida derives its freedom of action, its moral and physical strength or its will to fight. It is the destruction or neutralization of these things that brings about collapse. An attack is made by exploiting the enemy's critical vulnerabilities while protecting one's own, so the General must be aware of both his and his opponent's centre of gravity. In eighteenth- and nineteenth-century terms, the enemy's centre of gravity can usually be thought of as something physical, such as his army or capital city. However, it can be a group of people or a person – for the Germans in the Second World War it was indeed probably Adolf Hitler himself – or it can be a resource, either natural or industrial, or even something intangible like the will to resist.

From Napoleon onwards, there has been an inescapable connection between the campaign and the battle: the campaign is constructed to achieve strategic objectives and is designed to bring the enemy to battle, a battle that will be the decisive act of the war – as Clausewitz put it, 'the employment of battles to gain the end of war'. The purpose of battle is not merely to defeat the enemy's army – the operational centre of gravity – but to destroy it and thus end the war at one stroke. Jomini, who was at various times both a subordinate and an opponent of Napoleon, wrote that the General must concentrate on the battlefield

. . . the bulk of [his] force at the decisive point or against the section of the enemy line which one wishes to overwhelm, and ensuring that these forces are sent forward with vigour and concentration so as to produce a simultaneous result.

Clausewitz echoed this thought:

Our conviction that only a great battle can produce a major decision is founded not on an abstract concept of war alone, but also on experience . . . All fortunate generals, and not only the bold, the daring, and the stubborn, seek to crown their achievements by risking everything in decisive battles.

An army, by destroying that opposing it, can directly threaten the enemy's strategic centre of gravity, be it the capital city, vital resources or a key leader. Thus it must be apparent that while distinctions may be drawn between strategy, operational art and tactics using considerations of time, resources or geography, strategy and operational art have by no means been suspended when battle is joined.

III. WHAT BATTLES DECIDE

If all this is true, that the decisive acts of a war are contained within the context of a campaign, then in a book like this, which describes decisive battles, we must understand what it is that battles decide. First, there are battles that, on their conclusion, and probably with the benefit of hindsight, either marked the point at which a campaign changed direction or marked the passing of the initiative from one side to the other, as culmination was reached. From this point onwards, the side holding and maintaining the initiative began its inevitable victory. It is therefore not enough that a battle merely achieves operational objectives – that alone does not make it decisive.

In this category are battles like Gettysburg and Vicksburg (1863), Sedan (1870), Third Gaza (1917), Amiens (1918), the Arakan, Imphal and Kohima (1944), the Ardennes (1944) and Kuwait (1991) (all included in this book), as well as El Alamein, Stalingrad, the *Kaiserschlacht* and Okinawa. On the other side of the coin lies the Pyrrhic victory, which may cause the winner to seek compromise or otherwise modify its objectives.

Secondly, there are battles that marked the end of an era in warfare. These will usually have brought the termination of a campaign and, with it, the end of a period of total war; that is, war from which only one side could expect to emerge with its political system, its territory or its economy – or a combination of these – intact. In the aftermath of such a battle, both sides would recognize that a decision had been reached and agree on the resolution of the conflict – usually on terms favourable to the victor. Battles that brought only ceasefires or treaties that temporarily settled disputes cannot be classed as decisive.

Into this category fall, for example, Yorktown (1781), Waterloo (1815), (both in this book) and Berlin. In their aftermath, both the victors and the vanquished embarked on a new era in their history. After Yorktown, the USA emerged as a nation state, intent on dominating the continental land mass of North America, while the focus of the British Empire shifted irrevocably from West to East. Waterloo concluded more than 20 years of ruinous war with Revolutionary and Napoleonic France, restored the status quo ante, and, with the Congress of Vienna, instituted the system of alliances that would dominate Europe until 1860. Berlin finally ended the Second World War in Europe, brought to an end 100 years of German aggression on the Continent, and began the Cold War against Soviet Communism. Dien Bien Phu (1954) and Kuwait (1991) are other examples included here.

Of course, the results of a decisive battle may be achieved actively or passively. That is, they may be achieved as a direct result of the active victory by one side *and its exploitation*. The latter matters here: not for nothing (at least according to Livy) did the cavalry general Marhabal rebuke Hannibal for his refusal to march directly on Rome after the devastating victory of Cannae: 'You know how to win a victory, but you do not know how to use one.' Confederate General Nathan Bedford Forrest was similarly terse about Braxton Bragg: 'What does he fight battles *for*?'

Clausewitz expressed the same sentiment: '. . . the greatest strategic skill will be displayed in creating the right conditions for [the battle] . . . and making the fullest use of the results'. Alternatively, results may be achieved because one side loses rather than because the other wins: the Ardennes in 1944 was decisive because Hitler, in losing it, threw away the last army he had which was capable of delaying the Allied advance into Germany from the West or, if switched to the East, delaying the Russians in order to ensure that their Western Allies met them as far east as possible. The conflict reached culmination, the German Army falling into inexorable decline, and the war ended less than five months later.

Thus, the context of a decisive battle is not only its place within a campaign, but also its relation to strategy. Modern theories tend to separate strategy in its broadest sense – grand strategy, as it is called – from military strategy. The former can be defined very simply as the attainment of national or alliance objectives using all such ways and means as are available, appropriate and legal. It is about a state's external political objectives, its relations with other powers, and the coupling of security issues with the organization of the state in all its facets to ensure that its objectives can be met either through its own exertions or through alliance. The latter is the implementation, in the light of available resources, of the military aspects of a political decision to make war. Field Marshal Alanbrooke defined it thus:

> to determine the aim, which should be political: to derive from that aim a series of military objectives to be achieved: to assess these objectives as to the military requirements they create, and the pre-conditions which the achievement of each is likely to necessitate: to measure available and potential resources against the requirements and to chart from this process a coherent pattern of priorities and a rational course of action.

But there is a circular aspect to this, since although the decision to make war is a political one, no government takes such a course without having the means to do so. Military strategy is therefore, as Professor John Childs points out, a fundamental component in reaching the decision to go to war. Soldiers like Turenne, Condé and Vauban informed the political and military decision-making of Louis XIV alongside his civilian ministers. Hitler combined the functions of head of state with those of supreme warlord, as had, for example, William III of Great Britain and Ireland, Napoleon and Tsar Alexander I of Russia. It doesn't help, therefore, to be too rigid with these modern definitions. Moreover, the world is a more complex place now: the industrial and technological revolutions of the nineteenth and twentieth centuries have broadened both the bases of war and the means of conducting it. The Ardennes, as well as Yorktown, Dien Bien Phu, Okinawa and others, illustrate the great truth that if strategy is flawed, no matter how brilliant the tactical manoeuvres or how inspired the campaign, failure is inevitable: the decision will be handed to the other side.

IV. WHAT DECIDES BATTLES?

We have looked at the achievement of victory through physical destruction of the enemy, but the destruction of his will to fight is often a more efficient, if more indirect, means to the same end. As Napoleon himself remarked in his *Maximes*, 'More battles are decided by loss of hope, than by loss of blood': a battle is not necessarily decisive on account of its bloodiness. Loss of hope takes two forms: the collapse of the will of the General, and the collapse of the collective will to carry on the fight.

The will of the General may be the element of an opponent's ability to use force that is most amenable to influence. It is the glue that binds the other elements of this ability: his understanding or perception of the situation based on intelligence, and therefore vulnerable to deception; and his capabilities and their utility in a particular situation. Undermining it can be achieved through such things as pre-emption, dislocation and disruption; its means include firepower, superior force ratios, superior tempo, simultaneous action, and surprise. In 1942, the British and Empire army in Malaya and Singapore was out-fought and out-manoeuvred by a far smaller number of Japanese troops: General Perceval surrendered almost 100,000 men in Singapore, many of whom had recently arrived and not fired a shot, to a total Japanese force of no more than 65,000 after retreating 550 miles in 55 days. Perceval's force was capable of resistance, but Perceval *believed* himself to be beaten, and his will was therefore broken. The American General William Hull surrendered Detroit to a far smaller British assault force in 1812 for the same reason. Did the Dutch commander at Srebrenica in 1995 fall victim to the same belief and give in without a fight? Conversely, a General is not beaten until he himself knows it, or believes it – and the same goes for his army. At Albuhera in 1811, Marshall Soult famously remarked in exasperation of Beresford and his army: 'They could not be persuaded they were beaten. They were completely beaten, the day was mine, and they did not know it, and would not run.'

But what causes the loss of collective will? It is, of course, the accepted duty of any soldier to offer resistance to the enemy as long as he has the means to do so and he has not been incapacitated. Any soldier who does this, especially to the death, is performing his ultimate duty and fulfilling his contract. A soldier who runs away or surrenders while still armed, supplied and unwounded is of no use to his own side. These are the harsh facts of life and death in battle, but there is of course a world of difference between the theory, coldly stated or mulled over in a comfortable armchair in peacetime, and the actual conditions endured by men on the battlefield. Try to visualize, for example, the situation of a soldier in the British line during the German attack on 21 March 1918. Although he belongs to a platoon, a company, a battalion, what evidence does he see of this? Not much. His world is a few yards of trench or a lonely post, perhaps without a communication trench to the rear. The highest-ranking superior around is probably a corporal. A sergeant or an officer may appear from time to time and give a few words of encouragement before disappearing again. Then there is a five-hour bombardment that kills or maims men all around, and everyone is dazed, concussed, confused – perhaps shuddering and whimpering from shock. There is a thick fog, from which come all sorts of unnerving noises, and then the Germans are behind and all around him. He is, in his own view, as good as dead.

At this point, he feels much as soldiers in European and American armies have done throughout the term covered by this book. Soldiers are governed by the natural instinct for self-preservation shared by all humans, and the amount of courage and willpower they can summon. Historians and even Generals may write of 'fighting to the end', but armies do not usually fight on in the face of certain death, only in the circumstances already described. The real limit of a Western soldier's resistance is the point at which he feels that honour has been satisfied. If he cannot be certain of surviving battle, he will resist – for how long depends on the circumstances, the individuals concerned and the cohesion of their immediate group – but only to the point where individual honour is satisfied. The moment at which this threshold of resistance is reached varies from man to man and army to army, but not much over time. Consider the casualty figures of one British battalion, cut off and under attack: 59 killed, 180 wounded, 526 surrendered. A battalion in the forward zone on 21 March 1918? No: the Glosters in Korea in 1951.

Continuing the example of 21 March 1918, consider also the example of the 16th Manchesters. The regimental history records that of the defenders of Manchester Hill redoubt, 'Of the original garrison of eight officers and 160 other ranks, only two officers and fifteen other ranks survived.' Actually, the casualties cannot have been anything like that: official returns give the whole battalion's casualties that day as four officers and 69 men. The remainder, including at least three-quarters of the garrison of Manchester Hill redoubt, surrendered. The deciding elements seem to have been the death of the Commanding Officer, the knowledge of being surrounded and the impossibility of relief.

The 2nd/8th Worcesters tell a similar story of that day. Their divisional history says that 'they simply fought it out on the spot and their heroism will live forever . . .' But a former soldier, Private Bromell, said: 'When my position surrendered, we joined up with practically every man jack of our battalion who had been captured – transport, Red Cross, even the Band.

We were all marched into St Quentin.' The Commanding Officer, Lord Farnham, evidently decided that no relief could be expected, he could neither delay nor disrupt the enemy, and when the Germans brought up heavy guns and mortars the result would be dreadful bloodshed for no military gain.

'Fighting to the end' really means fighting until an honourable period of resistance has been offered and some delay or casualties have been inflicted on the enemy. But even in a well-disciplined unit, once the enemy is all around, or key leaders become casualties, or communication fails, morale suffers. The collapse of the collective will is therefore by no means a function of the number of casualties. In fact the reverse may be true, for when *all* hope is gone, when retreat is impossible and surrender not an option, men *will* fight to the end, as did the defenders of the Dunkirk perimeter in 1940. But the instances of this are rare, and usually a feature of warfare against savage opponents who obey no conventions of civilization, such as at Gandamack in 1840 or Isandlwana in 1879. The same is true of fighting today against jihadists in Iraq and Afghanistan: to such people, death is a welcome additional bonus of combat, not a risk to be avoided; and surrender to them or by them is out of the question. Every fight therefore tends to be a fight to the finish.

2

Yorktown, 1781: The World Turned Upside Down

I. THE WAR IN NORTH AMERICA

In January 1781, the war between Great Britain and the American Colonies, which had dragged on for six years since the opening shots at Concord, was effectively a stalemate. British military presence in North America, although 30,000 strong, was dispersed to a few coastal bases, all surrounded by hostile hinterland and threatened with attack. The main field army in the south had done well but it could no longer afford the rate of losses it had sustained during the previous campaigning season. Beyond North America, the war had become a world war as Britain had also to fight her old enemies, France, Spain and Holland, all of whom had scented the opportunity to make gain from their old rival's difficulties. British trade was suffering from the formation of the League of Armed Neutrality, and without trade Britain could not sustain her fleets and armies. The Americans were not in a particularly comfortable position either. Debts were huge, and shortages of equipment, ammunition and weapons were everywhere felt. Some states were openly questioning the cause, and much of the population was simply apathetic. America's relations with her allies were shaky. It was not so much a question of who was going to win the war, as who would first decide it was no longer worth the struggle.

British reverses in the northern theatre of operations had turned the ambitions of the Commander-in-Chief, Lieutenant General Sir Henry Clinton, towards the south, where he believed there to be a substantial but suppressed Loyalist interest. There had been little activity in the south during the early years of the war, but the British still held Florida, from where they could threaten Georgia. In March 1778, a British expedition had managed to capture Savannah and briefly threatened to reconquer the entire state of Georgia. Faced with a need for troops elsewhere, especially in the West Indies, Clinton found the attraction of raising troops from among the Loyalists a strong one.

II. THE BRITISH CAMPAIGN IN THE SOUTH

At the end of 1779, a more serious attempt on the South was made. Clinton sailed from his principal base, New York, with an army of 8,000 British, Hessian and Loyalist troops. Their objective was Charleston, capital of South Carolina, the fourth-largest city in the Colonies. After a siege that lasted from 1 April to 12 May 1780, Clinton captured the city and its 6,000-strong garrison – the biggest single capture of American troops during the whole Revolutionary War. The southern strategy appeared to be working. A proclamation of clemency looked as if it might restore British rule in South Carolina, making it the first state to return to the Crown. However, a second proclamation requiring those on parole to support all British measures, was too much for many men who might otherwise have stayed neutral: many returned to the American Colours.

At the end of June, news reached Clinton of a possible French attack on New York. Accordingly, he left the south, taking with him 4,000 men and leaving a small army under Lieutenant General Charles, Earl Cornwallis, to pacify North and South Carolina. South Carolina rapidly descended into chaos: many Loyalists did indeed come forward, but so did as many rebels. Moreover, the actions of the Loyalists, which were often rank banditry, induced many ex-rebels back into the field. Cornwallis was forced to establish a network of fortified garrisons across the state, which was a considerable drain on his limited resources. One of the British garrisons, at Camden, attracted the attention of the newly appointed American commander in the south, Horatio Gates. Cornwallis was able to reach Camden before Gates, and on 16 August 1780 inflicted a crushing defeat on the Americans.

This was the high point of Cornwallis's campaign in the South. In September, he launched an invasion of North Carolina, which had to be abandoned after the Loyalist force guarding his left flank was destroyed at the Battle of King's Mountain on 7 October 1780. In the following spring, Cornwallis launched another invasion of North Carolina. Once again, his campaign was stopped dead by the loss of a major detachment, this time at the Cowpens on 17 January 1781, where Lieutenant Colonel Banastre Tarleton's British Legion was badly mauled by the American forces of General Daniel Morgan. After a futile attempt to pursue Morgan, Cornwallis decided to retire southwards. The new American commander, Nathanael Greene, who had superseded Gates, followed Cornwallis with a larger force. On 15 March 1781, Greene offered battle, but although his army outnumbered the British two to one, the battle, fought at Guilford Courthouse, was a British victory. Casualties, however, reduced the number of fit men in Cornwallis's force to 1,600, all of them weary and very short of food. In his memoirs, published in 1809 in Dublin as the *Journal of Occurrences during the late American War*, Sergeant Roger Lamb of the 23rd Royal Welch Fusiliers recounts:

Sometimes we had turnips served out for our food, when we came to a turnip field; or arriving at a field of [Indian] corn, we converted our canteens into rasps and ground our Indian corn for bread; when we could get no Indian corn, we were compelled to eat liver as a substitute for bread, with our lean beef.

In such a situation, Cornwallis could no longer afford to maintain his army in the field.

Clinton had by now reached the conclusion that British interests would best be served by the establishment of a series of fortified bases along the eastern seaboard of North America. From these, military expeditions could be mounted into the interior. Such a strategy depended, of course, on sea control, which, like everyone else, Clinton took for granted. One such base was to be in Chesapeake Bay, from which operations could be directed in concert with moves from New York against Philadelphia and

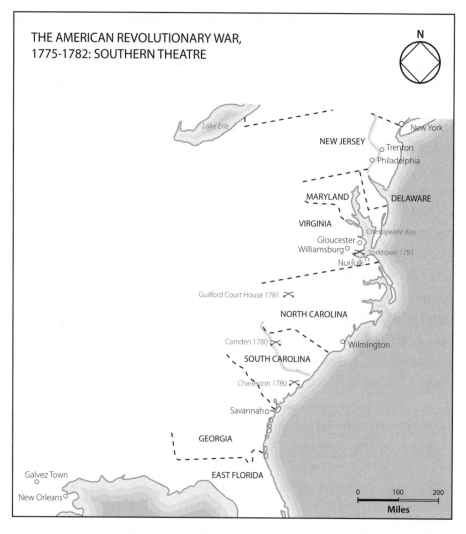

Map 1: The American Revolutionary War, 1775–1782

the centre of the rebellion. Late in 1780, Major General William Phillips was sent to take command in Virginia and begin surveying for this base. Cornwallis looked for a new strategy, and his mind moved to Virginia and the Chesapeake. At the beginning of 1781, British reinforcements commanded by former-American-turned-Loyalist General Benedict Arnold allowed Phillips to establish a firm presence at Portsmouth, on the coast of Virginia. Cornwallis, his position in the South now unten-able, proposed leaving a chain of garrisons in the Carolinas and moving north with his main force, to link up with Phillips and Arnold and effect a British concentration in Virginia. Virginia was the largest, most heavily populated and wealthiest of the Colonies, and provided food, reinforce-ments and supplies to the American field army as well as money through the export of tobacco. If he controlled the economy of Virginia, Cornwallis believed the Americans would have no choice but to move against him. With his large force, he thought that he could then bring the Americans to battle and achieve a decisive victory that would break the strategic and operational stalemate.

Cornwallis, with only about 1,000 men, crossed into Virginia on 10 May. The little army reached Petersburg at the end of the month, where Cornwallis learned that his friend William Phillips had died of typhus five days earlier, leaving all British troops in Virginia under the command of Benedict Arnold. Clinton's orders to establish a base on the Chesapeake but not to undertake any major action still stood – although Cornwallis's ideas were different. Clinton himself received news of Cornwallis's move by letter at about the same time as Cornwallis arrived in Virginia. Clinton dismissed Cornwallis's scheme, being far more concerned with the pos-sibility of an attack on New York by French troops, more than 8,000 of which had arrived at Newport, Rhode Island, in June 1780 under the command of Lieutenant General Jean Baptiste de Vimeur, Comte de Rochambeau. Clinton restated his orders to Cornwallis, telling him to 'establish a defensive post in any healthy situation' on the Chesapeake capable of sheltering ships of the line. These orders made sense: a chain of strongholds from New York to Charleston would indeed have allowed Clinton to strike at will along most of the American coast. Clinton also ordered Cornwallis to prepare to return some of his troops to New York for operations in Pennsylvania.

Cornwallis met little opposition in Virginia as he embarked on a series of raids to destroy economic and military targets and capture or kill key figures in the rebellion. The Marquis de Lafayette had arrived at Richmond, Virginia, in April 1781 with 3,000 men, tasked with preventing British raids and capturing Benedict Arnold. Realizing that he was vulnerable to annihilation by the superior British force, Lafayette avoided combat. Cornwallis, on the other hand, was determined to bring this about. On 6 July, a brigade of Pennsylvanian troops under Brigadier General Anthony Wayne, which had joined Lafayette on 10 June after a march through Maryland, was ambushed by Cornwallis at Green Spring, near Jamestown, and only escaped with great difficulty, losing two of its three guns. Only an incomplete pursuit saved Wayne from destruction. The siege that developed at Yorktown was not, therefore, inevitable at any point before the middle of September: Cornwallis could have marched south and out of danger. But after receiving a series of orders over the summer from Clinton, he decided to fortify the village of Yorktown with his entire force. On 2 August, the British began to entrench their base.

III. WASHINGTON AND ROCHAMBEAU

Four hundred miles north, the American army, under its commander, General George Washington, was still focused on New York. Rochambeau and the French were still at Newport, Rhode Island, and their naval squadron of eight ships of the line was now under the command of Admiral Jacques-Melchior Saint-Laurent, Comte de Barras. Rochambeau had decided to cooperate fully with Washington, even to the extent of accepting the orders of a man who was his social and professional inferior. Washington's plan for the spring of 1781 was to keep up the pressure on New York – not to effect the capture of the city, which was held by the most powerful British force in America, but to make Clinton bring troops from other theatres of the war. Rochambeau agreed to support this plan, but little came of it, for the British were too well entrenched and commanded all the approaches.

In June, news reached Washington that Rear-Admiral François Comte de Grasse had managed to evade the Royal Navy's blockade at Brest and was heading for the West Indies with a squadron of 21 ships. Washington immediately came to the same conclusion as Clinton had done: that the key to the war lay in control of the sea. It was possible that the combined French fleets would be able to gain this, at least temporarily. On 14 August, more news arrived: de Grasse, having picked up five additional ships and five frigates at Haiti, along with 3,200 men, was heading for Chesapeake Bay.

Washington saw his opportunity clearly. If he could move the American and French armies from New York and Newport to the Chesapeake, while Barras and de Grasse joined forces, Cornwallis would be trapped. If, however, the French fleet failed to gain control of the seas, Clinton would be able to move troops from New York and force a decisive battle on favourable terms. Washington decided to take the risk, and Rochambeau supported his decision.

IV. SURPRISE AND SEA POWER

The French squadron under de Grasse reached Chesapeake Bay on the last day of August and anchored inside the bay in three lines. Admiral Thomas Graves, commanding the British squadron on the American station, took his fleet of 19 ships of the line to find and attack the French. Just after 2.00 p.m. on 5 September, battle was joined off the Chesapeake. The British were outnumbered, and Graves's seamanship left much to be desired. Moreover, superior French gunnery did much damage to the badly handled British squadron. Despite these factors, the battle ended with only a slight French advantage, but it was the first time that the Royal Navy had been bested in a fleet action since the Dutch wars a hundred years before. Over the next two days, de Grasse moved northwards, drawing Graves after him and giving Barras's squadron the chance to slip into the Chesapeake. De Grasse turned back and on 11 September joined Barras, thus giving the French a two-to-one advantage over Graves in ships of the line. On 13 September, Graves decided to return to New York to repair his battered fleet. This was a decisive moment, if not *the* decisive moment, for, without sea power, Cornwallis's communications by sea from Yorktown were cut; but the main American and French armies had not yet arrived on the scene and Cornwallis could still have escaped by marching south. Graves's repairs were not completed until mid-October, and although there was a continuing debate in New York about an amphibious operation to relieve Cornwallis, it was not until 19 October that a reinforced squadron of 28 ships and eight frigates, with 7,000 troops embarked in transports, sailed south.

Meanwhile, the Allied armies had stolen two months, for they had begun to move southwards on 19 August. Had Clinton realized what was happening, he might have launched a counter-attack into their flank. To deceive him, therefore, Washington first feinted towards New York and then rapidly turned south, using speed to complete the dislocation of Clinton's forces. Clinton, in New York, was therefore uncertain about Washington's intentions until 2 September, by which time the Allied armies had already reached Philadelphia. On 14 September, Rochambeau and Washington met Lafayette at Williamsburg, where, it is said, 'no man ever greeted his mistress with more joy than did Lafayette and Washington greet each other'. On 28 September, having employed a combination of road movement and embarkation on ships, the Allied armies moved into positions around Yorktown. Cornwallis was now trapped.

V. YORKTOWN

The small town of Yorktown stood on bluffs 30 feet high overlooking the York River, and on a peninsula about 8 miles wide between the James River and the York River. The town had a harbour capable of berthing large merchant ships, troop transports and men-of-war. Two main roads led out of the town to Williamsburg, 12 miles westwards, and Hampton, 18 miles south-eastwards. A ferry crossed the York River to the village at Gloucester Point, 1 mile north-eastwards. The ground around the town was undulating but poor agricultural land, with few trees. The creeks around the town that drained into the York were all tidal, with steep, boggy banks.

As soon as he had arrived there, Cornwallis had begun to fortify

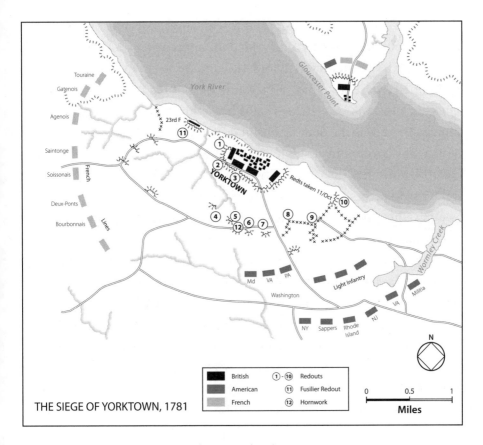

Map 2: *The Siege of Yorktown, 1781*

Yorktown and Gloucester, using all his men and a large number of slaves and freed slaves who had flocked to join him rather than stay with their American masters. The defences, however, were not of sufficient strength to stand a determined, formal siege in which heavy artillery could be brought to bear, being merely trenches and earthworks supplemented with log palisadoes.

An inner line of defence ran 500 yards from the edge of the town, but this line was still unfinished when the siege began. The outer defences were even less impressive. There were ten redoubts, linked by trenches and outworks. Redoubts 1 and 2 overlooked the Yorktown Creek and the road to Williamsburg; Redoubts 3, 4 and 5 overlooked the rear of the town;

the Hornwork, a more substantial fortification, covered the Hampton road; Redoubts 6, 7 and 8 commanded the approaches south-east towards Wormley Creek; Redoubts 9 and 10 were up to 300 yards beyond the main line. Twelve hundred yards south-west of the town was the Pigeon Quarter, a low hill where Cornwallis had built three additional redoubts. Finally, there was the Star, or Fusilier, Redoubt, north-east of Yorktown, which was covered by a single frigate, the *Guadeloupe*. The largest guns were 18-pounders dismounted from ships, but most of the 65 guns were lighter field pieces. Gloucester housed a further 20 guns.

Once the Allied armies closed up, Cornwallis found himself badly outnumbered as well as cut off. He had 6,000 British, Hessian and Loyalist regular troops, with another 1,500 drawn from the fleet to man the guns, but as many as one in four of the men were sick or wounded, and he needed to detach some troops to Gloucester. Facing him were 7,000 American regulars formed into five brigades, 4,000 militia, 5,000 French regulars formed into four divisions – really brigades – and 3,100 French marines: a total of 19,000 men, of whom 12,000 were regulars. The Allies had at least as big an advantage in numbers and calibres of guns. Cornwallis's only hope was that Clinton would send a relief force from New York – but that would have to happen quickly, for Yorktown could not hold out for long.

VI. THE SIEGE

Washington and Rochambeau decided on a formal siege, making best use of their superiority in artillery. On 30 September, however, they awoke to find that Cornwallis had abandoned the outer defences at Pigeon Quarter. This was rapidly seized and converted into a battery position; later the same day, Lafayette's troops seized two of the three redoubts overlooking the Hampton road. Under the direction of Major General Friedrich von Steuben, the Allied field artillery began bombarding Yorktown while preparing the entrenchments and works needed to invest the place. Within a week, 2,000 fascines, 6,000 palisado stakes and 600 baskets, or gabions, had been made; the heavier guns of the siege train also made their way up, having taken longer to complete the march south than the rest of the army. Morale was high among the attacking forces.

In accordance with the standard, formal practice of eighteenth-century warfare, von Steuben planned a series of parallels, or trenches and fortifications parallel to the defences, from which artillery and heavy mortar fire could be directed against the defenders. The first parallel, 600 yards from the British line, was started on 6 October. By 9 October the artillery was ready to open fire: the bombardment was devastating. At such short range, the French and even the American artillery were highly accurate. On the second day of the bombardment, the British were forced to stop firing during daylight to preserve their guns and ammunition.

Conditions inside Yorktown deteriorated rapidly. Nowhere in the town was out of range of the Allied guns, and even Cornwallis was forced to live underground. Having had time to prepare, the troops were not short of food, and the siege was too short for supplies to run low. Over the next days, the Allies continued to tighten the siege. A second parallel, only 300 yards from the defences, was begun on 11 October. This was very vulnerable at first, for Cornwallis had preserved his ammunition for just this moment and now ordered his guns to unmask, but over the next week the Allied artillery battered down the British resistance. On 14 October, a successful joint attack was launched on Redoubts 9 and 10, which were quickly integrated into the second parallel. The Allies were now in position to launch an assault on Yorktown itself. Cornwallis reported the loss to Clinton in a dispatch, concluding ominously that 'the safety of the place is, therefore, so precarious that I cannot recommend that the fleet or the army should run any great risk in endeavouring to save us'.

At this stage, Cornwallis decided on a sortie. On 15 October, a raiding party of 350 men drawn from the Light Companies of the Line Regiments, the brigade of Foot Guards and the 80th Foot broke into the second parallel and managed to spike seven guns before withdrawing back to their lines. It was brave but useless, for the guns were back in action six hours later. The next day, Cornwallis attempted to escape. The

French and American forces besieging Gloucester were not as strong or as well dug in as those around Yorktown, so Cornwallis tried to move as many men as possible across the river to attempt a break-out. Tarleton, who was commanding in Gloucester, sent over 16 boats, each capable of holding 100 men, and Cornwallis divided his force into three waves, which would move across in turn, leaving the 76th Foot and a contingent of Hessians from Ansbach to hold on as rearguard. The plan would have worked but for the intervention of nature: bad weather arrived after the first wave had crossed. By the time things settled, it was impossible for the remaining troops to be ferried across during darkness. As Sergeant Roger Lamb recalled:

> In pursuance of this design the light infantry, the greatest part of the guards and part of the 23d Regiment were embarked in boats and transported to the Gloucester side of the river before midnight, when a violent storm arose, which not only prevented the boats from returning, but drove them a considerable distance down the river.

Cornwallis reluctantly ordered the first wave to return to Yorktown.

VII. SURRENDER

As dawn broke on 17 October, 100 Allied guns and mortars of all calibres opened fire again on the defences of Yorktown. Just before 10.00 a.m., in accordance with the practice of the time for seeking parley, a drummer appeared on the British parapet, joined shortly afterwards by an officer with an improvised white flag. The gunfire slackened and died and the officer approached the Allied lines. He was taken, blindfolded, to Washington and Rochambeau's headquarters, where he delivered a sealed letter from Cornwallis suggesting a truce for 24 hours so that surrender terms could be discussed. Washington agreed initially only to two hours. Cornwallis asked that his force be paroled and returned to Europe, but Washington feared that a relief force might appear at any stage and insisted on the garrison becoming prisoners of war. Negotiations continued next day, and around midnight, terms were sent to Washington for approval: the garrison would march out and lay down its arms and Colours; but the Colours would remain cased – in fact, many were saved by being concealed under the officers' uniform coats. The formal surrender documents were signed by Cornwallis and Captain Thomas Symonds, the senior Royal Naval officer, on the British side, and by Washington, Rochambeau and de Barras on the Allied side.

At 2.00 p.m. on 19 October, Cornwallis's army marched out of Yorktown on the Hampton road. Tradition says that the fifes and drums played *The World Turned Upside Down*: a nice story but, like many stories, not based on any contemporary evidence. The British pointedly declined to recognize or salute the Americans' Colours – they were, after all, rebels – but paid the required compliments to the French. The troops were not led by Cornwallis himself, who pleaded illness, but by his deputy, Brigadier General Charles O'Hara. O'Hara offered his sword to Rochambeau, who declined and pointed to Washington. Washington in turn declined, indicating his own deputy, Major General Benjamin Lincoln. It was the aptly named Lincoln, therefore, who accepted the capitulation. The Gloucester garrison surrendered the next day.

In all, 7,247 troops – more than 300 of them wounded – and 840 sailors surrendered, along with 24 British and German Colours, 243 guns, 2,000 rounds of artillery ammunition, 8,000 muskets and rifles, more than 200,000 rounds of small-arms ammunition, 300 horses and mules, 43 wagons and a huge stock of food and liquor. About 150 British and German soldiers had been killed, and roughly the same number had died from sickness. On the Allied side there had been 76 killed and 190 wounded. The British and German soldiers, with 180 of their regimental officers, went into captivity for the remainder of the war; the more senior officers, as was usual, were paroled after a round of entertainments and courtesies with the French that excluded the Americans and left them feeling disgruntled, if not actually insulted by their allies. Four days later, the relief force, under Graves, arrived off the Chesapeake. The fleet lingered for five days, unwilling to accept that Cornwallis had surrendered, and then, against the wishes of Clinton, returned to New York.

VIII. AFTERMATH

The surrender at Yorktown certainly did not break the will of the British Army in America to continue the war, nor even convince Clinton that the game was up, despite the fact that some of his best and most experienced regiments had gone into captivity. There were still, after all, 30,000 troops and a considerable fleet in America. Nor did the Allies exploit their victory, for de Grasse sailed for the West Indies and Rochambeau and his troops went into winter quarters in Virginia. Washington was left to return to New York with his American army, believing that the war would enter another year.

The real decision of Yorktown took place in London. On 25 November, the news reached Lord George Germain, the Secretary of State for the American Colonies, in a letter from Clinton. He immediately told the Prime Minister, Lord North, who said, 'Oh God! It is all over!' The cost of a global war, the threat of invasion from France, the lack of any prospect of achieving a decision in America and a growing national debt were all looming large, and Yorktown was simply the last straw that broke the will of the British Government to continue. Even if Yorktown had been avoided and some sort of favourable outcome achieved, it is highly debatable whether Britain could have held on to all its colonies, faced as they probably were with a running insurgency.

Negotiations took place throughout the following summer while Sir Guy Carleton succeeded Clinton as the British Commander-in-Chief in America, with orders to undertake no offensive action but to plan for a complete evacuation. On the Allied side, success brought the re-emergence of individual agendas, as is so often the case with coalitions established to deal with a single enemy. Spanish ambitions in North America and French support for them, along with the naval defeat at the Battle of the Saints in April 1782, led the French to try to negotiate a separate peace with Britain.

In response, the Americans asked for effective British recognition of the United States through separate negotiations – something the British were willing to do to end the Franco-American alliance. The Treaty of Paris was eventually concluded in September 1783; however, the British evacuation had already begun: it was completed in November 1783. The French fleet and army left for the French West Indies, and 100,000 Loyalists left for Britain or Canada. The British turned their attention to founding a new empire in the East to replace the one lost in the West; and six years later, the ideals that had inspired many of the American revolutionaries broke into new and terrifying flames in the capital of their erstwhile ally, France.

3

Ligny, Quatre Bras and Waterloo, 1815:
The Hundred Days

I. NAPOLEON RETURNS

In March 1815, the victorious Allies of the Sixth Coalition – England, Prussia, Austria, Russia, Sweden, Spain and Portugal – were absorbed by the negotiations of the Congress of Vienna. Their deliberations were rudely interrupted by news of the escape of Napoleon Bonaparte from Elba, where he had been in exile since his abdication in 1814. Marshal Ney, now a servant of the Bourbons, was sent south with a large force to apprehend him – but the troops would not stand against their old master. To a man they went over to Napoleon, who marched north in triumphal progress, while men flocked to join his army. By 20 March, Napoleon was back in Paris and the Bourbons had once more fled. To his enemies, this was intolerable: the Corsican bandit, the tyrant, the thief of Europe, back once more on his throne!

A comprehensive Allied plan based on a convergent series of offensives was rapidly agreed. The English Field Marshal Arthur Wellesley, Duke of Wellington, and the Prussian General Gebhard von Blücher were to invade France through Belgium. The armies of Austria and Russia would assemble and invade from the east. But until the Allies could assemble overwhelming force and advance in concert, their strategy would be defensive. Napoleon rapidly mustered a French regular army of about 150,000 soldiers, and immediately began to raise more troops for an early campaign against the Allies: in eight weeks, repeating the fantastic efforts of 1813, he had increased the strength of the army by 80,000. By the end of April, he had decided to attack the British and the Prussians in Belgium, intending to defeat them before the Austrians and Russians could cross the Rhine and join in a concerted Allied march on Paris. Accordingly, at the beginning of June, he concentrated the Armée du Nord, approximately 120,000 men, close to the Belgian frontier, south of Charleroi. The concentration was a masterpiece of speed and secrecy, involving the movement of units and formations over distances of up to 200 miles. The army was grouped into three columns on a 20-mile front. It was therefore a professional and experienced army, with its morale high, which enthusiastically welcomed Napoleon at Beaumont on 14 June.

Napoleon at the age of 46, however, was no longer the confident, masterful and dominant genius of earlier years. He had put on weight alarmingly, and his health was not good. Following the best traditions of the subjective historical approach, different accounts, depending on the author's general opinion of Napoleon, have suggested that he was suffering from piles, cystitis, hepatitis and venereal disease. Whatever the accuracy of these various diagnoses, Napoleon, as he prepared to face Wellington and Blücher, was almost certainly suffering from the appalling pains of the duodenal-pyloric cancer which would eventually kill him. But on the battlefield, the dreaded cry of '*Vive l'Empereur!*' could still strike fear into the hearts of his enemies – except, that is, the English, who regarded him with a certain puzzled amusement which never turned into the kind of awe felt for the Emperor by Continental soldiers.

His Marshalate, too, was tired and depleted; a significant omission was his old Chief of Staff, Marshal Louis-Alexandre Berthier. Berthier had the master's touch as a staff officer and knew just how to translate Napoleon's concepts into clear orders. He had refused to serve Napoleon when he had returned from exile, and had died soon after. In his place Napoleon had appointed Marshal Nicolas Soult, who had no such talent. Much of the confusion of orders which characterized 16, 17 and 18 June in the French Army, and which contributed to its defeat, must be laid at the feet of Soult. Napoleon's choice of Marshal Michel Ney for an independent command is also extraordinary, given Ney's record, but he was extraordinarily brave and popular with the troops, and Napoleon still owed him a debt after his

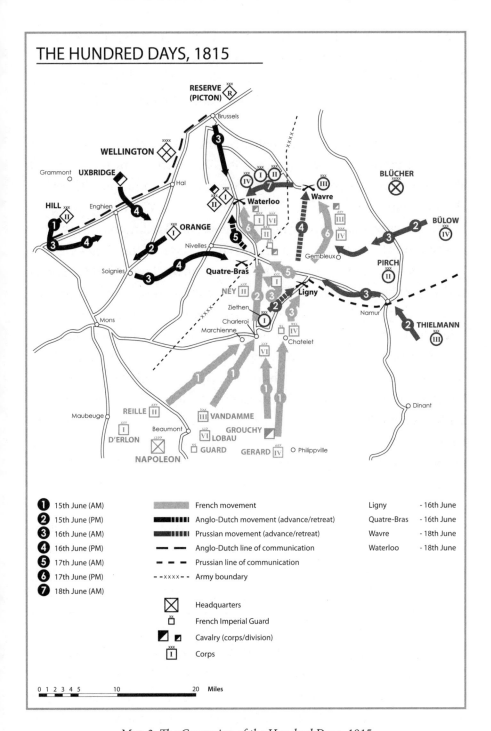

THE HUNDRED DAYS, 1815

RESERVE (PICTON) R

Brussels

WELLINGTON

Grammont   **UXBRIDGE**

Hal

HILL   Enghien

ORANGE

Nivelles

Soignies

Quatre-Bras

NEY

Ziethen

Mons

Charleroi
Marchienne

Chatelet

REILLE   **VANDAMME**

Maubeuge

Beaumont   **GROUCHY**

D'ERLON   **LOBAU**

GUARD   **GERARD**   Philippville

NAPOLEON

Waterloo   **Wavre**

BLÜCHER

BÜLOW

Gembleux

PIRCH

Ligny

Namur

THIELMANN

Dinant

❶ 15th June (AM)	French movement
❷ 15th June (PM)	Anglo-Dutch movement (advance/retreat)
❸ 16th June (AM)	Prussian movement (advance/retreat)
❹ 16th June (PM)	Anglo-Dutch line of communication
❺ 17th June (AM)	Prussian line of communication
❻ 17th June (PM)	Army boundary
❼ 18th June (AM)	

Ligny	- 16th June
Quatre-Bras	- 16th June
Wavre	- 18th June
Waterloo	- 18th June

Headquarters
French Imperial Guard
Cavalry (corps/division)
Corps

0 1 2 3 4 5   10   20   Miles

Map 3: The Campaign of the Hundred Days, 1815

handling of the rearguard in Russia. There was, too, political significance in giving high command to one who had renounced Bourbon service. Grouchy, too, was to prove an unwise choice. By contrast, the capable Marshal Joachim Murat and Marshal Louis Davout remained on the sidelines.

The Allies, in contrast to Napoleon's unified command, suffered from a divided command – the lessons of 1813–14 had not been heeded, although there was considerable exchange of liaison officers. There was also Prussian suspicion of England as a result of the Vienna Congress. The Prussian Army was relatively homogeneous, but Wellington's army was a mishmash: 21,000 British and 5,000 Hanoverians of the King's German Legion (KGL); 11,000 Hanoverians; 5,500 Brunswickers; 3,000 Nassauers; and 17,000 Dutch–Belgians. The quality of these troops varied considerably; among the British and KGL there were many veteran units and individuals from the Peninsular Army, but there were also large numbers of new men. Among the Allied troops, many were conscripts or *Landwehr* (militia), and some had been fighting for Napoleon until the previous year. For this reason, and to bolster the weaker contingents, Wellington grouped his British and KGL troops with Allied brigades – a practice he had used with his Portuguese troops in 1808–10. This measure also served another purpose – as a visible statement of Allied unity. At least Wellington had been appointed Commander-in-Chief of all these troops and had clear authority to issue orders.

The Prussians were led by the 72-year-old General of Cavalry Gebhard von Blücher. Blücher had fought Napoleon for years and had been beaten by him several times, most notably at Auerstadt in 1806 and again in 1814, but had also been present at Leipzig and played an important part in the Allied victory. Known to his troops as *General Vorwaerts* or *Alt Vorwaerts* (Old Man Forwards), he hated Napoleon like the devil and was determined to cooperate closely with Wellington, with whom, however, he could converse only in French. He was by now showing signs of mild eccentricity: when he met Wellington in London after Waterloo, he whispered confidently to him that he felt sure he was pregnant with an elephant which, horrible irony, had been fathered on him by a French soldier.

In both armies there was, therefore, a certain fragility. On the Allied side, this resulted from the nature of the coalition and the relative inexperience of the troops; on the French side, from a weakened command structure and also from a general mood of nervousness: there had been three changes of government in a year and this made the army prone to rumours of betrayal and treason. This was a cry that would be heard at the end of the day at Waterloo. But in Wellington, Napoleon had an opponent of the first rank, worthy of his own genius. Although he was dismissed by some as a mere sepoy general and by others as having conducted only a sideshow in Spain, a look at his campaigns tells a different story. The Campaign of Vitoria remains one of the great classics of manoeuvre, and his operational defensive against Soult's counter-attack against the Pyrenees is almost as impressive. He was by no means overawed by Napoleon: he stated openly that, had he commanded his old Peninsular Army, he would have attacked Napoleon at once.

II. PRELUDE TO BATTLE

No state of actual war existed between France and the Allies – under the Vienna System of collective security, Napoleon was merely treated as a criminal. Many on the Allied side considered that, faced with overwhelming odds, Napoleon would have no choice but to adopt a strategic and operational defensive: they little understood their opponent. Even with his back to the wall, it was not in Napoleon's nature to fight defensive battles. Moreover, he realized that his only chance of avoiding a second Leipzig was to destroy the various Allied armies before they could unite. Weighing the odds, he considered his best chance to be an operational defensive in the east and south to keep the Austrians and Russians at bay – they would in any case take some time to appear – while mounting an operational offensive to the north against the polyglot Anglo-Dutch and Prussian armies. This would allow him to pose his strength against the Allies' weakest formations, and to destroy the army of his inveterate foes, the English. With defeat, the English might be induced to sue for peace, and without their finance, no coalition would stand against him. Finally, the Netherlands and Belgium had for 20 years been part of France, and Bonapartist sympathies were strong, which would help Napoleon's prestige as well as increase his military potential in terms of recruits, horses, supplies and industrial capacity.

Looking more specifically at the positions of the Allied armies in the Netherlands, there were additional weaknesses to be exploited. The Prussians were centred on Namur, with their communications running eastward into Germany. The Anglo-Dutch army was centred on Brussels, with its communications running north and west. Wellington had remained to the west for two reasons. First, he wished to keep a close eye on the doubtful loyalty of the Dutch garrisons in the frontier fortresses; secondly, he felt that if Napoleon did attack, he would use his favourite strategy – envelopment – to march around the Allied right, cutting his (that is, Wellington's) communications with the Channel. In fact, Napoleon had discounted envelopment, since it would achieve what he sought to avoid: it would push the Anglo-Dutch and Prussian armies together. Instead, he had his eye fixed on the gap between Wellington and Blücher, a gap through which ran the great paved high road from Charleroi to Brussels. His intention was to employ the strategy of the central position: mask one and defeat the other, then turn and defeat the first. He wrote to Ney:

> I have adopted for this campaign the following general principle, to divide my army into two wings and a reserve. The Guard will form the reserve and I shall bring it into action on either wing just as the actual circumstances may dictate. Also, according to circumstances, I shall draw troops from either wing to strengthen my reserve.

Napoleon's two wings were those of Marshal Emmanuel Grouchy, commanding two army corps (General Dominique Vandamme's III and General Etienne Gérard's IV) and two cavalry corps (General Rémy Exelmann's II (Dragoons) and Count Pajol's I (Hussars and Chasseurs)), and Ney, with one army corps (Marshal Honoré Reille's II) and a cavalry division. Marshal Jean Baptiste Drouet D'Erlon's I Corps was also under Ney's command. In reserve, Napoleon held Count Lobau's VI Corps, Marshal Adolphe Mortier's Guard Corps and Count Milhaud's IV Cavalry Corps (Curassiers). Napoleon's operational plan, in accordance with the strategy of the central position, was simple. Ney, with Reille's corps, would seize the crossroads at Quatre Bras and hold it with a corps of observation of one division and some cavalry, thus masking Wellington. He himself, with Grouchy's two army and two cavalry corps, would attack the Prussians frontally so as to fix them. Ney's main body would then execute an enveloping manoeuvre on the Prussian right – designed to draw off the enemy's reserves – and the battle would be decided once the Prussian centre had been weakened, first by the devastating fire of massed artillery, then by the simultaneous attacks of the Guard Corps and the reserve cavalry. Lastly, Ney's second corps – that of D'Erlon – was ordered to march and join the Emperor at the main effort. It was a bold and simple plan – and it almost succeeded.

Having determined his plan, Napoleon moved with his usual rapidity. After concentrating his army in conditions of extreme secrecy and security, he crossed the River Sambre at Charleroi early on 15 June. A feint in the direction of Mons made Wellington hesitate for 24 hours – still worried about his right flank – but by 16 June, Napoleon's intention was clear. 'Napoleon has humbugged me, by God,' exclaimed the Duke.

III. LIGNY

By the night of 15 June, Napoleon's army was moving rapidly up the main Brussels and Liège roads, between the two Allied armies. After a great deal of confusion, Blücher decided to take up a defensive position astride the main Liège–Charleroi road and await the arrival of Wellington's army.

Prussian strength was about 84,000, including 8,000 cavalry, and 224 guns of the corps of Generals Ernst Graf von Zieten, Georg von Pirch and Johann Thielmann. The Prussian blocking position ran in general terms along the line of the marshy Ligny stream for some 7 miles, and incorporated ten hamlets, farms and villages as strong points. Four bridges, all dominated by strong points, crossed the river, and these were left standing, presumably to encourage the French attack to channel and thus be destroyed by defensive fire. Although a strong position, it was extensive for the number of troops: at Bautzen in 1813, the Allies had employed almost double the number to occupy a very similar position, and had spent a week fortifying it. Blücher had occupied a forward slope position using three of his available corps. On the left, holding the Charleroi road and beyond Tonginnes, was Thielmann's III Corps. On the right and the centre, Blücher had placed his main effort: the I Corps of von Zieten held Ligny, St Armand, Bussy Mill and Brye, with von Pirch's II Corps in echelon behind von Zieten from Sombreffe westwards to the junction of the Quatre Bras and Roman roads. Still approaching from the north was the IV Corps of Friedrich Count von Bülow, 29,000 strong.

At about 12.30 p.m. on 16 June, Prussian sentries spotted a group of officers riding horses with cut tails, which identified them without question as English. Half an hour later, Wellington met Blücher at the windmill in Bussy to survey the position. The Prussians were drawn up on the forward slope, and Wellington was heard to remark, as he observed the position, that 'If they fight here they will be damnably mauled'. He said more tactfully to Blücher and Chief of Staff August von Gneisenau: 'Everybody knows their own army best; but if I were to fight here, I should expect to be beat'. Gneisenau replied, 'My men like to see their enemy'. Wellington replied by promising that he would come to support the Prussians provided he was not attacked himself. He then started to ride back towards Quatre Bras; as he neared the crossroads he heard three cannon shots, repeated three times: it was the signal for Napoleon's attack.

On arriving to view the area of Ligny, Napoleon could hardly believe that Blücher, despite his nickname, had obliged him by concentrating so far forwards and out of touch with Wellington. His tactical plan was, therefore, typical of his battle system. His cavalry was ordered to pin the Prussian left, while the two corps of Vandamme and Gérard, supported by the artillery, made a frontal attack on the Prussian centre and right. This would fix the defenders, cause maximum casualties and draw in as many Prussian troops from the second echelon as possible. At the same time, D'Erlon would march from Quatre Bras and fall on the Prussian right wing. The day would be decided by the committal of the Guard Corps to smash the Prussian army irretrievably. The whole French army would then turn on Wellington.

It proved impossible, however, to launch an immediate attack on the Prussians, as the right wing and the reserve were still well spread out on the line of march. It was not until 2.00 p.m. that the corps of Vandamme and Gérard, the cavalry, and the 210 guns of the artillery had been brought up, increasing Napoleon's strength to 68,000. Significantly, no orders were issued to Lobau's VI Corps, back at Charleroi – a slip Napoleon would not have made five years before. The French cavalry attack began at 2.30 p.m., and the cavalry fulfilled its pinning role with great economy and effect all day. The infantry attack was preceded by a terrific bombardment from the French artillery, which inflicted heavy casualties on the Prussian first and second echelons. Despite this, the Prussian resistance was ferocious.

At 3.15 p.m., Napoleon sent the first of his messages to Ney, ordering him to march with all speed; but at about the same time, a message came in to say that Ney was fully engaged against 20,000 Allied troops. Napoleon, therefore, ordered only D'Erlon's I Corps to march on Ligny. He also remembered VI Corps, which had spent the day without orders around Charleroi: Lobau was ordered to march immediately for Fleurus. Meanwhile, the battle on the Ligny stream raged on, with villages changing hands repeatedly, but the Emperor's scheme was beginning to show signs of success. By 5.00 p.m., almost all Prussian reserves had been committed, while Napoleon had 10,000 fresh troops in reserve: thus, 58,000 French troops were successfully fixing 84,000 Prussians. This, Napoleon decided, was the moment to commit the Guard. He had, in fact, issued the order when a report came in of hostile troops – presumably Wellington – appearing from the direction of Quatre Bras. Napoleon accordingly suspended the attack, but it was 6.30 p.m. before he realized that it was actually D'Erlon's corps. Orders were sent to D'Erlon to attack the Prussian flank, but, in the meantime, D'Erlon received a new order from Ney to rejoin him, and retraced his steps towards Quatre Bras. Completely baffled by D'Erlon's movements, Napoleon turned his attention to retrieving the situation at Ligny.

But Blücher had not wasted the time which Napoleon's delay had given him. He had gathered up six battalions and a mass of other half-formed units and launched a sudden counter-attack towards St Armand. This certainly threw the French off balance, but the attack was unsupported, so that the French III Corps, although close to flight, was rallied by the Young Guard division of the Guard Corps. By 7.30 p.m., Napoleon was once more ready for his grand attack. Supported by 60 guns and both the light and heavy divisions of the Guard Cavalry, the two reserve corps smashed into Ligny itself, shattering what remained of the Prussian defence. By 8.00 p.m. the battle was almost won.

Blücher, however, had one more trick up his sleeve. Desperate to buy some space for his infantry to retire, he placed himself at the head of his whole available cavalry – 32 squadrons – and charged the Guard. The charge was easily held, but it did have the effect of halting the French attack. Blücher himself had his horse shot from under him, was thrown to the ground and was pinned by the horse's body. He was twice ridden over by French cavalry, but not recognized, before being rescued by an aide.

By 9.00 p.m., Napoleon had certainly achieved victory – but not the complete success he had hoped for. The Prussian centre had been smashed, true, but the final counter-attacks had allowed the flanking corps to extricate themselves and retire in relatively good order towards Wavre: had the battle gone according to plan and D'Erlon's corps enveloped the Prussians, the results would have been incalculable. As it was, the Prussians had lost 21 guns and sustained 16,000 casualties, and a further 9,000 deserted that night. The French, too, had lost heavily, so much so that Napoleon did not order the immediate pursuit that should have completed his victory. Thus the Prussian army, with the determined Blücher still at its head, was given the two days it needed to recover and appear at Waterloo.

Even so, on the evening of 16 June, the situation appeared reasonably satisfactory to Napoleon: the two Allied armies had been kept apart and Blücher had been well thrashed. He felt confident, therefore, that with two army corps and the Guard almost untouched, he would be able to do the same to Wellington. Meanwhile, what had been happening at Quatre Bras, and why had Ney not joined the battle at Ligny? Why, too, had D'Erlon not appeared? To answer these questions, we must examine Quatre Bras.

IV. QUATRE BRAS

The occupation of Quatre Bras was to have been a decisive point in Napoleon's campaign – but he was forestalled. Early on 15 June, realizing Napoleon's true intention, Wellington had given orders for his army to concentrate there. That evening he attended the Duchess of Richmond's ball in Brussels, by which time Prince Bernhard of Saxe Weimar, on his own initiative, had occupied the crossroads with 4,000 infantry and eight guns, thus forestalling the arrival of 1,700 French light troops. Tall corn concealed the relative weakness of the Prince's position so that the French did not push on, but by nightfall, the French were up at the position in strength. Fortunately, Prince William of Orange's chief of staff, General Constant de Rebeque, reinforced the position with the whole of one division in contravention of existing orders – but knowing the Duke's intention – and in so doing saved the army.

At 4.00 p.m. on 16 June, the rest of the Allied army began marching southwards from Brussels to Quatre Bras. Wellington himself rose at 5.30 a.m., and at 10.00 a.m. he rode into Quatre Bras. He found that the Prince of Orange had deployed Lieutenant General Baron Perponcher's Dutch–Belgian division – about 7,000 men and eight guns – in the Bossu wood, with a strong skirmish line out in front. This and the rolling country still concealed his weakness, and Ney now had Reille's complete corps of 21,000 men and 60 guns around Frasnes, 2 miles south. Approving these dispositions, and to fill time while the main army came up, Wellington rode over to meet Blücher at Ligny. When he returned, things had changed for the worse. By 2.30 p.m., the Allied strength had increased by only a further eight guns and a brigade of Brunswickers, while the French had captured Piraumont, Gemioncourt and the farm of Quatre Bras itself; only Bossu wood remained in Allied hands. It was a miracle that the French had taken as long as they had – owing partly to a lack of clear orders from Napoleon, and partly to lethargy on the parts of Ney and Reille, both of whom had a healthy respect for Wellington and feared that a large force was concealed on the reverse slope. This was a direct result of their experience in Spain and an excellent example of the importance of the psychological factor in war. Both agreed, therefore, that it would be best to await the arrival of D'Erlon's corps.

Wellington quickly realized the danger of his position. Lieutenant General Sir Thomas Picton's 5th Division and the Brunswick Division were within striking distance, and they were at once launched in a counter-attack which recaptured Quatre Bras and the line of the Nivelles–Ligny road. Thus, when – at about 4.15 p.m. – Ney received a dispatch from Napoleon ordering him to destroy immediately any force to his front and then swing right to envelop the Prussians, the Allies were strong enough to hold their positions.

The attack, by almost 20,000 French troops, was general along the Allied line: in the centre and left it was held, but the Dutch–Belgian troops in Bossu wood gave way. The Duke of Brunswick's leading brigade was committed to hold the position but it, too, broke and fled. The result would have been a disaster for the Allies but for the arrival of the two leading brigades of the British 3rd Division: Baron Ludwig von Kielmannsegge's 1 Hanoverian Brigade and Major General Colin Halkett's 5 Infantry Brigade. As they came up, Wellington directed the Hanoverians to extend the 5th Division's line south-east along the Ligny road as far as the wood of Paradis, and 5 Brigade was echeloned from Quatre Bras into Bossu wood, protecting the crossroads itself and guarding the rear exits from the wood. Thus, the flight of the Brunswickers and Dutch–Belgians, and the death of the young Duke of Brunswick while trying to rally them (his father had been killed at Auerstadt in 1806), had no permanent effect. The Prince of

Orange almost did, though, as he ordered the battalions of 5 Brigade to form line. Although Halkett countermanded the order, all three battalions were caught by French cavalry before they had completed forming square and were badly mauled. Only the steadfastness of the 5th Division held off Ney's attack.

Ney renewed the attack at 5.00 p.m., but his cavalry, led by Marshal François Kellermann, found the Allied infantry well prepared: the cavalry could only swirl around the Allied squares, subjected to devastating volley fire. The attack faltered and withdrew. As it did so, fresh reinforcements from the Brunswick Division and 1 Guards Brigade came up, and the crisis was over. The Allies now outnumbered Ney 36,000 men and 70 guns to around 17,000 effectives and 60 guns. It was Wellington's turn to attack.

At 6.30 p.m., the Allied bugles and drums sounded the advance. The exhausted French were driven out of Piraumont and Gemioncourt, but the Guards Brigade took heavy losses in clearing Bossu wood. Meanwhile, the French cavalry did sterling work covering the withdrawal of Ney's main body back to Frasnes, where he had begun. With no cavalry available – it had a march of 52 miles before it – Wellington could not press the pursuit, and in the end the battle must be accounted a draw. Both sides had prevented the other from achieving its objectives: Ney had kept Wellington from effecting a junction with Blücher, and Wellington had prevented the envelopment and destruction of Blücher, who was able to withdraw. Of the two accomplishments, however, Wellington's was by far the more significant.

The outcome of Quatre Bras – or Ligny – might well have been quite different if D'Erlon's corps had ever become engaged. It had not, having spent the entire day marching and counter-marching between Ligny and Quatre Bras. Napoleon's original plan called for D'Erlon to be detached from Ney's army and to march to reinforce the main effort at Ligny if summoned. D'Erlon was held back by Ney at Frasnes ready for this. But Napoleon's instructions to Ney at 4.15 p.m., telling him to begin his envelopment, did not make clear that Napoleon himself was facing the whole Prussian army and that D'Erlon's corps was urgently required. Ney therefore called up

D'Erlon to support his attack. D'Erlon started out, but never arrived. He was halted short of Quatre Bras by a message from Napoleon instructing him to march on Ligny – which he did, informing Ney that he had gone. When he received this news, Ney was practically beside himself with rage. To cap it all, he received a message from the Emperor telling him to look sharp and finish off the business at Quatre Bras: certainly, either Ney's or D'Erlon's arrival at Ligny would have led to the destruction of Blücher's army. Not unnaturally, Ney, in the face of mounting Allied resistance, once more summoned D'Erlon, who halted short of the Ligny battlefield, turned round and began marching back. He arrived too late – both battles had ended. The D'Erlon fiasco almost certainly robbed Napoleon of victory. It prevented him from achieving two decisive points in his campaign: the seizure of Quatre Bras – and thus the separation of the Allies – and the destruction of Blücher.

V. INTO POSITION

By 9.00 p.m. on 16 June, firing at Ligny and Quatre Bras had ceased. Wellington and his staff trotted back to Genappe, where supper was ordered at the Roi d'Espagne inn. He assumed that Blücher had repulsed the enemy: he had received a message in the late afternoon from Gneisenau, who said that although the villages north of the Ligny stream had not fallen, the best he could hope for was to hold his position until dark. It was not until early on 17 June that the true picture emerged: the Prussians had been beaten, but not routed, and had fallen back on Wavre, 18 miles to the north. Falling back on Wavre was the best thing they could have done, for, despite the distance, they were still able to keep in touch with Wellington. Had they withdrawn eastwards on their communications, they would not have been. Wellington, digesting the news, remarked:

> Old Blucher has had a damned good licking and gone back to Wavre, eighteen miles. As he has gone back, we must go too. I suppose in England they will say we have been licked. I can't help it.

But he knew that Wavre was only 7 miles east of the Brussels road, and that if he fell back to conform to the Prussians, a combined challenge to Napoleon was certainly still possible. Wellington has been criticized for adopting a static, defensive posture at Waterloo, but this is to misunderstand the bigger picture. He was operating as one wing of a multinational army. By the early hours of 18 June, he had received a promise of support from Blücher. He therefore knew that his task was essentially to fix the French with a defensive action – force Napoleon to commit himself to a set-piece battle, deprive him of his freedom of action – and set him up for a counter-attack by the Prussian army from the east.

It is sometimes said that Wellington had reconnoitred the Waterloo position a year before. Modern scholarship has cast doubt on this, but either way, the position was really the only viable blocking position south of Brussels. The low ridge dominated the two main approach roads only a mile south of their junction at Mont St Jean. The frontage was some 3,500 yards and so, given the size of force available, could be held in depth. It offered, too, a reverse slope, much favoured by Wellington. Closer country to the east would hinder any attempt to turn the Allied left, although it would also slow up the approach of the Prussians. The position had two weaknesses: on the Allied right, the ridge curved towards the French and petered out near the Nivelles road; and in the centre, a re-entrant broke the continuity. The weakness on the right was certainly a worry, and Wellington feared that Napoleon, using his classic battle system, would fix him with a frontal assault and then turn the Allied right flank. Accordingly, he detached to the area of Hal a strong flank guard of 17,000 men and 30 guns – a big detachment given the force ratios – under Prince Frederick of Orange. This force would be too far off to affect the battle if no flank attack emerged. A second force of divisional strength guarded the near right around Hougoumont at Braine l'Alleud, but this could be summoned within an hour if needed.

The main position on the ridge was held by four divisions. On the east side of the main road a small corps under Picton, consisting of the 5th Division, with four brigades, and two brigades of the 6th Division, was deployed in line on the reverse slope. The main effort was to the west side of the road, where a corps under Prince William of Orange held the centre, in line with Picton. First was the 3rd Division, which, like Picton's corps, found cover not only on the slope but also behind hedges (now gone) and along the Charleroi road, which was sunken where it crossed the Brussels road. Beyond the 3rd Division, the Guards Division, of two brigades, continued the line behind Hougoumont, with two cavalry brigades in immediate support. In front of these dispositions was placed the bulk of the Allied artillery, the guns spread out with muzzles just clearing the crest line, the gunners with orders to engage concentrations of infantry and cavalry and not engage in counter-battery against the superior French artillery.

Below the ridge, three groups of buildings were held as strong points in advance of the main line, to break up French attacks and anchor the skirmish line. On the extreme left, the village of Smohain and the farms of Papelotte and La Haye were held by a brigade of Nassauers, angled towards the French and providing a secure line of departure for the oncoming Prussians. In the centre, astride the main road, the farm of La Haye Sainte was held by a KGL rifle battalion, and on the opposite side of the road a large sandpit was held by a battalion of the 95th Rifles. This outpost protected the approach up the re-entrant. Finally, the substantial farm complex of Hougoumont Manor, with its farm buildings, walled gardens and orchard dominated the vulnerable Allied right. It was held by a provisional brigade made up of the light companies of the Guards battalions, a Hanoverian rifle battalion and a Nassau battalion.

Early in the morning of 18 June, Napoleon held a conference with key members of his staff. Soult suggested recalling Grouchy but this was rejected out of hand. General Antoine Drouot, the veteran commander of artillery, pointed out that heavy rain during the night had soaked the ground and made movement of guns impossible. Napoleon therefore agreed to a delay of all action until 1.00 p.m. – and it was this that would prove his undoing: it is very hard to believe that had he attacked at once Wellington could have held out long enough for Blücher to arrive.

Napoleon's battle plan was simple, and no time was to be lost in manoeuvre: Wellington was to be swept aside by a series of attritional sledgehammer blows. The attack order was only a few sentences. On the French left, Reille's II Corps was drawn up in front of Hougoumont, three divisions in line, with Kellermann's III Cavalry Corps in support. Reille was to pin the Allied left by attacking Hougoumont with only one division, that of Prince Jérôme Bonaparte, just before midday. In the centre and right, D'Erlon's I Corps, with four divisions, supported by a battery of 80 guns, was formed between La Belle Alliance and Papelotte. Behind him, on the main road, were Lobau's VI Corps (two divisions) and the Guard Corps. The remaining two cavalry corps, of General Count Edouard Milhaud and General Charles Lefebvre-Desnouettes, were in echelon behind D'Erlon's centre-right. At 1.30 p.m., the main attack would be launched under Ney's command. The artillery would blast Picton's corps, and D'Erlon and Reille would advance, smash through the centre and seize and hold Mont St Jean. Lobau, the Guard and the cavalry would be committed by the Emperor to finish the Allies and conduct any pursuit. It was a plan of simplicity and concentration, if not of economy or flexibility.

VI. WATERLOO

Jérôme Bonaparte's attack on Hougoumont opened earlier than planned, at 11.50 a.m. Contrary to the Emperor's intention, this developed into a major offensive, and it was halted by the defenders' fire. Wellington reinforced the batteries with a troop of howitzers to shell over Hougoumont into the wood and brought up a KGL infantry brigade from Major General Sir Henry Clinton's 2nd Division Anglo-German to reinforce the Guards Division. At 12.30 p.m., Bonaparte renewed the attack, reinforced by part of Major General Maximilien Foy's division. This time the French carried the wood and the orchard. As this threatened the safety of his outpost, Wellington sent in a battalion of Guards to clear the French; this succeeded, but one party of French managed to enter the manor house and open the gate, leading to the celebrated incident in which the gate

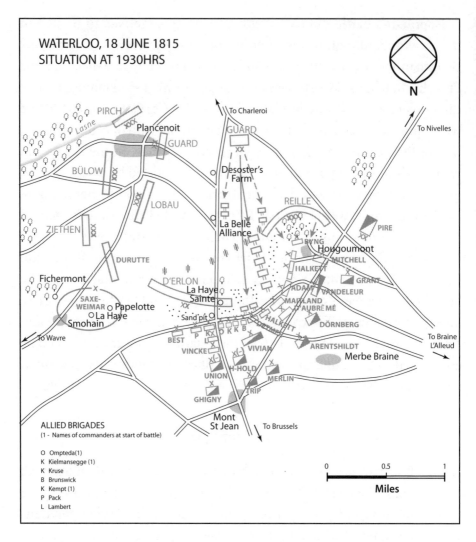

Map 4: Waterloo, 18 June 1815

was closed by the Guards, and to clear which another four companies of Guards were committed. Thus, Hougoumont acted throughout the day as a magnet for Reille's corps: some 14,000 troops – most of the corps – kept up a continuous attack, losing over half their number. By contrast, Wellington committed about 3,500 troops in the farm and thus tied up Reille most economically.

Behind the main Allied line, forming the second echelon, were seven brigades of cavalry deployed under the command of the Earl of Uxbridge, tasked with counter-attack and counter-penetration. Two heavy brigades – the Household and Union – covered the centre, either side of the main road. On the left, behind Papelotte, were three light brigades of British and KGL, and a further three Dutch–Belgian light brigades, which covered the right-centre behind Mont St Jean. Wellington's uncommitted reserves were, first, Clinton's 2nd Division and, second, the Brunswick Division, at Merbe Braine. Lieutenant General David Chassé's division, at Braine l'Alleud, was also available for rapid deployment. Thus, although narrow, the position was held in some depth: 1½ miles from the skirmish line in front of the strong points to the cavalry in front of Mont St Jean. This depth shows clearly Wellington's intention: to hold his position, soaking up French attacks and setting Napoleon up for Blücher's flank attack.

The Emperor established his command post at the farm at La Belle Alliance, where he could see the front of the Allied position but not its depth, nor the valley between him and it. He was much impressed by those Allied troops he could see:

> How steadily those troops take the ground! How beautifully those cavalry form! Look at those grey horses! Who are those fine horsemen? These are fine troops, but in half an hour I shall cut them to pieces!

Napoleon was aware that Blücher was still capable of action, but clearly did not appreciate the old man's determination to settle accounts. Napoleon was therefore obliged to divide his force in order to extend the strategy of the central position. On 17 June, Marshal Grouchy, with Vandamme's III Corps, Gérard's IV Corps and Pajol's I Cavalry Corps – more than one-third of the whole French army – had been ordered to pursue the Prussians towards Wavre. At 10.00 a.m. on 18 June, Soult sent further orders:

> His Majesty desires that you will head for Wavre in order to draw near to us, and to place yourself in touch with our operations, and to keep up your

communications with us, pushing before you those portions of the Prussian army which have taken this direction and which have halted at Wavre.

This was neither a recall nor an order to pursue independent action – and it was late being sent. Its effect will be seen later, but both it and Napoleon's intentions regarding Grouchy have been argued over by historians ever since.

In the Prussian camp, the army had regrouped at Wavre. Gneisenau, even after ten years of fighting for and against Napoleon, had still not grasped the strategy of the central position and did not understand that Grouchy's force was designed to keep the Prussians pinned down while the French main effort destroyed Wellington. Blücher, however, understood this perfectly, and although Gneisenau tried to keep the bulk of the Prussian army at Wavre, Blücher ordered the army to march. In a letter to Wellington he wrote:

> I will march at the head of my army to attack without delay the right flank of the enemy, if Napoleon should attempt anything against the Duke. In case the French do not attack today, I am of the opinion that we should attack the French army tomorrow.

Accordingly, von Bülow's corps had begun to march at daybreak, since it had not been engaged at Ligny and was unmauled. It was, however, the furthest east of Blücher's formations, so time was lost while a passage of lines was effected. It was followed by von Zieten's and von Pirch's corps. Thielmann's corps was left at Wavre. Grouchy, meanwhile, had begun a slow pursuit on 17 June and by nightfall had reached Gembloux. Here, early on 18 June, his patrols detected Prussian movement towards Waterloo; by making an early start, he would certainly have been in a good position to strike the Prussians in the flank, but he did not do so: the army only moved off at 8.00 a.m., by which time the two leading Prussian corps were well on their way. Grouchy himself was taking a late breakfast at 11.30 a.m. when the sound of the opening cannonade at Hougoumont was heard. Gérard at once urged that the army should march to join Napoleon, but Grouchy refused; thus, both the chance of intercepting the Prussians and the chance of unity with Napoleon on the battlefield passed.

While the attack against Hougoumont was under way, so too were preparations for the main attack. Just after 1.00 p.m., a battery of 84 guns opened up from the spur just east of the main road. This battery consisted of 24 twelve-pounders from the Guard, 40 eight-pounders from I Corps and 20 twelve-pounders from II and VI Corps. The effect was minimal, for most of Wellington's troops were concealed on the reverse slope; only a Dutch–Belgian brigade under Major General Willem van Bylandt, through an error, had been positioned on the forward slope.

D'Erlon's corps was forming up for the attack when movement was seen away to the east. Soon after, a patrol report came in: the movement was not, as had been thought possible, Grouchy, but the Prussian corps of Bülow, which was appearing in the direction of Chapelle St Lambert. Napoleon could not ignore this unexpected threat to his right wing, but equally clearly he was determined not to abandon the battle. He sent off new orders to Grouchy to rejoin the main army, and detached the Young Guard division, the Guard's heavy cavalry – two divisions – and Lobau's VI Corps to form a strong flank guard where Bülow's men were pushing in. This was alarmingly close, and cannon balls were already whisking into the French right flank.

This is important: the main attack on Wellington was to have been delivered by the three corps of Reille, D'Erlon and Lobau. The result of Reille's action at Hougoumont, and of Bülow's appearance, was that the force ratios for the attack shifted in the Allies' favour: instead of 3:1, the attack was effectively 1:1.

At 1.30 p.m., D'Erlon's corps began its advance towards the still unseen enemy; it was formed in unwieldy battalion columns, each division with 200 men in the first rank and followed by 27 files. Only one division, that of Major General Count Durutte on the extreme right, adopted mixed order. The artillery preparation was inadequate, and only one brigade of cavalry had been allotted in support; it was an attack, therefore, that lacked the vital ingredient of simultaneous action.

Preceded by a cloud of skirmishers, D'Erlon's men struggled across the 1,300 yards of muddy, uphill ground. As they did so they took terrible punishment from the Allied skirmish line and artillery. At first, however, it seemed that the attack might succeed: Bylandt's exposed brigade broke and fled; a German battalion on the main road was cut to pieces by the French cavalry; the sandpit was carried; and, on the extreme right, Papelotte and Frischermont were captured from the Nassauers. Had proper cavalry and horse-artillery support been allocated, who can say what would have happened? As it was, the attack ran out of steam, and Picton's 5th Division, moving up to the crest, shattered D'Erlon's columns with murderous volley fire – even though Picton himself was killed. The defeat of D'Erlon was completed by the famous charge of the British heavy cavalry. The Household Brigade charged the cuirassiers on the main road, then wheeled into D'Erlon's left flank. At the same time, the Union Brigade charged the front of the French column. The effect was devastating: 3,000 French surrendered, two eagles were captured, 1,000 men were killed and, within minutes, the remaining 9,000 men of the corps were fleeing in disarray.

Had the counter-attack stopped there, it could have been held up as a superbly contrasting example of the successful simultaneous effect of artillery, infantry and cavalry on suitable ground. But it did not stop there. The wildly excited British cavalry plunged on across the valley and into the French artillery battery. Although the guns were reached, the horses, given the bad going, were blown, and Napoleon, judging the moment with customary skill, launched a strong force of Polish lancers and cuirassiers in a counter-charge. The result was that 1,000 out of 2,500 men in the Union Brigade were felled. A similar fate befell the Household Brigade, as it also did Major General Sir John Vandeleur's light cavalry brigade, which was dispatched from the Allied left to help extricate the survivors. In all, some 2,500 Allied horsemen were lost, and so, although Wellington had succeeded in pinning down Reille and routing D'Erlon, his cavalry's rashness had deprived him of much of the striking power of the second echelon of the defence. But, above all, the Allies had gained what they most needed: time.

In the lull following the repulse of D'Erlon's attack and the Allied cavalry action, Wellington reoccupied the sandpit, reinforced the garrison of La Haye Sainte, and re-formed Picton's corps under the command of Sir John Kempt. Bylandt's brigade was also re-formed, and an additional brigade brought into the line from the 2nd Division. On the far left, the Allies also reoccupied Papelotte. Napoleon, meanwhile, was becoming increasingly anxious. It was quite obvious now that Grouchy would not appear but that the Prussians would. He was faced, therefore, with the choice of either abandoning the battle or flinging everything he had left at Wellington. There was no doubt which course he would pursue.

At 3.30 p.m., Ney was ordered to take La Haye Sainte at any cost, and the Guard Corps was moved forward to where Lobau's VI Corps had been ready to exploit any break-in. Ney led forward one weak division of D'Erlon's corps – all that had so far rallied – to take the farm, but was thrown back. As he withdrew, he was sure he could see signs of an Allied retreat. What he saw, in fact, was wounded men going towards the rear, ambulances and ammunition wagons, and a regiment of Dutch–Belgian cavalry in disarray. To Ney's overheated brain it seemed as if victory was imminent. Carried away with excitement, he ordered up a brigade of cuirassiers to turn the supposed retreat into a rout. In the excitement, this cavalry attack very quickly got out of hand. First, the whole of one division joined in, then the entire heavy cavalry corps, then a division of light cavalry. By 4.00 p.m., 5,000 horsemen were attacking the Allied centre unsupported either by infantry or, because of the direction of attack, by artillery.

With no threat of simultaneous action, the Allied line rapidly formed square. As the French cavalry charged up the ridge, they were subjected to a dreadful canister fire from the Allied artillery, whose gunners then sought shelter in the squares. The impetus of the charge broke: no effort was made to carry off or spike the Allied guns, and the cavalry had no means to shake the solidity of the infantry. As the force of the charge waned, the remnants of the Allied cavalry counter-attacked and threw back the French. But they re-formed and came on again – to receive the same treatment. Even so, some of the squares received severe handling: one young officer wrote:

> During the battle our squares presented a shocking sight, inside we were nearly suffocated with the smoke and smell of burned cartridges. It was impossible to move a yard without treading on a wounded comrade, or upon the bodies of the dead, and the loud groans of our wounded and dying was most appalling.

Napoleon looked on, first in disbelief and then with anger. Even so, he was forced to commit, at Ney's request, the remainder of his cavalry to extricate the rest. But the prevailing air of excitement was too much, and these horsemen, too, were carried away in the charge. Altogether, eight charges were made, and all were repulsed. By 5.00 p.m., Napoleon had no formed body of cavalry uncommitted, and by 6.00 p.m., the French cavalry was a spent force. And yet there were several uncommitted French infantry divisions available; only at 6.00 p.m. did Ney remember them, collect a division-and-a-half of Reille's corps and lead them forward. But these troops never reached the Allied position: the British artillery inflicted 1,000 casualties in ten minutes, and this was enough.

In the wake of the failed cavalry attack, Napoleon was forced to take account of Bülow's Prussians, who had pushed Lobau's VI Corps back around Plancenoit. This was alarmingly close, and Prussian artillery fire was now whistling onto the Charleroi road. Next, Napoleon realized that his only chance of victory – or, at least, of avoiding defeat – now lay in capturing La Haye Sainte and, from there, smashing Wellington's centre. Ney, despite all his ineptitude so far, was again ordered to take the farm. This time, probably accidentally, he attacked with an infantry division supported by cavalry and guns: the simultaneous, coordinated attack succeeded where all else had failed, and both the farm and the sandpit were captured. Ney at once sited his guns only 300 yards from the Allied centre and opened a devastating fire. Success now really was a possibility, for Wellington's centre was wavering. Ney sent an urgent message to Napoleon for troops – and Napoleon refused him. This was indeed the moment of crisis, when an all-out attack by the Guard would certainly have succeeded. But Napoleon could not oblige: Bülow had succeeded in routing the Young Guard, and another division of the Guard had to be detached to shove up the French right. This it succeeded in doing, but the move allowed the crisis in the Allied centre to pass. The earlier troop movements to support Hougoumont had placed Wellington's immediate reserve much closer in, and he was thus able to bring the Brunswick Division quickly into the centre to shore up the position. Of equal importance, the leading element of von Zieten's Prussian corps were now coming up on the Allied left, behind Smohain, tipping the force ratio decisively.

It was now around 7.00 p.m., and Napoleon, believing the situation on his right to have been stabilized, felt that he could turn his attention back to the centre. His last remaining reserve was the uncommitted part of the Guard Corps: one division of nine battalions – the Old Guard. As the Guardsmen moved forward, dark masses of troops could clearly be seen; Napoleon had his aides announce that they were Grouchy's men, but incoming cannon fire soon turned the French troops' elation to fear. All eyes turned to the Guard.

Wellington was ready. The centre was now strengthened, and von Zieten's corps was moving into position on the left. Accounts of the actual attack vary considerably, but it seems that the attacking column veered towards the Allied right-centre and, as it did so, became spread out. The battalions at the rear then came up on the left, forming two columns. Thus, the main attack came in with La Haye Sainte on the Guard's right and Hougoumont on its left, up against the British Guards Division and 3rd Division. Each of the two columns was dealt with sequentially by Wellington. The column facing the 3rd Division found all three brigades in line and was met by concentrated artillery fire and musketry. The attack ground to a halt. Farther west, the British Guardsmen were lying down behind the road. When the French column was only 60 yards away,

Wellington himself gave his celebrated order: 'Stand up, Guards'; then, 'Now Maitland, now is your time.' At 20 yards, the Guards poured in a series of volleys: the Grenadiers of the Guard stopped, then fell back.

But the attack was not yet over. The Chasseur battalions of the Guard were still moving forward, and these came up on the extreme left. Waiting for them was Major General Sir Frederick Adam's light brigade, which Wellington had moved forward from the reserve. One of its battalions, the 52nd, generally reckoned one of the outstanding infantry regiments of the period, was ordered to change formation so as to take the French in the flank. It is probable that no other infantry regiment could have done this at speed, but the 52nd did. As the Chasseurs came up, they too were subjected to devastating close-range volley fire. They halted, and Wellington ordered an immediate charge with the bayonet. In the ensuing mêlée, both sides lost heavily, but the French had lost all momentum and were unable to deploy. Within a short time, the Guard was in full, if controlled, retreat.

Why was the invincible Guard defeated? It was an army corps in its own right, with infantry divisions, light troops, cavalry, artillery and engineers. At its height it numbered some 40,000 men. During the Battle of Waterloo, it had been committed piecemeal to shore up Napoleon's position, so only a maximum of nine battalions remained for the final attack: not enough to achieve a decision. Moreover, in the past it had invariably been committed against an already penetrated and partly beaten enemy; yet here it was put against unbroken infantry with their hearts fully in the business, in an excellent defensive position: the Guard could not win.

This was the moment in which the battle was won. The French army could see both von Zieten's and von Bülow's corps in the attack, and the unbelievable sight of the Guard in retreat was too much: with cries of 'Sauve qui peut!', the army began to break and flee. As it did so, Wellington waved his hat, ordering a general advance; the whole Allied army gave a loud hurrah, and the men threw themselves on the beaten French. Napoleon did what he could to stem the rout. He formed three squares from available units of the Guard to check the Allied advance. The Guard, both here and around Plancenoit, certainly preserved perfect discipline and covered the flight of the rest; the last square of the Middle and Old Guard famously preferred death to surrender when offered the choice by Maitland. But it could not check the Allied advance. Napoleon, narrowly avoiding capture, made off for Genappe.

At about 9.00 p.m., Blücher and Wellington met at last at the inn at La Belle Alliance. It was immediately settled that the Prussian cavalry would conduct the pursuit, for the main Allied army was exhausted and, besides, had suffered 15,000 casualties against the Prussians 9,000. Gneisenau himself pressed the pursuit, going as far as the River Dyle before breaking contact. As for the French, the Emperor rallied the army at Phillippeville, but it was a spent force. It had lost 25,000 casualties, 8,000 prisoners, 8,000 deserters and 220 guns. Including the casualties of Ligny and Quatre Bras, losses amounted to nearly half the army. Grouchy had fought an inconclusive battle with the Prussians at Wavre. As the French fell back, the Allies followed up with skirmishes and sieges. Napoleon had no choice but once again to abdicate. On 4 July, Paris surrendered, and on 8 July, Louis XVIII once more sat on this throne. The long struggle of the Revolutionary and Napoleonic Wars was over at last: Waterloo had decided it. In its aftermath, the Congress of Vienna laid down the system of collective security in Europe which maintained peace for the next 50 years.

4

Gettysburg and the Siege of Vicksburg, 1863: Confederate High Tide

I. WAR IN THE INDUSTRIAL AGE

By the spring of 1862, the leadership of both sides in the American Civil War had had to confront the fact that the war was going to be longer and bloodier than anyone had predicted. In the wake of First Bull Run, President Abraham Lincoln called for an increase in volunteers from 70,000 to 400,000, to serve for three years rather than the three months that, in the tradition of the Continental Militia, had previously been required. Faced with the prospect of secession by Maryland, the state that effectively hosted the Federal capital, Lincoln had declared martial law there early in the war; in the succeeding months, he extended this throughout other border states, such as Kentucky, Delaware, Missouri and West Virginia, where opinion was divided between secessionist and unionist. This caused many – the so-called Copperheads – to question the value of preserving a union on the basis of enforcement: perhaps it would be better just to let the Southern states go. On the other hand, the Radicals saw the war as the chance to achieve social change in the South – in particular, to abolish slavery.

The Confederate Congress had required a one-year enlistment from its first recruits – a year that was about to expire. Volunteers were already harder to come by, for the Confederate population was a fraction of that of the North: 9 million – including 4 million black slaves – as against 22 million. Moreover, the Confederacy had been founded on the principles of State rights over Federal powers, individualism and limited government. Many state governors, therefore, tended to keep hold of their troops for local defence, rather than commit them to the Confederate field armies. On 16 April 1862, the Confederate Congress passed the Conscription Act, obliging all white males between the ages of 18 and 45 to register for military service. The Confederacy and its President, Jefferson Davis, were finding out the hard way that the demands of total war on one hand and of limited government on the other posed a dilemma that could not be solved.

As apparent as the disparity in population between North and South was the disparity in industrial production. Since the end of the Napoleonic Wars, the full impact of the Industrial Revolution on war had begun to be felt: rifled muskets, modern fusing of shells, the percussion cap, the railway and the telegraph were all increasingly evident. There is, of course, a relationship between the introduction of new technologies and the battlefield employment of troops. This relationship is not constant, because military technologies do not advance in complete capability leaps: cutting-edge and legacy equipments coexist, and this gradual process of transition tends to obscure tactical or operational innovation. In 1863, the influence of Napoleon on warfare was profound: every general, including Lee, wanted to be him – to crush the enemy's army in a great battle and march into his capital, achieving thus the elusive goal of decisive victory. So although the armies of the civil war were armed with a different generation of weapons, their tactics were still those of Leipzig and Waterloo. The results were the casualty rates of Antietam, Fredericksburg and Gettysburg.

But the disparity in the industrial capacity of the two sides was marked. The Federal Quartermaster General's office, headed by Montgomery Meigs, employed over 7,000 clerks and was an administrative machine that kept the Union armies clothed, fed and supplied with ammunition: it had no effective counterpart in Richmond. Throughout the war, the North produced 90 per cent of its own requirements for manufactured goods, and 97 per cent of its own armaments. The comparable Confederate figures were 10 per cent and 3 per cent. This meant that, as the war progressed, commanders like George Brinton McClellan on the Union side and Robert E. Lee on the Confederate handled responsibilities far greater than, for example, Irvin McDowell, P. G. T. Beauregard or Joseph Johnston had done. The generals of 1861 had commanded armies of up to 35,000 men: McClellan and Lee commanded armies of up to 150,000. McClellan has been criticized for the failure of his Peninsular Campaign, but the very act of transporting an army of more than 120,000 men to the peninsula and maintaining it in the field was a formidable achievement, requiring a level of staff work beyond the capability of any organization that had existed in 1861.

The events of the first year of war had led both sides to make changes in the senior levels of their military commands. In the North, Major General Henry Wager Halleck, known as Old Brains, was brought to Washington in 1862 to serve as Commander-in-Chief of the Union armies. McClellan, a superb organizer and very popular with the troops, commanded the Army of the Potomac. Despite his administrative skills, including the creation of a proper military staff, he was cautious, even timid, about committing his army to battle. Undoubtedly, his talents in training, drill and logistics brought about the creation of the powerful Union army that eventually delivered victory, but he was less skilled in wielding that army in battle. It was his caution and lack of battlefield skill that caused Lincoln to dismiss him in early 1863 and replace him with Ambrose Burnside. But Burnside did not last long against Lee and in turn was replaced by 'Fighting Joe' Hooker. Hooker fared no better, and, after the Wilderness, he was succeeded by George Gordon Meade – 'Old Snapping Turtle'.

In the South, General Robert E. Lee succeeded to the command of the Army of Northern Virginia when Johnston was wounded at Fair Oaks. Almost immediately he began the offensive that became known as the Seven Days, and drove McClellan from the gates of Richmond. Lee's assumption of command was perhaps more significant to the destiny of the South than McClellan's organizational innovations were to that of the North. Lee instituted for the first time a Napoleonic corps system, dividing his army into two corps, each of three divisions, under Lieutenant Generals James Longstreet and Thomas 'Stonewall' Jackson. But Lee's greatest contribution was his personal qualities and style of leadership, including his ability to manage Jefferson Davis and the Confederate Congress. While both Beauregard and Johnston had quarrelled with Davis and each other, Lee's tact did much to reduce the tensions in a society engaged in a revolutionary struggle. Moreover, in contrast to McClellan, Lee was always willing to take risk: to divide his numerically inferior army in the face of an enemy in order to outflank or envelop his opponent; and to launch frontal attacks against strong positions in the belief that superior moral qualities would make up for inferior troop numbers and firepower. Often he was right; but the Confederacy could not afford the drain on its manpower that Lee demanded, haunted as he was by the ghost of Napoleon.

By early 1863, the effects of this drain on manpower, and especially on its officers, had begun to be sorely felt by the Confederacy. In an age when little was demanded of a regimental officer save that he see to the men's welfare and be brave in action, the sense of honour held by many Southerners frequently led them to expose themselves to enemy fire at the head of their men. The result was a heavy loss of life among battalion, brigade and divisional commanders and staffs. The death of 'Stonewall' Jackson after the Battle of Chancellorsville, in May 1863, was only the most serious of a long list of casualties that deprived the Confederate armies of many of their best commanders. But Lee's army in Virginia was still a formidable force; and news of the Confederate victory at Chickamauga, in northern Georgia, renewed Southern hopes that Confederate arms might yet triumph.

II. THE CAMPAIGN IN MARYLAND

Despite all the difficulties, a string of Confederate victories – the Wilderness, Fredericksburg, Chancellorsville, Chickamauga – were giving strength to the Copperhead cause in the north. One more big setback for the North might just do what Yorktown had done nearly a century before: persuade the dominant power that the war was not worth the expenditure of more lives and treasure. There were other factors, too. The Union blockade was closing Confederate ports and the Southern economy was increasingly fragile. The war in the West was going badly, too, with the Union in control of much of Louisiana and Tennessee, and with Vicksburg under siege. There was also the dim Southern hope of foreign intervention. One reason Lee sought a decisive engagement in the North during July was the hope that such a victory would convince Britain or France, or both, to provide active military and naval assistance to the Confederacy. But the fact was that Lincoln's Emancipation Proclamation after Antietam had made it impossible for the British to intervene, and Napoleon III would not move on his own.

The beleaguered Confederacy's best hope of survival was, it seemed, one big decisive battle in the East. Lee was therefore determined to seize the initiative and take the war to the North. Maryland, with its strong Confederate sympathies, offered an obvious target: by marching into the state he might not only raise more troops – and even detach the state from the Union – but directly threaten the Federal capital as well. Such a threat would be bound to bring the Union army to a pitched battle: a battle that Lee was sure he could win. There was also the matter of supply. Confederate troops were always hungry and short of supplies. Marching north would allow Lee to feed his army from the rich farmland of Maryland and to seize Union stores of war materiel. In such a situation, the Confederacy might just be able to dictate the terms of a favourable peace.

Longstreet's corps rejoined the Army of Northern Virginia after the siege of Suffolk in late May. His two divisions raised Lee's strength to around 75,000 men – its greatest since the Seven Days, a year earlier – and this, along with Jackson's death, obliged Lee to reorganize his enlarged army. Longstreet retained command of I Corps, with the divisions of Lafayette McLaws, John B. Hood and George Pickett; Richard S. 'Dick' Ewell, whom the troops called Old Bald Head, was given II Corps, with the divisions of Major Generals Jubal Early, Robert Rodes and Edward Johnson; and A. P. Hill was promoted and given command of the new III Corps, with the divisions of Henry Heth, Dorsey Pender and Richard

Anderson. Each corps comprised three divisions plus artillery. J. E. B. Stuart retained command of the cavalry division. Next, Lee shifted his base of operations westward from the Wilderness to Culpeper on the Orange and Alexandria Railway. From there, Stuart's 10,000-strong cavalry force would act as a screen as the army moved into the Shenandoah Valley, keeping the Union scouts at bay.

III. OPENING MOVES

Stuart held a great review of his cavalry at Brandy Station, just north of Culpepper, on 5 June and was so pleased with it that he repeated it two days later for Lee. But news of the parade reached Union Major General Alfred Pleasanton, whose orders from Hooker were to 'disperse and destroy' Confederate forces. In obedience to those orders, he took about 11,000 troopers of his own to Brandy Station on 9 June, catching Stuart's men off guard. After a hard fight, the Confederate cavalry drove off Pleasanton's troopers in what was the largest cavalry action of the war. But Stuart's pride had been wounded, and a residual feeling of resentment would determine key actions in the coming campaign.

A week after the clash at Brandy Station, Lee ordered his three corps to begin the march north. Ewell's corps moved first, passing through Chester Gap on its way toward Winchester. On 14 June, Ewell surprised a Union brigade of about 5,000 at Winchester and inflicted a crushing defeat, taking almost the entire force prisoner. Ewell then marched on towards Sharpsburg, while Longstreet moved northward, east of the Blue Ridge Mountains, towards the passes of Ashby's Gap and Snicker's Gap.

Hooker, who at this point was still in command of the Army of the Potomac, had by now received enough reports from his cavalry to have guessed something of Lee's design. He therefore recommended to Washington an immediate attack to destroy Hill's corps, followed by a rapid descent on the Confederate capital of Richmond, which Lee had left uncovered. Lincoln, however, rejected this proposal on the ground that 'Lee's army, and not Richmond, is your true objective'. Grumbling loudly,

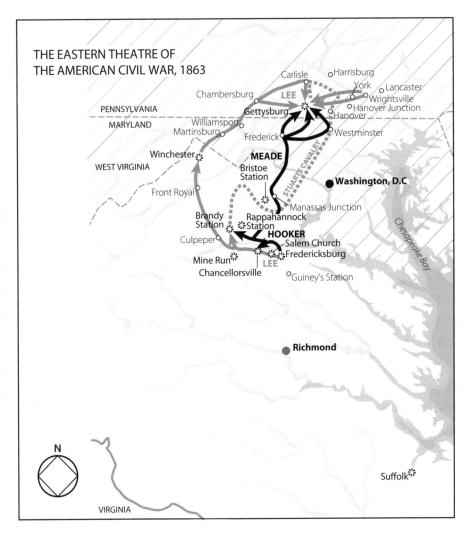

Map 5: The Eastern Theatre of the American Civil War, 1863

Hooker started north, keeping his army between Lee and the Federal capital.

Longstreet held his corps close to the passes into the Shenandoah Valley until it became clear that Hooker was heading north. Meanwhile, Hill's men moved on past Longstreet and followed Ewell across the Potomac River. While the infantry laboured north in the summer heat, Stuart's cavalry were hard at work keeping the Union cavalry at arm's length. But with his job almost finished, Stuart asked Lee's permission to mount a raid to plunder in the Union rear. Through Longstreet, Lee gave conditional approval, but stipulated that when Hooker crossed into Maryland, Stuart must rejoin the main army.

Stuart moved off on 25 June with about half his division, determined to ride right round the Union army just as he had done before the Seven Days and again after Antietam. But Hooker was also on the move, so Stuart had to ride a great distance to do this. Though he accomplished great deeds on his raid, throwing Washington into a panic and capturing 125 fully loaded Union supply wagons, he left Lee without eyes and ears as the army moved further into enemy territory. Once in Pennsylvania, without Stuart's reports to provide him with intelligence on enemy dispositions, Lee was blind and deaf.

Now leading the Confederate advance, Ewell's men had marched through Chambersburg. From there, Ewell dispatched one division, under Early, eastward towards the small college town of Gettysburg, while he took the rest of his corps north to Carlisle. Early's men met only scattered resistance from militia units and so pushed through Gettysburg to York and finally to Wrightsville, on the Susquehanna River. Early rejoined Ewell on 30 June north of Gettysburg.

On the Union side, Hooker had become embroiled in yet another dispute with his superiors, this time over the garrison of Harper's Ferry, and had threatened to resign. Already displeased by Hooker's performance and manner, Lincoln surprised him by calling his bluff and accepting his resignation. When the Union army reached the vicinity of Frederick, a courier informed Meade that he was now in command of the army. Meade was neither a strategist nor a master of campaigning, but at least he knew his own limitations. He continued to move the army northward on a course parallel to Lee's – towards Gettysburg.

IV. THE ARMIES CONVERGE: 1 JULY 1863

Lee learned of the change of Union commander, and of the proximity of the Army of the Potomac, on 28 June. He immediately ordered his corps commanders to concentrate either at Cashtown or the more centrally located Gettysburg. Meanwhile, the brigades of Union cavalry under Major General John Buford, riding ahead of Meade's main body, entered Gettysburg from the south on 30 June. Buford studied the ground north and west of the town and decided that a gentle tree-covered ridge, dominated by the white cupola of a Lutheran seminary, was defensible. He dismounted his men and took up a position just in front of the ridge on a low rise known locally as McPherson's Ridge. He knew that dismounted cavalry unsupported by artillery could not stop a determined infantry attack, but he hoped to hold on until he received support from Major General John Reynolds's I Corps, which was the leading formation of Meade's main body. The first contact between the two armies took place that afternoon, when a foraging Confederate brigade in search of shoes and hats became aware of Buford's cavalry. The news was soon carried to Confederate Major General 'Harry' Heth, who commanded the lead division of Hill's III Corps, west of Gettysburg.

The next morning, Heth had his division on the road by 5.00 a.m.: he meant to push the Union force – which he assessed to be of no great size – out of his way. Arriving outside the town at about 8.00 a.m., he deployed two brigades and sent them across Willoughby Run and up the ridge. Buford's troopers fought hard, and losses mounted on both sides. After nearly two hours of combat, the lead elements of Reynolds's corps arrived on the ridge. Reynolds himself rode to the front to assess the situation and was killed almost instantly by a Confederate sniper. But the rebels had not expected to encounter the veteran troops of the Army of the Potomac, and after another hour of close combat they pulled back, leaving the ridge in Union hands.

Lee arrived on the field at about 2.00 p.m., while Heth was reassessing the situation. Lee was, to say the least, surprised to find Union infantry at Gettysburg; what their strength was he could not tell. He was on the verge of calling off the action altogether when the lead elements of Ewell's corps, coming south from Carlisle, arrived on the Union flank. As quick to recognize an opportunity as ever, Lee decided to allow both corps to attack, and gave orders for a general advance.

On the Union side, Meade had by now a fair idea of Lee's dispositions and was moving towards Gettysburg. His army comprised no fewer than seven corps, plus a cavalry corps and artillery, which, even though Union corps were generally of only two divisions, meant that he had at least 95,000 men against Lee's 75,000 – assuming the Confederate cavalry showed up. Abner Doubleday's I Corps held a position due west of Gettysburg on McPherson Ridge, facing Hill, while Oliver Howard's XI Corps was falling in to Doubleday's right, facing Ewell. It was hoped that Henry Slocum's XII Corps would arrive soon. At first, Ewell's men made no progress, but around 2.30 p.m. Heth's division joined the attack from the west. This developed into one of the bloodiest struggles of the entire war. The Union line was well positioned, but the Confederate troops worked round to the flanks, decimating the Union regiments. The Union line withdrew through the town, pursued by the Confederates, onto the slightly higher ground of Cemetery Hill. A determined attack on Cemetery Hill that evening would undoubtedly have pushed the Union troops off, allowing the Confederates to adopt a strong defensive line which the Union forces would have been obliged to assault: another Fredericksburg would probably have been the outcome. But Lee had given orders that corps were not to become decisively engaged until the whole army was concentrated, and Longstreet's corps was still approaching along the Chambersburg Pike. Despite their heavy losses, Ewell's divisional commanders urged him to attack anyway, saying that Lee surely did not mean him to let such an opportunity be missed. But Ewell was not to be budged. The opportunity thus afforded the Union troops was not wasted, and by midnight, General Winfield Scott Hancock, the commander of II Corps, who had been sent ahead by Meade, had secured the position. The Confederates had had the best of the day, to be sure – but they had not won the battle.

V. THE BATTLES OF 2 JULY 1863

Meade, meanwhile, was at Taneytown, 9 miles south of Gettysburg, where he received a stream of dispatches and, late in the evening of 1 July, word from Hancock that the Gettysburg position was secure. Hancock also recommended that the Union army fight there, and not fall back to an alternative position at Pipe Creek. Meade accordingly sent word to his corps commanders. Slocum's XII Corps had arrived just as the day's fighting had ended; Dan Sickles's III Corps arrived after dark; Hancock's II Corps was bivouacked close by; and George Sykes's V Corps could be expected from Hanover early on 2 July. Only John Sedgwick's VI Corps, marching up from Manchester, Maryland, would not be available until the afternoon of 2 July. At 11.30 p.m. that night, Meade himself arrived on Cemetery Hill and placed his corps in a curving arc about 3 miles long, stretching from Culp's Hill on the right, across Cemetery Hill, along Cemetery Ridge, to two hills known as the Round Tops.

At about the same time as Meade was making his dispositions, Lee visited Ewell, on the Confederate left, to discuss the next day's operations. Lee suggested that Ewell might be able to turn the Union right flank, but Ewell replied that the Union positions were too strong. Lee considered occupying a defensive position on Seminary Ridge and inviting a Union attack; he also considered Longstreet's suggestion that the army move south, occupy a more favourable position and thus force a Union assault; yet another option he considered was retiring to the passes and awaiting developments. However, he rejected all these ideas in the belief that he had to maintain the initiative and make a breakthrough before the Union army gathered its full strength and the odds became insuperable. He therefore decided that Ewell should make a demonstration against Culp's Hill, and if the situation seemed favourable, he should develop a full-scale assault. The Confederate main effort, however, would be with Longstreet's corps on the right.

As dawn broke on 2 July, the armies faced each other on parallel ridges across an open plain. Both sides had been reinforced overnight. Longstreet had arrived with two of his divisions, those of McLaws and Hood, bringing the Confederate strength to around 50,000. Only Pickett's division, still on the march, and Stuart's cavalry were missing. Stuart was in fact moving north, to the east of Gettysburg, towards Carlisle, Pennsylvania. Longstreet's arrival, however, did not change the overall force ratios, since Lee was faced by three Union corps with a fourth closing on Gettysburg, so that the Union army now numbered at least 60,000 men. Without knowledge of these movements, which his cavalry should have provided, Lee decided to attack.

The position of Ewell's corps was by now well known to the Union troops on Culp's Hill, and so, believing his enemy to be fixed, Lee decided to strike from the south. There were, it seemed, no Union troops so far on the Round Tops; Lee therefore ordered Longstreet to attack in echelon up the Emmitsburg Road, in the expectation that he would strike the Union army in the flank and rear. Lee intended this move to begin early, but the orders did not go out until 11.00 a.m., a delay that was compounded by Longstreet's conviction that the Confederate army should slip past Meade's left and take up a position in his rear, thus forcing Meade to attack prepared positions. Longstreet was well known for his belief that, given the imbalance of forces, the Confederates should generally adopt a tactical defensive even when operationally they were on the offensive, since fighting from prepared positions gave the advantage to the defender. Thus, knowing Lee's intention but hoping to change it, he delayed his preparations for the attack; and even after he had begun to move, it took several hours to shift the troops southward, screened from Union view by Seminary Ridge, to their new assault positions.

On reaching those positions, Hood and McLaws were dismayed to find an entire Union corps deployed right across their axis of advance: Sickles had decided independently to advance his corps to the Emmitsburg Road from Cemetery Ridge, and in doing so had created an exposed salient that was now to bear the brunt of the Confederate attack. Lee's orders called for an attack in echelon of divisions sequentially from right to left, preceded by a bombardment from all the artillery within range. Hood's division went first, at about 4.00 p.m., attacking into the Devil's Den – a mass of elephant-sized boulders which soon made keeping formation impossible. Fighting quickly became hand-to-hand. Several Confederate regiments were able to bypass the worst ground and came close to the summit of Little Round Top. They were just beaten to it by Colonel Joshua Chamberlain's 20th Maine Regiment, and a meeting engagement developed. Hood's Texans put in three determined charges over the next hour, all of which were beaten off, and as they were withdrawing, Chamberlain's men counter-attacked, sweeping the Confederates off the hill and back into the Devil's Den.

At about the same time – it was now about 5.00 p.m. – Longstreet sent McLaws's division in to the attack. It swept over the Peach Orchard, shoving the defenders unceremoniously aside, and pushed on into the adjacent wheat field. Here the fighting was again hand-to-hand. Though McLaws's men had the better of this struggle, Confederate losses mounted to the point where the attack stalled on the banks of Plum Run. Now Anderson's division attacked. Hancock, who had charge of the Union centre, had thinned out this part of the line to support Sickles, and it was towards this weakened centre that Anderson's three brigades came charging in. One brigade actually reached the crest: for a moment the men looked down on the Union rear. A desperate Hancock ordered the 1st Minnesota Regiment, which had arrived, from Cemetery Hill, to counter-attack. The regiment lost more than 80 per cent of its strength, but its attack slowed the Confederate assault long enough to allow Hancock to establish a new defensive line. This line held, and Anderson's men began the long retreat back across the valley, having gained nothing for all their effort.

At the other end of the line of battle, Ewell had waited all day to put in his attack, which was to begin when he heard the guns firing to signal Longstreet's advance. One division assaulted Culp's Hill, and the second the saddle between Culp's Hill and Cemetery Hill. Both attacks made early progress, and for a moment a breakthrough again seemed possible. In the gathering dusk, Early's division actually broke through the Union line, but unsupported and faced with counter-attacks, it had to withdraw.

Both sides lost at least 10,000 men killed, wounded or missing that day.

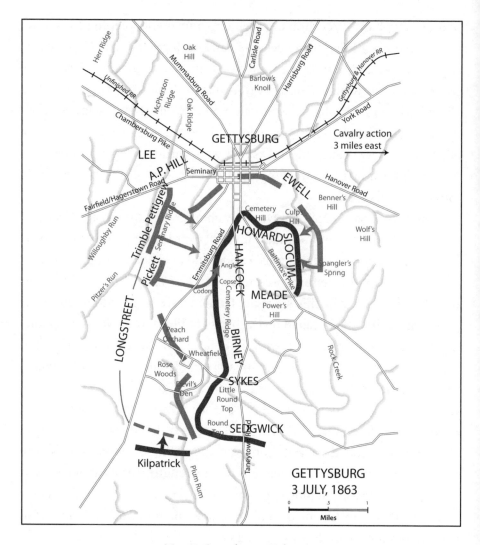

Map 6: Gettysburg, 3 July 1863

Lee had not broken the Union line, but he had come close three times. Meade was aware just how close, and called a conference that night to discuss a possible retreat; but his corps commanders were united in their determination to hold firm. He therefore turned to analyzing Lee's options and concluded that, having attacked both the left and the right and failed, Lee would try to force the Union centre. He was right.

VI. CLIMAX: THE BATTLES OF 3 JULY 1863

Turning over the events of the last two days in his mind, Lee believed success had only just eluded him and was yet within his grasp. Moreover, his remaining troops had now arrived: Pickett's Virginian division and, at last, Stuart's cavalry. He met Stuart with an uncharacteristic flash of anger; a less generous commander would have dismissed the man. Lee's army would not get any stronger; in fact, the longer he left things, the more likely it was that the Union force would increase. He had tried on the left; he had tried on the right. Should he try one of his famous night marches to envelop the enemy's flank and rear? No. Instead, he determined on a classic Napoleonic grand assault, massing all his forces at one point and trusting to morale, speed and momentum to break the enemy's will. Longstreet was horrified.

Lee's orders for 3 July called for an attack on the Union main position, led by Pickett's fresh division and reinforced by two brigades from Anderson's division. To Pickett's left, four of Heth's brigades were placed under the command of Johnson Pettigrew; Heth himself was wounded and out of action. Behind Pettigrew, two brigades of Dorsey Pender's division were left under Isaac Trimble, who had taken command after Pender's death in action the previous day. Altogether the assault corps would number 12,500 men: an impressive force but, as Longstreet observed, one-third smaller than the force that had attacked the Union line the day before and failed. Lee, however, argued that the earlier attacks had been neither properly coordinated nor properly supported by cavalry and guns. All the Confederate artillery within range –140 guns – would bombard the position before the assault, chiefly to silence the Union batteries, beginning at 1.00 p.m. But they would not fire during the assault, for Confederate ammunition was notoriously unreliable, and overhead fire, too, often caused more casualties among the gunners' own troops than among the enemy. When Lee outlined his plan, a protesting Longstreet tried everything short of outright disobedience to change his mind. Pickett, on the other hand, was delighted. His division had not taken part in the battle to date, and he fretted for the chance of glory.

The Union army, too, had been reinforced overnight. Sedgwick's VI Corps – the largest in the Army of the Potomac – brought Meade's strength to more than 70,000. Despite his belief that Lee would attack the centre – and perhaps because he most feared Lee's usual tactic of envelopment – Meade placed Sedgwick on the left, behind the Round Tops. However, the first action of 3 July took place neither on the left nor in the centre, but on the right, around Culp's Hill, where Slocum's corps, reinforced by men from I and VI Corps, faced the Confederate foothold on the southern spur. At dawn, five batteries of Union guns opened a devastating fire for half an hour, after which the Confederates tried three times to take the position by storm. But by now, the defenders had erected strong breast-works and the odds were too great. The battle swayed to and fro until about 10.30 a.m., by which time a final attempt by the Stonewall Brigade and a North Carolina brigade, and a half-hearted counter-attack by two Union regiments, had failed. The Confederates were at last forced to retreat back across Rock Creek. A pause followed, while the Confederate assault formed up and Meade watched in astonishment as his enemy prepared to take him head-on.

At 1.00 p.m., the Confederate artillery opened up, forcing the defend-ers to take cover, while the Union artillery fired back. After an hour, the Union fire slackened, deceiving the Southerners into thinking that the enemy's guns had been silenced. The Confederate guns also ceased fire, and, as the smoke of the cannonade slowly cleared, the assault divisions moved forward: 11 brigades, 42 regiments, 12,500 men, on a front of nearly a mile, advancing steadily at 100 yards every minute up the gentle slope. It was three-quarters of a mile from the Confederate guns to the Union breastworks, with barely a scrap of cover. The axis of the attack was a clump of trees in the centre of the Union line. As they closed on the enemy, the brigades executed a series of left obliques, which Longstreet had hoped would confuse the enemy and spread them out. As the range closed further, the line began to take artillery fire from Cemetery Hill and Little Round Top, but still the assault came on. Closing more now, the assault reached the Emmitsburg Road, and the Union guns on Cemetery

Ridge switched from ball to canister, a dreadful weapon like a huge shot-gun cartridge that – literally – ripped men to pieces and tore great holes in the ranks of the advancing regiments. The gaps were filled, and the assault frontage was now reduced to half a mile, but still the line came on, and now the Union infantry joined in with volley fire. It was as if the assault had been struck by a meteor. Whole regiments were swept away, leaving only a few men standing. At least 7,500 men – 60 per cent of the force – lay stricken on the field. But the tide was not quite spent: the dreaded rebel yell broke from the smoke as the remnants of Lewis Armistead's brigade, led by their general, broke into the Union position and went for the nearest Union battery. They reached the guns – the high tide of the Confederacy – but Armistead was shot dead and only a remnant of the 300 men who had pierced the Union line made it out again. As they went, the Union soldiers could be heard shouting in unison, 'Fredericksburg! Fredericksburg!'

What was left of Longstreet's corps went streaming back down the slope: the attack – known to history as Pickett's charge – had failed. Of Pickett's 5,000 men in the centre of the attack, only 800 were left fit for duty; over the three days of fighting, the Confederate army had lost 28,000 men – a third of its strength, and men it could not replace. Lee and Longstreet rode out to meet the survivors, conscious of the need to rally them for Meade's expected counter-attack. Lee would have launched one had he been in Meade's position, but Meade was content to watch Lee draw off. In any event, his own army was close to exhaustion, having lost 23,000 men over the three days.

The next day was 4 July, the 86th anniversary of the founding of the republic. Early in the day, in pouring rain, a wagon train stretching nearly 17 miles went off, bearing the Confederate wounded. At noon, covered by his cavalry, Lee began the long retreat into Virginia. On 5 July, he found the Potomac River too swollen by rain to cross near Hagerstown, but by the night of 13 July he was able to throw a pontoon bridge over the river and cross. Meade's pursuit, slow and hampered by rain, arrived to find the enemy gone. Lee never again went on an operational or strategic offensive; and he never again tried a Napoleonic grand attack against prepared

positions. That same day, the news came in that the Confederate fortress
of Vicksburg had fallen.

VII. VICKSBURG

The Confederate fortress of Vicksburg lay on a high bluff, dominating
a great horseshoe bend in the Mississippi River. From this position, its
powerful batteries, along with those at Haynes' Bluff, Drumgould's Bluff
and Grand Gulf, dominated and controlled both the east–west ferry crossing and the north–south traffic on the river. It was also the terminus of
two railway lines: the Vicksburg, Shreveport and Texas Railroad, running
westwards from the far bank opposite Vicksburg through Louisiana and
Texas; and the Southern Railroad of Mississippi, running eastwards to the
industrial manufacturing town of Jackson, where it connected with the
north–south New Orleans, Jackson and Great Mississippi Railroad. On
these railways were moved the food supplies from the western states on
which the Confederate field armies and major cities depended. Thus, the
Mississippi was both an obstacle and a highway: an obstacle to movement
across the continent, especially between the eastern and western states
of the Confederacy; and a trade highway between the city of St Louis
in the North and the Gulf of Mexico, where the Union now once more
controlled the port of New Orleans. Confederate President Jefferson Davis
called Vicksburg 'the nail head that holds the South's two halves together'.
Abraham Lincoln was equally clear about its importance: 'Vicksburg is the
key. The war can never be brought to a close until the key is in our pocket.'

The position of the city, high on the bluff on what was known as the de
Soto Peninsula, made it impossible to approach by amphibious assault.
North and east, the approaches were protected by the swamps of the Yazoo
Delta, stretching 200 miles from north to south and 50 miles from east
to west. To the west, the terrain of Louisiana was low-lying and marshy,
traversed by many creeks which were prone to flooding in winter. The
only good approach lay to the south-west, from territory controlled by the
Confederates. In addition to the natural defences, the Confederates had

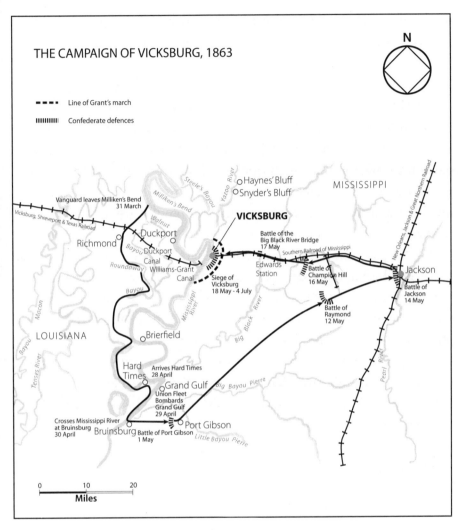

Map 7: The Campaign of Vicksburg, 1863

erected earthworks and dug trenches around the western and southern perimeter, dominated by a series of eight forts or redoubts. Confederate forces in the west were commanded by General Joseph Johnson and divided into three: the Army of the Mississippi, which included the Vicksburg garrison, under John Pemberton; Johnson's own Western Department troops – about 6,000 men centred on Jackson; and Braxton Bragg's Army of Tennessee. Pemberton's command consisted of 40,000

men in five divisions of varying sizes, under Major Generals William
Loring, Carter Stevenson, John Forney, Martin Smith and John Bowen,
plus river batteries.

After the fall of New Orleans, Union Admiral David Farragut sailed
up the river and on 18 May 1862 demanded the surrender of the city. He
was rebuffed and, having few troops embarked, was obliged to turn back.
He returned with a flotilla on 26 June and bombarded the city for three
days, again without results. Periodic shelling throughout July and some
engagements with Confederate vessels followed; at the same time, a landing force tried to dig a canal across the de Soto Peninsula but on 24 July
the project was abandoned.

In November, Halleck indicated to General Ulysses S. Grant, who had
succeeded him in command of Union troops in the western theatre, that
a major move down the Mississippi to seize Vicksburg was required.
Grant's Army of Tennessee was divided into five corps of varying sizes:
John Parke's IX Corps with two divisions; John McClernand's XIII Corps
with four divisions; William Sherman's XV Corps with three divisions;
Cadwallader Washburn's XVI Corps with three divisions; and James B.
McPherson's XVII Corps with four divisions and a black brigade of four
Louisiana battalions and two Mississippi battalions, all freed slaves. Grant
developed a series of operations from December 1862 to January 1863
which succeeded in capturing the Confederate position at Fort Hindman,
north of Vicksburg. Following these otherwise inconclusive moves, Grant
launched a series of seven offensive moves between January and March
1863, known as the Bayou Operations. These were aimed at constructing
alternative waterways so that troops could be moved close to Vicksburg
without requiring a direct approach. All failed.

Grant was left with one final option: to march the army down the
western side of the Mississippi, cross the river south of Vicksburg, capture
Port Hudson, and then invest and reduce Vicksburg. The Mississippi
was too broad to be bridged at this point using the technology of the
time, so Grant's naval commander, Rear Admiral David Dixon Porter,
would have to brave the fire of the Confederate batteries to get enough

barges and gunboats below the city to effect a crossing. At the same time, McClernand's corps would have to build a corduroy road across swamps and numerous creeks to get the army with its artillery, ammunition and stores wagons down the 70 miles from Grant's advanced base at Milliken's bend to the crossing site at Hard Times, Louisiana. McClernand's men began their mammoth task on 29 March, and within the amazingly short time of 20 days they had constructed enough of a road for the main body to begin its march.

With this project progressing well, Porter made his move on the night of 16 April, in the dark of the moon. Seven gunboats and three transports loaded with stores made the run. The Confederate batteries sighted them immediately and began a furious fire – furious, but ineffective. All the boats but one made it through. On 22 April, another six boats full of stores made the run; all but one made it through. The final refinement in the plan was to draw off Confederate forces with a series of diversions. Sherman's XV Corps made a demonstration against Haynes' Bluff, Drumgould's Bluff and Snyder's Bluff, north of Vicksburg, which was largely ineffective. However, Colonel Benjamin Grierson's famous cavalry raid drew off Loring's division and much of the available Confederate cavalry, which were never able to return to the fight. More of Pemberton's forces were tied down when Porter attacked the Confederate batteries at Grand Gulf, where Grant had been intending to land his force; the batteries proved too strong for him to do this, but Pemberton was further diverted from the defence of Vicksburg.

With Grand Gulf out of the question, Grant decided on the village of Rodney, Mississippi, as his bridgehead; however, advice from a local slave made him change his mind and select Bruinsburg instead. On 30 April, the corps of McClernand and McPherson were ferried across the river; on the same day, Grant sent a dispatch to Sherman telling him to move south down the road to rejoin the main army. With two corps over the river and a third on the way, Grant began to move north-east towards Jackson. The first contact with the Confederates came on 1 May, at Port Gibson, less than 5 miles east of the bridgehead, where Pemberton had moved part of his force to block the Union advance. The contest was an uneven one, and Pemberton was pushed north. Sherman's corps caught up on 8 May, and on 12 May, another Union victory was won at Raymond after six hours of heavy fighting.

Johnson himself arrived at Jackson on 13 May and took personal command of the troops there. Grant had initially intended to turn north and west following the railroad from Raymond, but Johnson's presence on his flank, and a rumour that Beauregard's army was approaching, made him decide to deal with the threat to his flank before turning on Vicksburg. Grant's force arrived at Jackson the following day and fought a sharp engagement against the Confederate rearguard, for Johnson had ordered the evacuation of the town. Johnson's command was pushed east and prevented from moving to join Pemberton; had he hung on, he would have had 11,000 men at his disposal on 14 May and another 4,000 the following day – probably enough to stop Grant. Even worse, his retreat allowed Sherman's men to destroy the heavy industrial works at Jackson and tear up the railroad. In two weeks, Grant's men had advanced 130 miles, won three battles and effectively isolated Vicksburg. Grant now turned west, following the railroad to Vicksburg.

As Johnson had retreated he had sent word to Pemberton to move from Edwards Station and attack Grant at Clinton. Pemberton, however, felt that this was too dangerous and decided instead to march south-east and cut Grant's supply line between Grand Gulf and Raymond. In the small hours of 16 May, he was on the road when another order came from Johnson, reiterating that he attack at Clinton. Pemberton had to turn his march column round, making his supply wagons his advance guard. By 7.00 a.m., his force was in a hastily drawn-up defensive line on a ridge overlooking Jackson Creek, and astride Grant's intended line of advance. To prevent a Union envelopment of his left flank, Pemberton posted a brigade on Champion Hill. This position was assaulted by Grant at 10.00 a.m., and by 1.00 p.m., the Union troops had advanced to the Confederate main line. A desperate fight ensued as both armies attacked and counter-attacked, but in the end Pemberton's men could not stand. Brigadier General Lloyd

Tilghman's brigade had to be sacrificed to hold open the escape route, and by midnight, Grant held Edwards, and the Confederates were in full retreat towards Vicksburg. A holding action was fought the next day at Big Black River Bridge between McClernand's corps and three Confederate brigades under Brigadier General Bowen; the Confederates again could not hold the position, and after burning two bridges to prevent close pursuit, they retreated with the loss of 1,800 sorely needed men.

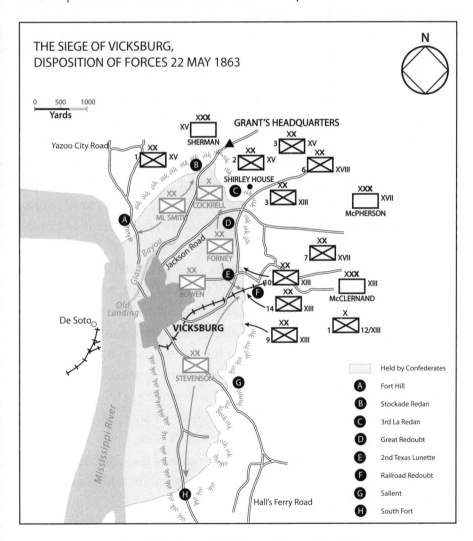

Map 8: The Siege of Vicksburg, May to July 1863

On 18 May, the Union army formally invested Vicksburg. Grant tried two hasty assaults, on 19 and 22 May, but without success, and so settled down to bombard the city and starve it into submission. Sherman, with IX Corps and part of XV Corps, was given the task of screening Johnson, who was gathering forces at Canton. Johnson sent word to Pemberton to evacuate the city and save the army, but Pemberton thought it impossible. No part of the city was outside the range of the Union guns, and the inhabitants bore as much of the effects of the siege as did the garrison as many wooden buildings were set ablaze by artillery and mortar fire. Many people burrowed into the bluffs for shelter and not a few were buried alive when their makeshift caves collapsed under bombardment. Meat ran out at an early date; flour, corn, dried peas and rice soon also became short, especially as speculators took to hoarding to increase prices. Even the most basic foodstuffs were rationed, and the ration included the meat of dead horses and mules. Clean water, too, was difficult to find, and this had an even more serious effect than shortage of food. On 3 July, after a six-week siege, Pemberton raised a white flag for parley, and after a personal conference with Grant – the two had been personal friends before the war – he surrendered the city and his army.

Confederate wounded and killed in the siege amounted to 2,800 – relatively light casualties by the standards of the war. Grant lost almost 5,000 men but captured an entire Confederate army: 29,500 men surrendered, although most were soon paroled, along with significant quantities of guns, small arms and ammunition. To the Confederacy, the surrender of the city on 4 July – Independence Day – was a bitter blow indeed, although Union troops generally behaved well in the aftermath of the siege, sharing rations with the hungry garrison and civilians. Black marketeers were forced to stand by as their stores were broken out and given away.

The Confederacy was indeed now cut in half and the Union had control of the Mississippi River: Port Hudson surrendered on 9 July, and a week later, a Union steamer arrived in New Orleans from St Louis. Johnson, having failed to defeat Sherman, withdrew, leaving all of central Mississippi under Union control. Grant went on to rescue Union forces besieged at

Chattanooga, after which he replaced Halleck as Commander-in-Chief of the Union armies. Pemberton became probably the most hated man in the Confederacy, and Johnson, out-generalled by Grant, lost the initiative for the rest of the war.

VIII. CONCLUSIONS

Lee's target at Gettysburg had been more the will of the Federal Government to continue the struggle than the mere destruction of an army. Whether one more big defeat would have changed the views of those in the North who were fighting the war for ideological reasons must be open to question, for even another Chancellorsville would not have been fatal to the Federal war machine. Its materiel and manpower were huge, and anyway, the Union had already shown that it could face down defeat and carry on the struggle. The South, meanwhile, was in no such position. To achieve a shift in the balance of power between North and South as a result of one battle was simply beyond its capabilities. During the American Civil War, as from that point onwards in history generally, entire campaigns – and, indeed, sequences of campaigns – were required to deliver victory through coercion in what was increasingly an age of mass manufacture and mass information. It would take the combination of the loss of Vicksburg, the withdrawal from Pennsylvania and Maryland, Sherman's campaign in Georgia and defeat in the western theatre to persuade the Confederacy that it was beaten. Gettysburg and Vicksburg, therefore, were decisive only in the context of a four-year war that was fought in a thousand places.

5

Sedan, 1870: Birth and Death of Empire

I. FRANCE AND PRUSSIA

The years following the Prussian victory over Austria at Königgratz brought or revealed new political tensions between Prussia and France. The French were well aware of Prussia's rise to pre-eminence in Central Europe and were uneasy at the prospects it raised. Emperor Napoleon III wished to add to his territories along the Rhine, but Prussia refused to cede any land and, moreover, thwarted his attempt to purchase Luxembourg from the Netherlands. After these rebuffs, the Emperor was willing to look for any pretext for war, despite his country's poor state of preparation compared with Prussia's. The main question that preoccupied Prussian Chancellor Otto von Bismarck, War Minister Field Marshal Albrecht von Roon and Chief of the General Staff Field Marshal Helmuth von Moltke was how France would react to the emerging national identity of Germany based on the North German Alliance (*Norddeutscher Bund*), founded by Bismarck. They agreed that war was inevitable, but Bismarck was against making a pre-emptive attack, while von Moltke urged that this could and should be what they did. In the end, von Moltke had to accept that war would be fought only if the vital interests of the emerging German nation were threatened. In keeping with his general principles, his war plan was, first, to mobilize all the German armies, then to concentrate them, and then to advance rapidly, covered by a large force of cavalry, to seek out, separate and destroy the French field formations as rapidly as possible by envelopment. This would open the way for an advance into the heartland of France, the capture of Paris and the imposition of a peace on terms highly favourable to Germany.

On 18 September 1858, von Moltke was appointed Chief of the Prussian General Staff. Originally in the Danish service, he had transferred to the Prussian Army in 1821. He had subsequently served with the Turks, after which he had been appointed as Chief of Staff of IV Corps at Magdeburg. In 1855 he had become personal aide to Prince Frederick of Prussia, later Emperor Frederick III. As Chief of the General Staff he supervised Prussia's wars against Denmark and Austria. He was well aware of the effect of the Industrial Revolution on weapons technology, especially artillery, on transport and logistics and, indeed, on the whole science of war. His thinking adapted Napoleon I's methods of bringing large military formations towards potential battlefields. He understood the usefulness of railways and of the telegraph and did his best to integrate these into strategic planning: Prussia had the densest railway network of any country in Europe, France the fifth-densest. When looking at Prussia's likely opponents, von Moltke mechanized Napoleon's methods, and in the case of France turned them on the former Emperor's own nation: large armies could now advance along multiple routes and concentrate rapidly at the point of decision. By developing the *Krumpersystem* of Napoleonic times, he used universal conscription to produce a field army of 1,200,000 men from Prussia and her allies, of whom 500,000 could be put into the field in three weeks.

Von Moltke's General Staff was organized into four divisions, three of which planned operations in different European theatres; the fourth was the railway department. He trained the staff and the staffs of his armies, corps and divisions to proceed on the basis of simple directives and statements of intent, rather than detailed orders. Detail would follow when and as required, but speed would be more important. For communicating this intent, the telegraph was useful during the initial stages of a campaign but of little or no use at the tactical level on the battlefield. Even though armies and battlefields had expanded to the point where it was now no longer possible for a general to view the whole field of battle from one or two positions, he still had to communicate with his subordinates by dispatch rider once battle was joined. This combination of factors gave birth to the German system of *Auftragstaktik*, or mission orders, which would remain the basis of German military practice right up to the present day and would in time be adopted by all Western militaries.

Moltke's staff system was not, however, simply a development of the Napoleonic model. Napoleon never instituted a staff college or educated his subordinates. His staff was a cabinet based on his personal requirements: Moltke's staff was a wholly military institution operating methodically on the basis of information and intelligence analysis. Not for the Prussians the flashes of Napoleonic intuition and the dictation of a plan on the basis of a few moments' thought. As historian Martin van Creveld has put it, Napoleon's system relied on command from the front, Moltke's on management from the rear.

In France, stable government had returned after revolutions in 1830 and 1848 with the establishment of, first, the Second Republic, and then, under Napoleon III, a nephew of the great Emperor, the Second Empire. The economy had been improved, a successful war had been fought against Sardinia, and a working relationship had been established with Britain; indeed, despite the invasion scare that led to the building of Palmerston's massive system of fortifications around the main British naval bases, the two countries had fought as allies in the Crimea. However, by the late 1860s, Napoleon III was seriously ill and his reputation had been tarnished by an ill-fated adventure in Mexico.

Napoleon feared the rising power of Prussia: its huge army, the way it had harnessed emerging technology, and its ambitions. The French Army was nominally a conscript force; however, the conscription system, based on quotas and ballots, produced a relatively small peacetime strength of about 280,000 long-service *moustaches*. Napoleon therefore instituted changes to increase the available number of trained men. The memory of Napoleon I's ravages was still very much alive and the legislature did not receive his proposals kindly. It was only the unavoidable menace of Prussia that allowed Napoleon to push his plan through. Even so, France would

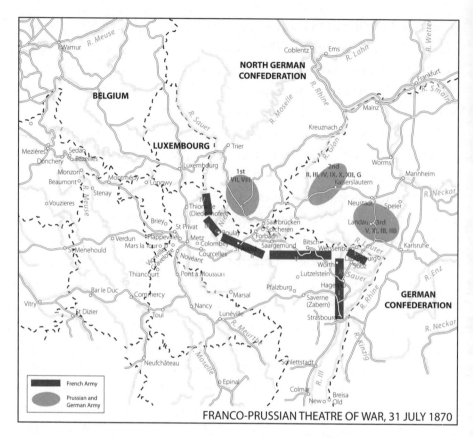

FRANCO-PRUSSIAN THEATRE OF WAR, 31 JULY 1870

Map 9: The Franco-Prussian Theatre of War, 31 July 1870

not field a trained strength of 1,000,000 until 1875. In 1870, it could, at a pinch, field about half that number.

Faced with the prospect of a German army that would not only outnumber them but also outface them technologically, the French Government, starting in 1866, allocated money to replace the infantry rifle with the chassepot, its response to the Prussian needle gun. With a range of 1,600 yards, rapid reloading and greater accuracy than even the Enfield rifled musket, the chassepot would confirm the ascent of firepower over mass on the battlefield. Money was not allocated to improve or replace the French field artillery, however, and here the Germans held a significant advantage with the breech-loading rifled guns manufactured by the great firm of Krupp. Both armies had analyzed the Prussian victory over Austria but had paid far less attention, it seems, to the lessons of the recent American Civil War. Modern weapons extended the killing zone of the musket, so that mass charges could no longer be effective and the preferred tactic would have to be the envelopment or outflanking attack. There had therefore been some modification in battlefield tactics, but no radical shift; this was in part due to the fact that the artillery was still a direct-fire weapon rather than indirect-fire and thus could not provide cover for the infantry or cavalry from dispersed or distant fire-bases. In defence, the infantry awaited the attack in prepared defensive positions so as to bring concentrated fire to bear at maximum ranges. The French found it hard to subordinate their natural inclination to the offensive to the demands of reality, but in effect the French Army accepted a primarily defensive doctrine in recognition of the superiority its enemy enjoyed in numbers, technology and the ability to manoeuvre. In the attack, the German infantry – without the cover of the creeping barrage, which would have allowed it to advance unscathed by keeping the enemy's heads down – still moved forward in massed formations, relying on discipline and accepting casualties in order to close and finish the fight at close quarters. The cavalry, too, still clung to the traditional tactics of the charge, and it was here that the flair and élan of the French Army was still most apparent.

The actual *causus belli* between the two opponents was the Spanish succession – a cause of war in Europe in earlier times. A military coup in September 1868 deposed the debauched Queen Isabella II and left the throne of Spain empty. The family nearest in line able to meet the required criteria – Catholic but non-Bourbon – was German. The Cortes therefore offered the crown to Prince Leopold of Hohenzollern-Sigmaringen, a cousin of King William of Prussia. The prince was understandably reluctant to accept, but Bismarck recognized the opportunity to engineer a confrontation and ordered him to do so. Napoleon objected on the grounds of Prince Leopold's relationship to the royal house of Prussia, and did actually obtain from King William the withdrawal of Prussia's consent to Leopold's candidacy; but when the Emperor also demanded a promise that never, in any circumstances, should Leopold accept the Spanish crown, William refused. The famous Ems telegram – so-called because William received it from the French Ambassador at Bad Ems – allowed Bismarck to deceive the French into believing that the King had insulted their ambassador. The French population demanded war.

II. THE WAR OPENS

France declared war on 15 July 1870. A pre-war plan laid out by the late Marshal Adolphe Niel called for a French offensive from Thionville towards Trier and into the Prussian Rhineland. This was discarded in favour of a defensive plan put together by Generals Charles Frossard and Bartélémy Lebrun, which called for the Army of the Rhine to remain on the defensive close to the German border ready to repel any Prussian offensive. Since France expected Austria, Bavaria, Württemberg and Baden to join in a war of revenge against Prussia, the French I Corps would invade the Bavarian Palatinate and liberate the South German states in cooperation with the Austrians. Held in reserve, VI Corps would reinforce either army as needed. Unfortunately for Frossard's plan, the Prussian army mobilized far more rapidly than expected, the German states all fell in alongside Prussia, and the Austrians remained neutral.

By the time the French had issued their declaration of war, the reserves of Prussia and her client and allied states had been called up and the war budget agreed. The formal Prussian declaration was drafted on 17 July and delivered two days later. The German mobilization was the pre-eminent example of von Moltke's organizing genius. By August, the army of the North German Alliance consisted of 982,000 men and 209,402 horses. Bavaria and her neighbours also joined the Prussian cause, in contrast to the wars against Napoleon I, bringing another 200,000 men and 40,000 horses. The field formations of this huge army, greatly outnumbering the French in manpower and capability, were moved on 13 railway lines to their concentration areas near the Rhine, as dictated by the master plan. These lay within an area 95 miles wide and 50 miles deep. Von Moltke and his small General Staff moved there on 31 July, along with the King and the Chancellor and their headquarters of more than 1,000 men, in three special trains.

The German forces were formed into three armies. The First Army, under the 74-year-old General Karl von Steinmetz, comprised I, VII and VIII Corps, under Generals Edwin von Manteuffel, Adolf von Zastrow and August von Goeben respectively, and two cavalry divisions – a total of about 60,000 men. The Second Army, under Prince Frederick Charles of Prussia, consisted of the 134,000 men of III Corps, under General Eduard von Fransecky; IV and X Corps; and the Guard Corps, under Prince August of Württemberg, with three cavalry divisions. The Third Army, under the Crown Prince of Prussia, consisted of the 130,000 men of V Corps, under General Hugo von Kirchbach; VI Corps and one division of XI Corps; the Württemberg–Baden Corps of two divisions; I and II Royal Bavarian Corps; and two cavalry divisions. The remaining two divisions of XI Corps and XII Royal Saxon Corps were held in reserve. In von Steinmetz and Prince Frederick Charles, von Moltke had two very different subordinates. Steinmetz had emerged from the war with Austria with a reputation as a determined and energetic commander, but he was also obstinate, impatient and given to insubordination; he resented the small size of his command and made little effort to understand von Moltke's intentions. Frederick Charles, on the other hand, was a loyal, reliable, intelligent and analytical professional soldier, although with something of a reputation for caution.

In France, there was no equivalent General Staff organization to deliver rapid mobilization. By early August, two armies had been formed out of the 270,000 available men in the French Army's eight corps – not all of which were ready for deployment. The Army of Alsace, commanded by Marshal Patrice de MacMahon, consisted of the three corps stationed on the southern frontier with Germany: I Corps, under General Abel Douay; V Corps, under General Pierre Failly (later General Emmanuel de Wimpffen); and VII Corps, under General Félix Douay. The Army of Lorraine, under Marshal François Bazaine, comprised another four corps:

II Corps, under General Charles Frossard; III Corps, under Bazaine himself; IV Corps, under General Paul de Ladmirault; and VI Corps, under General François Canrobert. The Imperial Guard, under General Charles Bourbaki, was in reserve behind the Army of Lorraine.

On 4 August, the German Third Army advanced against MacMahon's leading corps, which had only a single division deployed on the River Lauter. This action, the Battle of Weissenburg, resulted in 1,600 French and 1,550 German casualties as well as MacMahon's immediate withdrawal and adoption of a defensive posture. Two days later, at Fröschwiller – or Wörth, as it is also known – battle opened with a German reconnaissance in force by the Crown Prince. This was thrown back by MacMahon, but the Crown Prince reinforced his initial attack with artillery, and MacMahon, despite a cavalry charge of suicidal bravery, had to fall back towards Châlons-sur-Marne.

III. THE BATTLES OF AUGUST 1870

The Battle of Fröschwiller opened the route through the Vosges and thus towards Paris. The Third Army continued its advance towards the River Meuse, while Steinmetz and Prince Frederick Charles advanced into Lorraine against Bazaine. Coming unexpectedly upon Bazaine's II Corps, under Frossard, on the Spichern Heights, Steinmetz impetuously launched a frontal attack not planned by von Moltke. This was stopped dead in its tracks by concentrated French rifle and artillery fire, before the threat of an enveloping movement caused Frossard to pull back. It was, however, a Pyrrhic victory for the Germans, for it cost them nearly 5,000 men to the French 2,000.

Reviewing the situation, von Moltke decided that the Crown Prince should continue to fix MacMahon's army while Steinmetz and Prince Frederick Charles pressed on and completed the destruction of Bazaine. The German advance was characteristically rapid and bold, and by 12 August, von Moltke's main force was between the two French armies and threatening their communications. Bazaine was left with no option but to fall back towards Metz. At the same time, Napoleon, a sick man, relinquished his overall command to MacMahon. Because of the position of the German First Army, Bazaine was obliged to cross the Meuse and make for the fortress of Verdun; however, in so doing, he was stopped by the Second Army at the Battle of Borny. Bazaine repositioned his army with its left flank against the fortress of Metz, where Frederick Charles found him and immediately attacked with his leading corps. Having established the position of Bazaine's centre around Mars-la-Tour, Frederick Charles concentrated his forces against that place, pouring in more and more guns and men and a series of wild cavalry charges. This battle was probably the hardest-fought of the entire war, with each side losing more than 16,000 men killed, wounded, taken prisoner or missing. At its close, Bazaine regrouped his army closer to Metz, facing towards the west, while Frederick Charles closed on Rézonville.

Von Moltke now began to exercise much closer control over the German armies. He himself firmly believed that Bazaine would cling to Metz; however, Prince Frederick Charles believed he would try to make for Verdun. Von Moltke therefore had to plan for both possible situations while gathering intelligence. When Bazaine's position was established, there was considerable consternation among the General Staff that, should the German armies move to attack Bazaine from the west, their line of withdrawal back towards the Rhine could be severed should things go wrong. Indeed, this view was put before the King of Prussia by von Roon, who advised against fighting such a battle. Von Moltke, however, thought differently and his view prevailed. The battle, known afterwards as Gravelotte-Saint Privat, opened with a German attack at 10.30 a.m. on 18 August and lasted until midnight. It was dawn before von Moltke could be sure of the outcome. Had Bazaine attacked the Germans with all his available strength, he should have been able to break up von Moltke's developing encirclement; instead, he withdrew into Metz, leaving 13,000 dead and wounded and 5,000 prisoners on the field, alongside 20,000 German casualties.

IV. THE RESCUE OF BAZAINE

The fortress of Metz was now in effect besieged. Von Moltke had not expected such an outcome and so had to pause in order to carry out a major regrouping exercise. Prince Frederick Charles was left to mask Metz with the whole of Steinmetz's First Army, detachments from the reserve, and one corps of his own Second Army – a total of 150,000 troops. A new army, the Fourth, was formed from the 138,000 men of the remaining three corps of the Second Army and placed under the command of Crown Prince Albert of Saxony. The Third Army, under the Crown Prince of Prussia, was reinforced from the reserve to a strength of 223,000 men, and both formations were given axes of advance towards Paris.

MacMahon, meanwhile, had received word from the French War Minister to the effect that if he did not relieve Bazaine, there would be a revolution in Paris. MacMahon therefore rapidly formed a new force, the Army of Châlons, in order to raise the siege of Metz and rescue Bazaine. The army comprised 202 infantry battalions, 80 squadrons of cavalry and 564 guns. MacMahon led it in a march to the north-east, around the left flank of the Prussian army, towards the Belgian border, in an indirect approach aimed at avoiding battle with the main Prussian force before striking south to link up with Bazaine; battle could then be sought on favourable terms with the combined force of the two French armies.

Some French Generals considered MacMahon's plan to be unsound: the Prussians had repeatedly shown during their series of victories in August that they could out-manoeuvre the French through better intelligence, a higher tempo of decision-making and implementation, better logistic support and better transportation; there was no reason to suppose that anything had changed. Moreover, it was felt that the proposed route of the march spread out the French force and left both flanks exposed. Von Moltke soon detected the movement and realized its purpose – which was not difficult. He decided to catch the French while they were on the move, in an enveloping movement or pincer. He moved the Third and Fourth Armies first to the west, and then north. These two armies comprised 222 infantry battalions, 186 squadrons of cavalry and 774 guns – around

250,000 men – thus seriously outnumbered the French. Von Moltke's prediction was that battle would be joined on 30 August.

Von Moltke caught up with the French a day earlier than he had predicted, at Beaumont, and continued the action the following day at Nouart and Bazeilles. After a series of hard-fought battles in which the French lost 5,000 men killed, wounded or missing, as well as 40 guns, MacMahon withdrew towards the city of Sedan, on the River Meuse. His intention was to rest the army after its long march, resupply it with food and ammunition and then retreat to more favourable defensive terrain rather than giving battle in the town.

V. SEDAN

While Failly's V Corps was still fighting at Beaumont, and before the rest of the French army had crossed the Meuse, MacMahon gave orders that all forces were to concentrate on Sedan. He then intended to withdraw towards Mezières, where General Joseph Vinoy was to meet him with the newly formed XIII Corps. To hold off any further advance by the Germans, I Corps, which had arrived at Carignan early in the afternoon of 29 August, detached two of its divisions to Douzy in the evening.

The French retreat towards Sedan soon turned into a rout; it was just as well that the river was swollen and a hard pursuit by the Germans thus not possible. The troops were worn out and short of food; moreover, they had little confidence in the high command. Nor had the series of defeats they had suffered done anything for their self-confidence. MacMahon probably realized that the only chance of safety for his army, or even a part of it, was to continue the withdrawal at once, yet he delayed; the danger was that the Crown Prince of Prussia's army, which controlled all the crossings over the Meuse, would attack his flank and then pursue him to the Belgian frontier, little more than a mile away, where he would have to lay down his arms and be interned. However, the fact that he did not move straightaway was probably more to do with the state of the army than his analysis of the situation.

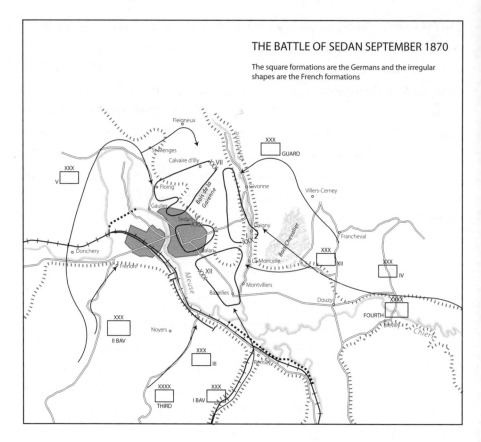

Map 10: The Battle of Sedan, 1 September 1870

Von Moltke still believed that the French would make for Mezières. The Fourth Army was therefore ordered to attack MacMahon and fix him where he was, and the Third to advance on the right bank of the river, leaving one corps on the left. The French rear was protected by the fortress of Sedan. The Meuse and the valleys of the Givonne and the Floing were formidable obstacles, and the combination of features provided a strong defensive line if it could be held. The Calvaire d'Illy and the Bois de Garennes in its rear, from where a ridge extends to the village of Bazeilles, offered cover from view and from fire. Bazeilles also provided a useful strong point to anchor the line facing the Givonne, but after the loss of the bridges across the Meuse it was open to attack from two sides.

To maintain contact with the Fourth Army and fix the French, General von der Tann, commanding I Bavarian Corps, opened the attack, sending a brigade across pontoon bridges at 4.00 a.m. on 30 August to attack Bazeilles. A thick mist covered the approach, but as the troops closed up to the little town they found the streets barricaded and took fire from every house. The leading company pushed on despite appalling casualties, but the rest of the brigade was driven out of the western part of Bazeilles by the arrival of 2 Brigade of the French XII Corps. However, the Germans held on to the buildings at the southern end of the town and from there kept up the attack. Fresh troops were constantly coming up on both sides; the French were reinforced by one brigade of I Corps and one brigade of V Corps. The fighting went on for hours; even citizens took part, and, according to the custom of the time, those found with arms were shot out of hand.

The German gun batteries drawn up across the Meuse could not be brought to bear on the crowded streets of Bazeilles, now on fire in many places; but when, at 8.00 a.m., the Prussian 8th Division arrived at Remilly, von der Tann ordered his last brigade into action. The walled park of Monvillers was stormed and enough of a bridgehead made to allow the artillery to cross the bridges an hour later. The 8th Division was then moved south of Bazeilles to support the Bavarians.

Prince George of Saxony had dispatched an advance guard of seven battalions from Douzy towards La Moncelle at 5.00 a.m. They drove the French from the village, pushed on to Platinerie and the bridge there, and, in spite of heavy fire, took the houses on the other side of the Givonne. The 8th Division was able to make contact with the Bavarians, and guns were moved into position to provide fire support; but the French were able to prevent infantry reinforcements being brought forward.

Early in the fighting, at around 6.00 a.m., MacMahon had been hit by a shell splinter at La Moncelle. He sent word to General Ducrot, now commanding I Corps, that he should assume command of the army, passing over two generals with more seniority. When Ducrot received the news at around 7.00 a.m., he issued orders to the corps commanders to concentrate the army at Illy and then make an immediate withdrawal back towards Mezières. He dispatched General Joseph Lartigue's division from his own corps to cover the crossing at Daigny; the divisions of Generals Henri de Lacretelle and Bassoigne he ordered to attack Prince George's Bavarians and Saxons to buy time and space for the rest of the army to break contact and withdraw. The divisions forming the second line immediately began to move north.

However, the Minister of War had appointed General Emmanuel de Wimpffen, recently back from Algiers, to command V Corps, and had also given him authority to assume command if MacMahon were disabled. De Wimpffen knew from cavalry reconnaissance that the army of the Crown Prince was deployed around Donchery, so that a retreat to Mezières would be impossible. Instead, he determined to force a way through to Carignan, certain that he could push the Bavarians and Saxons aside, and so effect a junction with Bazaine. When he heard Ducrot's assessment of the situation and, at the same time, saw that an attack on the Germans in La Moncelle was going well, he decided to insist on his right to command. Ducrot submitted without protest. The divisions of the second line were ordered back, and the Bavarians and Saxons were again attacked.

One regiment of the Saxon advance guard had marched to La Moncelle at 7.00 a.m.; the other had been tied down by the advance of Lartigue's division on the right. Here the firing soon became fierce. The regiment had marched without knapsacks and was running low on ammunition; the repeated and violent attacks of the French Zouaves, mainly against the right flank, had to be stopped at the point of the bayonet. On the left, Prince George had managed to position a strong concentration of artillery, which by 8.30 a.m. amounted to 12 batteries. But Lacretelle's division was now approaching and, within half an hour, masses of *tirailleurs* forced the German batteries to retire. They withdrew only a short distance, however, before turning and reopening a heavy fire, which was enough to force the French back so that the batteries could again take up their original positions.

Meanwhile, 4 Bavarian Brigade had reached La Moncelle, and 46 Saxon

Brigade was coming up, so that the limited progress made by Bassoigne's division was stopped. The right wing of the Saxon contingent, which had been hard pressed, now received much-needed support from the 24th Division; they at once assumed the attack. The French were driven back on Daigny, losing five guns in the struggle. Then, joining the Bavarians, who were pushing on through the valley to the north, the men of the 24th took Daigny and the bridge and farmstead of La Rapaille.

It was now about 10.00 a.m., and the Prussian Guard Corps had arrived at the Upper Givonne. The corps had marched before dawn, in two columns. When the sound of heavy firing had been heard from Bazeilles, the pace had been forced. The shortest route for the left column would have traversed two deep ravines and the wood of Chevallier, which would have reduced the rate of advance; the column had therefore taken a longer route, through Villers-Cernay, bringing it behind the right column, which had already passed in time to take part in the battle between the Saxons and Lartigue's division.

The divisions ordered back by Ducrot had by now resumed their positions, and the leading batteries of the Guard's artillery opened fire on them from the east. At the same time, the Prussian IV Corps and 7th Division arrived at Lamecourt, and the 8th Division at Remilly, on the opposite bank of the Meuse from Bazeilles. The first French attempt to break through eastwards to Carignan ended in failure; the line of retreat to Mezières in the west was cut by V and XI Corps of the German Third Army, which, with the Württemberg-Baden Division, had moved north on that route. These troops had also marched before daybreak, crossed the Meuse at Donchery and found the road to Mezières clear of the enemy. Heavy shelling could be heard from the direction of Bazeilles, which made it seem highly likely that battle had been joined at Sedan. The Crown Prince therefore ordered V and XI Corps to march to the right towards St Menges and the Württembergers to mask Mezières. Von Kirchbach, commanding the V Corps, identified Fleigneux as the next objective, the occupation of which would cut off the retreat of the French into Belgium and maintain contact with the right wing of the Fourth Army.

The narrow road between the hills and the river leading to St Albert, about 2,000 yards away, was not guarded by the French. It was not until the Crown Prince's advance guard reached St Menges that the Prussians encountered a French detachment, which soon withdrew. The Germans then deployed in the direction of Illy, two companies on the right taking Floing, which they held unsupported for two hours against repeated French attacks.

The first Prussian batteries to arrive had to fight hard against the larger number of French artillery around Illy. At first they were protected only by cavalry and a few companies of infantry, and they soon came under direct attack. One French cavalry division had reached the Illy plateau at 9.00 a.m.: General Gaston, Marquis de Galliffet, formed his three regiments of *Chasseurs d'Afrique* and two squadrons of lancers into three divisions and gave the order to charge. The Germans allowed the cavalry charge to come as close as 60 yards before firing a volley. The charge did not stop, and the leading French division rode on, then wheeled outward to both flanks. As they did so, the horsemen came under fire from German infantry in a large copse. The Prussian batteries now fired canister from close range. Unable to drive the Germans away, the French cavalry withdrew out of range.

By 10.00 a.m., at the same time as the French attacks at Bazeilles and Daigny were being repelled, fourteen German batteries of XI Corps were in position around the hills south-east of St Menges; the batteries of V Corps soon joined them. Thus, with columns of German infantry advancing on Fleigneux, the noose was being drawn ever tighter round Sedan. Von Moltke believed that the Bavarian Corps and the artillery reserves remaining on the left bank of the Meuse would be enough to repel any French attempt to break through in that direction. Five corps were standing on the French right flank, ready to attack.

The Bavarians and Saxons, reinforced by the advance guard of IV Corps, moved out of the burning town of Bazeilles and from La Moncelle and drove regiments of the French XII Corps from the east of Balan back to Fond de Givonne. This gave the Germans possession of the spur of Illy, but a French counter-attack was sure to be made to retake it, so the Germans consolidated and reorganized in preparation. Then 5 Bavarian Brigade advanced to Balan; the troops met only light resistance in the village, but it took a hard fight to occupy the park of the castle. Soon after midday, the leading battalion got close enough to the walls of the castle to exchange fire with the garrison.

The French were now moving into position at Fond de Givonne, and both sides opened a heavy fire. At 1.00 p.m., the French received reinforcements, and when, after a preliminary bombardment, they went over to the attack, 5 Bavarian Brigade was forced back. Supported by 6 Brigade, however, the German troops counter-attacked and regained their old position after an hour's hard fighting. Meanwhile, the Saxon Corps had continued to advance steadily towards Givonne, where the leading companies of the Prussian Guard Corps were already established. Heavy fire from the superior Prussian artillery put many French guns out of action and forced the French batteries to change their position several times. To try to reverse matters, the French repeatedly sent out battalions of skirmishers and light troops; Givonne was briefly recaptured and ten guns were moved into the village, but these were taken when the place again changed hands before they could even unlimber.

The French tried again to break through at Floing; but the weak German screen there had gradually been reinforced, so that the attacking French were driven out of the area as fast as they had entered. Now the fire from the twenty-six batteries of the Fourth Army was joined by that of the Guard Corps, which took up a position on the eastern slope of the Givonne Valley. The effect was devastating. French batteries were destroyed and many ammunition wagons blown up. De Wimpffen at first thought the advance of the Germans from the north was a feint, but he soon recognized his mistake when he went to see things for himself around noon. He therefore ordered two divisions in the second line, which were behind the Givonne front of I Corps, to move to the high ground above Illy and support General Douay. On rejoining XII Corps, he found it in full retreat towards Sedan, and so sent word to Douay to dispatch urgent support to Bazeilles. A brigade marched there at once, soon followed by another.

All these marches and counter-marches took place in the area immediately south of the Bois de Garennes and under continuous fire from
German artillery on two sides. The retreat of the French cavalry heightened
the confusion, and several battalions returned to the doubtful protection
of the forest. Douay's men, reinforced by brigades of V Corps, actually
retook the Calvaire d'Illy but by 2.00 p.m. had been forced to abandon it
following shelling of the forest by sixty guns of the Prussian Guard.

General Alphonse Liebert's division alone had so far held its strong
position on the hills north of Casal. At 1.00 p.m., however, the leading
regiments of the German V and XI Corps began to scale the hill, while
other troops moved round to the south toward Gaulier and Casal and yet
more marched down from Fleigneux. These regiments became so mixed
that no detailed orders could be given to individual units, and the fighting
was fierce for at least an hour. Liebert's men, shelled and attacked on both
flanks, eventually gave way. As the reserves of the French VII Corps had
already been redeployed, it fell to the French cavalry to try to save the day.

General Jean-Auguste Margueritte, with five regiments of light cavalry
and two of lancers, charged out of the Bois de Garennes. He was one of
the first to fall, mortally wounded, and Galliffet took his place. The charge
traversed very difficult ground, and even before the division had begun to
move, the ranks had been thinned by heavy flanking fire from Prussian
artillery. Still, with reduced numbers but unflagging courage, the squadrons charged on 43 Prussian Infantry Brigade hurrying up from Fleigneux.
Some of the German infantry on the hillside were lying under cover, others
were exposed. The cavalry broke their line at several points, and one troop
even forced its way past the fire of eight guns. However, German reserves
checked any further progress. A troop of cuirassiers, coming out from
Gaulier, fell on the German rear but were met by Prussian hussars and
driven off. Other detachments forced their way through the infantry as
far as the narrow road by St Albert, where the battalions holding it gave
them a bad time. Others again got into Floing, only to be shot down by
Prussian jaegers.

Two further French cavalry attacks were mounted during the next hour but with steadily diminishing success. The short-range rifle fire of the Prussian infantry and the canister shot fired by the German guns strewed the whole field with dead and wounded. Many fell into quarries or over steep precipices; a few may have escaped by swimming the Meuse, but scarcely more than half of these brave troops were left to return to the protection of the fortress. This magnificent sacrifice did not change the outcome of battle. The Prussian infantry returned to the attack against Liebert's division but sustained heavy losses; three battalions of the 6th Infantry Regiment ended the day being commanded by lieutenants. After a dogged resistance, the French withdrew at about 3.00 p.m. to their last refuge – the Bois de Garennes.

An hour earlier, the fighting round Bazeilles had seemed to be going well for the French. De Wimpffen had returned to his original idea of pushing through the Bavarians and making for Carignan with I, V and XII Corps, covered by VII Corps. However, the orders for this move never reached the corps commanders – or, if they did, they arrived too late to be carried out. The French army was close to its last gasp. Three divisions, those of Generals Bassoigne, Gozo and Grandchamp, were still uncommitted. At 3.00 p.m., the last two of these advanced from Fond de Givonne over the eastern ridge and attacked the 23rd Saxon Infantry Division, which was marching in the valley on the left bank of the Givonne. With the support of the left-column of the Prussian Guard and its artillery, this last attack was soon beaten off. The French soldiers at this point suddenly seemed to lose all moral strength and surrendered in whole companies. As soon as the hills on the west of the Givonne had been secured, German artillery was set up there; by about 3.00 p.m., 21 batteries were ranged in line between Bazeilles and Haybes.

The Bois de Garennes still remained in French hands. After a short barrage, the 1st Division of the Prussian Guard attacked uphill from Givonne, supported by the Saxon battalions and by the left wing of the Third Army pressing forward from Illy. Chaos ensued: some French troops resisted, others surrendered by the thousand, and it was not until 5.00 p.m. that the Germans had secured control of the fortress. Meanwhile, long columns of French troops could be observed pouring down on Sedan from all the neighbouring hills. Unformed bodies of soldiers massed in and around the walls of the fortress, and shells from the German batteries on both sides of the Meuse exploded among them. Fires broke out in the city, and the Bavarians were about to assault the palisades at the gate when, at about 4.30 p.m., flags of truce were raised on the towers. Napoleon III had refused to join de Wimpffen in his attempt to break through the German lines; instead, he had told him to negotiate with the enemy. Suddenly, the French army ceased firing.

VI. SURRENDER

General Count Reille made his way under a flag of truce to King William. He carried a signed letter from the Emperor, whose presence in Sedan had until now been unknown to the Germans. Reille surrendered his sword to William as a symbolic act of personal submission. The Prussians' answer to the Emperor's letter demanded that a senior French officer come to the German headquarters, fully empowered to negotiate with Field Marshal von Moltke for the surrender of the French army. This task fell on de Wimpffen. The negotiations were held at Donchery during the night of 1–2 September. The Germans insisted on the disarmament and imprisonment of the entire army, with only the officers freed on parole. De Wimpffen found it impossible to accept such hard conditions; the negotiations were broken off and the French returned to Sedan at 1.00 a.m. Before their departure, they were given to understand forcefully that unless the German terms were accepted by 9.00 a.m., the action would be renewed. After conferring with the Emperor, and with further resistance imposs-ible, de Wimpffen signed the articles of surrender early in the morning of 2 September. The battle had cost the Germans 460 officers and 8,500 men. The French losses were far greater: 17,000 killed and wounded – most by artillery fire, presaging events 40 years on – and 21,000 taken prisoner. Another 83,000 surrendered after the capitulation.

Napoleon III also surrendered to the Prussian King. The following day, the German Third and Fourth Armies marched on Paris. However, the capture of the French Emperor left the Prussians without an opposing government willing to make a quick peace. Indeed, two days after news of the Emperor's capture reached Paris, the French Second Empire collapsed in a bloodless revolution. A provisional government, willing to carry on the war, took power, and for five more months it spared no effort to try to turn the situation to advantage – or at least rescue some self-respect. The effort was in vain. The defeat at Sedan and the capture of Napoleon sealed France's doom. With his empire overthrown, Napoleon was permitted to leave Prussian captivity for exile in England, while, within a fortnight, Paris was formally invested. The city eventually capitulated on 27 January 1871, and those French forces that remained in the field were dealt with rapidly by the German armies.

VII. AFTERMATH AND CONCLUSIONS

Even though the war dragged on for another five months, Sedan was the decisive moment when the campaign was won and lost. After it, with Bazaine's army still cooped up in Metz and the remaining French forces either in German prison camps, isolated garrisons or hopelessly outnumbered, the initiative lay irreversibly with the Germans. Once Paris had fallen, it only remained to complete the formalities of the Treaty of Frankfurt. Signed on 10 May 1871, this gave formal expression to the new German Empire with the King of Prussia as its Emperor. The border provinces of Alsace and Lorraine, long-disputed territory, passed to the new Germany.

For Chancellor Bismarck, the victory over France complemented those over Denmark and Austria and established the new empire as the dominant power in Central Europe, at last eclipsing the old rivals. With its powerful army – an army that seemed made for victory – its huge industrial potential and its limitless self-belief, Germany from now on would be unstoppable short of complete destruction. The victory decided the future course of European history until 1945, ensuring that France would do all in its power to rebuild and take back what it had lost. It set Germany on a collision course with Britain, too; not only through its quest for an overseas empire and a high-seas fleet, but also because British foreign policy since the mid-sixteenth century had sought, through a system of alliances, to prevent any one power becoming dominant on the mainland of Europe. To counter-balance the power of Germany, Britain was inevitably, at some point – and despite all her instinctive wishes to avoid continental involvements – going to be driven into alliance with her old enemy, France.

6

Third Gaza, 1917:
Strategic Diversion, Tactical Deception

I. THE MIDDLE EAST CAMPAIGN

Turkey had entered the Great War on the side of the Triple Alliance on 5 November 1914. For much of the time, the Turks faced enemies on several fronts: the Russians in the Caucasus and the British, Anzacs and Indians in the Sinai and Mesopotamia and, plus the French, at Gallipoli. Operations against the Turks in the Middle East had been, since early 1916, the responsibility of General Sir Archibald Murray, commander of the Egyptian Expeditionary Force, and his subordinate, General Sir Charles Dobell, who commanded most of the fighting troops, which were formed into a provisional corps known as Eastern Force. During 1916, Turkish attempts to sever the vital Suez Canal had been thwarted, and by January 1917, Dobell had pushed his force into the Sinai to the southern limits of Palestine, with the objective of capturing Jerusalem and then Damascus. This, combined with the British advance in Mesopotamia, which had captured Baghdad, would bring about the collapse of Turkish power in the Arab lands. In the aftermath of the Gallipoli expedition, Egypt and Palestine had been regarded as an economy-of-force sector, but Murray had agitated for resources sufficient to take the offensive.

In this region, the climate and terrain posed severe problems for a military force before ever the enemy took a hand. Murray had built a railway and a pipeline to carry the all-important fresh water needed by his troops, and by their horses, mules and camels, from the Suez Canal to his forward operating base in southern Palestine. Both were great feats of engineering, but they had the unintended effect of tying the force to within range of the railheads and pumping stations.

Before further progress could be made, the Turkish defensive lines around the city of Gaza would have to be cracked, and this presented formidable problems. The city dominated the main coast road and had been heavily fortified by the Turks. Their line then extended south-east to the village of Beersheba, which provided the last access to water before the desert stretched away towards the Dead Sea and beyond. Two attempts in March and April 1917 both ended in costly failure.

At this point, the War Office in London removed both Murray and Dobell from their commands and sent out General Sir Edmund Allenby, formerly General Officer Commanding-in-Chief of the Third Army in France. Allenby was under something of a cloud, having been criticized by Field Marshal Sir Douglas Haig, commander of the British Expeditionary Force, for failing to exploit opportunities at the Battle of Arras. He had, moreover, the reputation of a butcher general – he was commonly referred to as 'the Bloody Bull' – although two famous subordinates, Archibald Wavell and T. E. Lawrence, both asserted this was undeserved. His imaginative, manoeuvrist approach in the campaign that now lay ahead also belies this label.

Allenby arrived in Cairo on 27 June 1917, and with him came significant reinforcements, so that his army comprised 88,000 men in three corps. XX Corps, under Lieutenant General Philip Chetwode, who had commanded a division under Dobell, consisted of one New Army division – the 10th (Irish), under Major General John Longley – and three Territorial divisions – the 53rd (Welsh), under Major General S. F. (Stanley) Mott, and the 60th (2nd London), under Major General Jimmy Shea, both second-line, and the 74th (Yeomanry), under Major General E. S. (Eric) Girdwood. XXI Corps, commanded by Major General Edward Bulfin, consisted of two Territorial divisions – the 52nd (Lowland), under Major General John Hill, and the 54th (East Anglian), under Major General Steuart Hare – and a composite division – the 75th (Territorial and Indian), under Major General Philip Palin. The third formation was the Desert Mounted Corps, under Lieutenant General Harry Chauvel, the first Australian to command a corps. This comprised the Australian and New Zealand Army Corps (ANZAC) Mounted Division, under the New Zealander Major General Edward Chaytor; the Australian Mounted Division, under Major General Sir H. W. (Henry) Hodgson; and the Yeomanry Mounted Division, under Major General Sir Edmund Barrow. These three divisions, which included cavalry and mounted infantry formations, and the Imperial Camel Brigade, under Brigadier General Clement Smith VC, were the most experienced and best trained. They were in marked contrast to many of the infantry divisions, which were still raw or newly formed and, as well as Territorial units, contained many New Army battalions. The weakness in artillery which had plagued Murray – who had had only 170 guns of all calibres, of which only 10 per cent had been medium or heavy – was made up by reinforcements to a total of 460 guns, and augmented on the western side by naval gunfire from ships offshore. More tanks and aircraft of all types were also made available. These reinforcements came in the teeth of opposition from Sir Douglas Haig, who insisted, rightly, that all such diversions of resources from the Western Front were detrimental to the achievement of the decisive effort of the war – the defeat of the German field army in the West.

Allenby arrived to find that Chetwode had written an appreciation of the situation and an outline plan for an offensive operation: *Notes on the Palestine Campaign*. Liking what he saw, Allenby set about implementing Chetwode's recommendations. There was probably a good deal in the plan that chimed with Allenby's experiences of dispersed, mobile war against the Boers in South Africa. This would also explain Allenby's immediate support for Lawrence and the Arab Revolt.

At about the time of Allenby's arrival, the Turks also conducted a reorganization. The former German Chief of the Imperial General Staff, General Erich von Falkenhayn, had recently arrived. Falkenhayn, like Allenby, was also under a cloud, after the costly failure of the Verdun offensive to deliver victory, and his move to the Middle East came in the wake of his replacement by the partnership of Field Marshal Paul von

Hindenburg and his deputy, General Erich Ludendorff. Originally intending to put his main effort into the recapture of Baghdad, Falkenhayn had had to abandon this and concentrate on Palestine. He organized his 35,000 men into two Turkish armies: the Seventh, under General Feusi Pasha, and the Eighth, under General Friedrich Freiherr Kress von Kressenstein. Despite their successful repulse of two British attacks, the Turks were in a poor state: short of food, fodder, ammunition and transport. Desertion rates were high, indicating low morale.

The Eighth Army was divided into two corps, with confusingly similar numbers to the British: XX Corps was thinly spread, with only three divisions holding the front between Gaza and Beersheba, astride the Wesh Sheria, a seasonal watercourse, and another division in reserve. XXII Corps defended Gaza itself with two divisions. To the east of the main north–south railway line from Beersheba, the Seventh Army had originally been intended for operations against Baghdad, and most of its troops were concentrated around Aleppo, in Syria. Many of them never reached the Gaza area in time for the coming battle; thus, the Army defended Beersheba with the two divisions of II Corps in the town and another division covering the flank. The Reserve Corps was held under Seventh Army command some 25 miles north but able to move forward by train. The Turks were outnumbered by the British by about three to one in infantry, eight to one in mounted troops and about three to two in guns; moreover, they were in the midst of their reorganization. However, they enjoyed a strong defensive position.

II. CHETWODE'S PLAN

Chetwode was well aware of the strength of the Turkish position and the uselessness of throwing infantry at it. Even if this had succeeded in breaking *into* the position, it would have been unlikely to break *through*, as any exploitation would have been vulnerable to flanking counter-attacks. Instead, he decided to exploit the British advantage in mobile troops to get around the Turkish left, or eastern, flank. Here, the Turks were relatively weak, there was an inter-army boundary that could be exploited, and the Turks clearly believed that scarcity of water would make enemy operations impossible. Chetwode saw that, once round the flank, the attackers could threaten to encircle Gaza by striking towards the coast and cutting the roads and railways north. He also saw that deception would be vital to this manoeuvre. The Turks would have to believe that the next blow would fall directly against Gaza, so preparations for such a move, and feint attacks, would have to be overt and convincing, while preparations and preliminary moves near Beersheba for encirclement would have to be carefully screened. The plan therefore called for Bulfin's XXI Corps to demonstrate against Gaza, Chetwode's XX Corps to demonstrate elsewhere on von Kressenstein's Eighth Army's front, and then for Chauvel's Desert Mounted Corps and XX Corps to attack Beersheba from the south and east. These moves would be assisted by a squadron of Bristol fighters, newly arrived, which would clear the Turks' reconnaissance aircraft from the skies, and by the famous Meinerzhagen ruse. Other measures would also assist the deception: a heavy patrol programme was to be initiated around Beersheba; troops moving towards Beersheba were to leave their camps standing at Gaza, well lit by night; and even the construction of the railway and water pipeline were to be left to the last safe moment.

The critical factor against which this course of action had to be tested was resources: in order to supply a force of two corps in the east, the railway would have to be extended from the coast to double its length; water brought forward to fill ancient cisterns, including a new half-million gallon reservoir; wells drilled; and ammunition, food and fodder stockpiled. Once the offensive had been launched, the attack force would be reliant on pack animals, so further wells and cisterns would have to be captured at Beersheba on the first day of the operation. Preparations began at once, with D-Day set for 29 October.

III. BEERSHEBA

The demonstrations began as planned on 29 October, preceded by a two-day naval bombardment and fire from the guns of Bulfin's XXI Corps. On the night of 30–31 October, 47,500 men of Chetwode's XX Corps and the 11,000 men of Chauvel's Desert Mounted Corps moved to their forming-up points for the attack on Beersheba; these moves were detected by the Turks, but the demonstration at Gaza was so effective that

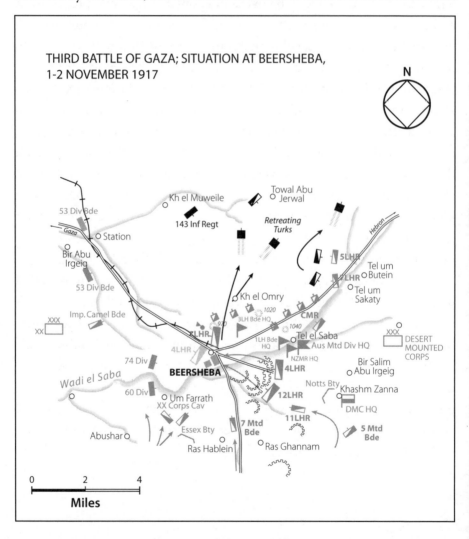

THIRD BATTLE OF GAZA; SITUATION AT BEERSHEBA, 1-2 NOVEMBER 1917

N

Map 11: Beersheba, 27 October 1917

von Kressenstein believed the force directed at Beersheba to be no more than two divisions in strength. The mounted divisions had the furthest to go, a night march of up to 30 miles, in order to attack Beersheba from the east. Closest were the infantry divisions, which would attack from the south. Between the two assault forces, Barrow's Yeomanry Division would act as a link. The sequence of the main attack was to be as follows: first, the infantry divisions of XX Corps would secure the outlying Turkish strong points to the south and east of Beersheba, driving the Turks back into the main position; then the Mounted Corps would attack, followed by a diversionary attack on Gaza in order to draw the Turkish reserves away from the eastern flank. It would therefore be up to two days before XX Corps mounted its main attack.

With the support of all 242 guns in range, the 60th and 74th Divisions had cleared the outer defences of Beersheba by late afternoon on 31 October; to the east and north-east, Chaytor's ANZAC Mounted Division secured the redoubts at Tel as Sakaty and Tel es Saba after some fierce fighting. Shortly afterwards, the Anzacs began to work in to Beersheba from the north. Even so, the attack was moving too slowly, and Chauvel knew that he had to make up time. His solution was simple: a cavalry charge by 4 Light Horse Brigade, supported by 5 Mounted Infantry Brigade – a famous event. Executed with speed and daring, it carried the Light Horse straight through the deadly zone of enemy fire and into the main position. Then it was hand-to-hand combat – but the Turks would not stand. The Light Horse lost 31 killed and 32 wounded but took 1,000 prisoners and nine guns. Just as important, they prevented the Turks from destroying all but two of the 17 vital wells and cisterns. Along with the capture of two large reservoirs, and an unexpected rainstorm, this was enough to sustain the operation. By 4 November, engineers were producing 390,000 gallons a day at Beersheba; however, the Turks still controlled the water supplies to the north.

Chetwode pushed a strong guard force northwards to protect his flank, moving Mott's 53rd (Welsh) Division, Chaytor's ANZAC Division and Smith's Imperial Camel Brigade towards Khuweilfe and along the Hebron road. Over the coming days, the Turks were drawn to these formations, with the result that an effective, coordinated counter-stroke became impossible anywhere along the line.

IV. GAZA

While the mounted troops had been in action at Beersheba, the bombardment of Gaza in support of the deception operation had begun on 27 October with 218 guns plus those of the ships offshore, concentrated on 5,000 yards of front running inland from the sea. The assault was fixed for the night of 1–2 November, in two phases. The first phase, the break-in, was to be undertaken by Hare's 54th Division, reinforced with a brigade of Hill's 52nd Division and six tanks. The attack was a complete success: the dominating feature of Umbrella Hill was taken before midnight, with all other objectives secured soon afterwards. The second phase – the main attack – began four hours later. After only two-and-a-half hours, a penetration of 3,000 yards had been achieved. This obliged the Turks to commit reserves (as had been intended) to shore up the position; however, the depth of the penetration effectively opened up the flank of the prepared positions around the town.

A pause now followed, while operations at Beersheba were developed and water and supplies replenished. The decisive attack was timed for 6 November, against the central stretch of 8 miles of Turkish trenches running eastward from the village of Sheria to Hareira, known as the Qawuqa system. Three divisions of XXI Corps were to be committed: Longley's 10th (Irish) in the west, Shea's 60th (2nd London) in the centre and Girdwood's 74th (Yeomanry) in the east, attacking on an axis which would at first be oriented eastwards and then swing north and east, rolling up the Turkish line towards Gaza. There would be a 15-mile gap between XX and XXI Corps, which would be covered by Hodgson's Australian Mounted Division.

The 74th Division was the first to attack, and the Turks defended their positions with great determination. However, by mid-afternoon, the

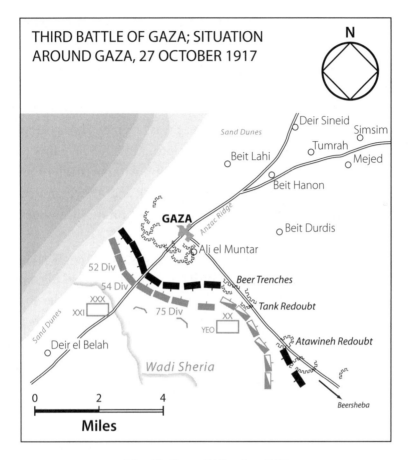

Map 12: Gaza, 27 October 1917

division had advanced 5 miles, securing the necessary break-in, and had taken all its objectives. The 60th and 10th Divisions were able to exploit the break-in, working across the main Qawuqa system, supported by the massed fire of the corps artillery. By 4.30 p.m., Shea's men, who had captured the railway station at Sheria, began their swing to the north to capture the Turkish redoubt on the hill of Tel-el-Sheria, but continued stubborn defence by the Turks, and the coming of night, halted operations. However, the Turks had lost heart and were burning their stores and blowing up ammunition dumps.

During the night, a retreat began. The next morning, 7 November,

Bulfin directed XXI Corps to return to the attack on Gaza itself, with Hare's 54th Division attacking from the sand dunes to the east, and Palin's 75th Division attacking the strong point of Ali Muntar from the west. The attacking British troops found Gaza all but abandoned, and all objectives were taken with comparative ease; the corps cavalry brigade entered the city at 9.00 a.m. Tel-el-Sheria was taken by Shea's troops soon after dawn, and Hareira Redoubt was captured with heavy loss after an attack by Irish battalions of the 10th Division without artillery preparation. The final positions, based on the old Tank and Atawineh Redoubts, held by the Turkish 54th Division, were taken on 8 November by the 75th Division.

With the Turks' main position broken open, Allenby was anxious to switch to pursuit. Accordingly, he ordered Chauvel to push his mounted formations north-west towards al-Jammama and Huq in order to secure the supplies of water there and so further extend the range of his troops. Once this was done, Allenby intended the Mounted Corps to cut the Turks' line of retreat across the Plain of Philistria by advancing to the coast. Accordingly, Chaytor's Anzacs moved on al-Jammama while Hodgson's Australians, supported by Shea's Londoners, moved on Huq. For the plan to work, Huq and its water supplies had to be reached on 7 November; however, in the time available for the move the two mounted divisions for this operation, the Mounted Corps could muster only four brigades out of the ten in its order of batle – should they encounter sustained resistance they would be unable to deal with it rapidly enough to meet this time-line.

After consolidating Tel-el-Sheria, the 60th Division pressed on northwards, but an action by a strong Turkish rearguard stopped the advance. Four Light Horse Brigade, with two regiments, mounted a hasty attack off the line of march but could not close with the enemy. It was not until later that evening that a deliberate attack by the 60th Division cleared the way. The advance on Huq was resumed the following morning, but again, a strong Turkish rearguard, supported by machine guns and artillery, was encountered. This time, a cavalry charge by the Warwickshire and

Worcestershire Yeomanry Regiments managed to reach the guns, despite heavy losses. In doing so they destroyed the last Turkish force in front of Huq, and the village was entered later that day. Chaytor's Anzacs fared less well, not reaching al-Jammama until 9 November; however, they held the village in the face of a strong Turkish counter-attack.

These various engagements prevented the pursuit gaining the momentum required to complete the destruction of the Turkish army.

V. THE RESULTS

Third Gaza was a triumph of tactical deception, meticulous planning and logistic preparation. For the British, it at last unlocked the main Turkish defensive line, which had held them up for nine months. It cost nearly 20,000 British and Imperial casualties, of whom the great majority were wounded – cheap by the standards of the Western Front in 1917, where the dreadful grind of Third Ypres–Passchendaele was reaching its appalling climax at roughly the same time. The Turks lost heavily in killed, wounded, deserters and prisoners: by December, half their force was gone, of whom 12,000 were prisoners – losses they could not replace. The defeat also sowed the seeds of considerable dissention between the Turkish Army and its German allies. Von Kressenstein was relieved of his command before the end of the year, and the Turks thus lost the services of a capable and sympathetic commander. The renowned General Otto Liman von Sanders arrived to take charge in February 1918, but too late to stop the inevitable. By contrast, Allenby's reputation was restored by his success.

In the weeks that followed the battle, the Turks fell back 75 miles: the flame of the Arab Revolt was fanned; Jerusalem fell on 9 December after further hard fighting; and the way was opened for the conquest of Syria, the fall of Damascus and, with it, the loss of all Turkey's provinces in south-west Asia. But in the end, Haig was probably right. The surrender of Turkey came only days before the collapse of Germany. It would have taken a far earlier defeat of Turkey to have allowed the transfer of Allied effort to the West; and to have generated the extra divisions needed to produce such a collapse would have entailed considerable risk. Palestine, in military terms, remained a strategic diversion. In the context of world history, however, it gave rise to the Balfour Declaration of 1917, the British Mandate in Palestine and the eventual birth of the state of Israel.

7

Amiens, 1918: The Black Day of the German Army

I. THE WAR IN 1918

On 8 August 1918, the corps of the British Fourth Army – the Canadian, ANZAC and III British – supported on its right by the French First Army, launched the decisive battle of Amiens. It was a truly combined-arms operation in the modern sense, in which artillery, infantry, horsed cavalry, armoured cars, tanks, armoured personnel carriers, gas, motorized supply, railways and aircraft were integrated to a degree that bears comparison with the early years of the Second World War. When the operation was closed down three days later, the Germans had been pushed back 8 miles; more importantly, the will of their commander, General Erich Ludendorff, had been broken. From then until November, the record of the British and Empire armies was to be one of unbroken success against an enemy who, although not the power he had been, was still capable of maintaining a resolute and well-ordered defence up to the moment of the Armistice, having carried out that most difficult of operations, a fighting withdrawal in contact.

In terms of the level of coordination required, this operation represents an object lesson in the effectiveness of late-war British tactics and the competence of the British Expeditionary Force in putting them into practice. The technology involved demonstrated the effects of the Industrial Revolution as it approached its climax, with all the ingredients of modern war before the technological revolution of the 1960s brought the full exploitation of the electro-magnetic spectrum into play, save one: tactical radio. Radios there were, to be sure, but not below divisional-headquarters level, so coordination was still dependent on pre-arranged timings and phase lines, and on messages passed by telephone, runner or light. Cutting-edge technologies, like aircraft, coexisted and cooperated with horsed cavalry – a legacy of organization from an earlier age of warfare. Even so, this was an army that looked much more like that of 1940 than of 1914.

By the summer of 1918, the Germans' last throw – the series of offensives, known collectively as Operation MICHAEL, that had begun on 21 March – had petered out with appalling losses. They had shaken the Allies, they had broken *into* Allied territory – but they had not broken *through*. They had, moreover, forced the Allies to accept at least an embryonic supreme command under Marshal Ferdinand Foch, and Foch was in a position at least to coordinate Allied moves. The French and American operations in Champagne had been planned for July, and the Amiens plan as proposed to him was attractive, for it gave him the chance to switch pressure points across the front, keep the Germans off balance, oblige them to move reserves and, above all, make them react. In short, it allowed him to maintain the initiative.

In the medium term, Foch had the prospect of a huge, fresh American army to take up the fight, but even without it, the casualties sustained by the Germans during their spring offensives had decisively changed the force ratios on the Western Front. In July 1918, the Germans disposed 202 infantry and four cavalry divisions, but most were badly under strength and, as prisoners captured by patrols attested, their morale was shaky. Against them were ranged 194 Allied infantry and nine Allied cavalry divisions: even odds, but the Allies had the ability to concentrate where they wished. The Allies were also, for the first time, better equipped than the Germans in artillery and in aircraft, and benefited from important technical advances in ammunition, especially the fusing of artillery shells.

II. RAWLINSON'S GRAND DESIGN

The course of the River Somme northwards from Péronne, where it changes its course in a sharp turn from north-south to run east–west, lay 20 miles from the line just east of Villers Bretonneux on which the Germans had been halted in April. The ground there – rolling chalk down-land – was perfect tank country, and especially favourable during June and July because of dry weather. It stretched 7 miles from the east–west stretch of the River Somme near Villers Bretonneux to the River Luce, a marshy stream which provided some flank protection to an attacker. A mile or so east of the German lines lay the old fortifications of the Amiens Inner Defence Line; 6 miles further east the old Amiens Outer Defence Line provided a clearly defined objective. Both these lines were seamed with old wire obstacles, trenches and dugouts; but another 5 miles to the east, running roughly north–south, stretched the broad belt of the old Somme battlefield, from which the Germans had withdrawn in early 1917. This was a veritable labyrinth of trenches, shell holes and craters, with thick belts of wire and other obstacles, all now covered in a rank growth of rough grass. Within this belt stood Lihons Ridge, commanding a fine view in all directions and especially over the railway junction at Chaulnes, where met the four lines on which the maintenance of the German armies between the Somme and the River Oise depended. Across the area ran two great paved roads from Amiens, one to St Quentin and the other to Roye, both granite surfaced, lined with poplars and straight as a die. North of the Somme, the ground became much closer and more wooded, with a series of spurs reaching down to the river and dominating the southern side. On these spurs, with steep valleys either side, tanks could not be used, and an attacker faced a series of complex problems; for example, what might seem obvious to an observer on the southern side was hidden to anyone on the north. These, then, were the major geographical features which would dictate the form and course of the coming battle.

The commander of the British Fourth Army, which was to make the attack, was General Sir Henry Rawlinson. Nicknamed 'the Fox', he was a man possessed of subtlety, imagination and vision to a degree not shared by any other army commander except Sir Herbert Plumer. Alone among his fellows, Rawlinson was an infantry officer – but he made a point of being always faultlessly dressed and being an accomplished horseman and polo player. He had available the Canadian Corps, made up of four Canadian divisions and one British division; the Australian and New Zealand Army Corps (ANZAC), which, despite its name, comprised five Australian divisions; and the III (British) Corps, of four British divisions and one US division. He was also allocated the three divisions of Cavalry Corps from General Headquarters Reserve. These forces would be supported by the entire strength of the Tank Corps: 244 fighting tanks in nine battalions of Mark Vs and Mark V*s. The Mark V* was longer than the standard tank, designed to cross wide obstacles like trenches, ditches and belts of wire, and it carried infantry Lewis gun teams. There were also 120 supply tanks; two battalions of 48 Whippet light tanks (96 in total); over 2,000 guns; and, from the Royal Air Force, 800 aircraft of all types and eight observation balloons.

Rawlinson's staff had analyzed the experiences of Cambrai, of the German spring offensives and of Hamel in July. What Rawlinson had proposed, and Haig had accepted, from this analysis was a surprise attack, using the Canadian Corps and ANZAC as the main effort between the Somme and the Amiens–Roye road, close to the boundary between the German Second and Eighteenth Armies. The scheme of manoeuvre would be to capture on the first day the Amiens Outer Defence Line, 6 miles ahead, and subsequently the western edge of the old Somme battlefield west of Chaulnes, breaking the Second Army in that area. To increase the surprise, the Canadians, now at Arras, would be brought in on the right of the attacking force at the last possible moment, with their left on the main railway line from Amiens and their right near the Amiens–Roye road, connecting with the French. The French were to attack in concert and capture Moreuil from the Eighteenth Army.

To the left of the Canadians, the Australians were to form up between the railway and the Somme, and III Corps north of the Somme. The immediate objectives of the assaulting corps were set about 4 miles into

German territory, beyond which the Cavalry Corps would move by forward passage of lines, exploit to the old front line and hold until the infantry of the assault corps closed up.

The ANZAC and Canadian Corps would each employ four divisions in their attack echelons. In reserve, the Australians had their 1st Infantry Division, and the Canadians the 32nd (British) Infantry Division. Each of these two corps was allotted a brigade of four battalions of tanks, each comprising 108 Mark Vs, 36 Mark V*s and 24 supply tanks – a total of 168 tanks per corps. The remaining battalion of tanks was allocated to III Corps. The ANZAC was also allocated a battalion of armoured cars, and the Cavalry Corps, in addition to its three divisions, was given the two battalions of Whippets. In terms of guns, the Canadian Corps and ANZAC had a combined allotment of 490 guns, including 8-inch howitzers and 60-pounders, in addition to their standard 48 guns per division, bringing the total to 922. All this – infantry, cavalry, tanks, armoured cars, guns, plus the mighty stocks of ammunition needed – had to be squeezed into the triangle east of Amiens formed by the 6-mile-long arms of the Somme, the Avre and the front line. There was not much scope for concealment on these rolling uplands; much of the area was under direct observation by the enemy, and in dead ground movement was still observable from the clouds of smoke and dust thrown up.

To achieve his grand design, Rawlinson employed a blend of bluff and secrecy well in keeping with his reputation. He employed two complementary aspects of deception; the first was security and the second, diversion. To achieve security, only the corps commanders were initially told of the plan, and information was kept on close hold throughout the preparations. To divert the enemy's attention, a number of measures were employed: the first was to transmit indications that the Canadian Corps, which had been in reserve since the success at Arras in 1917, had been transferred north for an offensive. Two Canadian battalions were actually put into the line there, the corps wireless link was opened up behind them, and casualty clearing stations arrived in the rear area where spies would be sure to see them. None of the troops thus employed knew that they were engaged in subterfuge. The RAF contributed to the diversion by undertaking great activity in the north and constructing dummy airfields. Both security and diversion were needed to cover the extension of the Fourth Army sector as far as the Amiens–Roye road. This was where the Canadians were to attack, and it was currently occupied by the French. Although a relief in place of the French was feasible, Rawlinson decided to extend the Australian line into that area to give the impression that the Australians were taking on more of the line and going on the defensive. Indeed, it might have been expected that the French would ask for relief, as they were heavily engaged on the River Marne. By dawn on 2 August, therefore, the Australians had handed over the line north of the Somme to III Corps, and a single brigade had taken over the 4 miles of French line south of Villers Bretonneux.

Previous attempts at using the Canadians and Australians together had not worked well, as at Ypres in October 1917; however, commander of the British Expeditionary Force Field Marshal Sir Douglas Haig had long considered using the two corps together as a striking force. Why? The conventional Australian and Canadian view was that their troops represented an élite. Certainly they were a cut above the general run of soldiers in 1918: the Australians were all volunteers, there being no conscription back home; and although conscription had been introduced in Canada, no conscript soldiers had yet made it to the field army. The men of both countries were individualistic, non-deferential and in good physical shape. They had no time for social standing. Their morale, fighting experience and capability were high. From the British point of view, however, they were scruffy, lackadaisical and poorly disciplined. There was some truth in the last as regards the Australians: the crime rate in Australian divisions was 8.5 men per 1,000 in jail in 1918, compared with 1.0 per 1,000 British, Canadians and New Zealanders, and 2.0 per 1,000 South Africans. Cases of venereal disease were 15.3 per 1,000 Australians as against 5.0 per 1,000 British and 3.0 per 1,000 Canadians. Discipline, though, was firmly in the hands of Australian and Canadian officers and their governments – it had been so since the 'Breaker' Morant episode in South Africa – and there was no death penalty. Moreover, the Australians had only five divisions in total, the Canadians four and the New Zealanders one. Set against the 50 British divisions in France and Flanders, six in Italy and 30 in the Middle East, one has to conclude that, however high their quality, in terms of numbers, the view that these men won the war cannot be sustained.

Canadian divisions were still at a strength of 12,000 fighting men, so the Canadian Corps was far stronger than the average British corps – and most German divisions were no more than 4,000. As for the Australians, it was only after Gallipoli – where there had been a single Australian corps – that they had been reinforced from home and formed into two ANZACs: I ANZAC under Sir William Birdwood with the 1st, 2nd and 5th Australian Divisions; and II ANZAC, the 3rd and 4th Australian and the New Zealand Division, under Sir Alexander Godley – both of these Generals were British. In late 1917, all five Australian divisions were concentrated into a single corps, which became the ANZAC, II Corps was re-designated as XXII British Corps and the New Zealand Division was transferred to IV Corps of Byng's Third Army. This concentration was made necessary by the Australians' politically motivated refusal to break up formations after heavy casualties, in order to keep others up to strength. The ANZAC Corps with five divisions was in numbers, therefore, equivalent to a British Corps of three divisions. Maintaining a distinct national corps was of considerable importance to a young country like Australia (and an older but determinedly independent one like Canada), still in the process of nation building. This partly explains why, despite losses, the Australians insisted on maintaining the structure of five divisions when manpower dictated that they should probably reduce to three. In contrast, the two Irish divisions were never allowed to form a corps, nor were the Scottish or Welsh – this would have been far too dangerous. The ANZAC was now commanded by Lieutenant General Sir John Monash, a pre-war Australian militia officer who became Australia's best-known officer during the war.

The view of most colonial troops was that British divisions could not and did not fight, and that they (the colonials) were always given the hard jobs. In reality, however, there were plenty of British divisions of high quality; and, in fact, the colonials were often given easier tasks because of political sensitivities with the Dominion governments. But no one doubted that they could fight. An inscription on a rough wooden cross seen on the battlefield of St Quentin in 1918 recorded: 'Here lie six Bosches. They met a Digger.'

III. THE GERMANS

What of the Germans? Their last gasp had failed, it was true, but their situation was not irretrievable, especially if a respite could be secured for the troops by making a clean break and withdrawing to the fortifications of the *Hindenburg–Stellung* Line. Doing so would shorten the front and save a number of divisions to be brought into reserve. This was the view of the line's architect, and Chief of Staff of the army group concerned, General von Lossberg. It was a view shared by other senior German generals, including Prince Rupprecht of Bavaria – who commanded the army group opposite Rawlinson – and even the Kaiser himself. If this was done, they reasoned, morale could be restored and the opportunity created to inflict such losses on any Allied attack as would shatter the will of the people and their governments to continue the war. At the very least, the prospect of another winter of war with their armies having to endure badly sited, waterlogged and shelterless positions might be enough to induce the British and French to agree to a compromise peace, whatever the Americans might say.

But Ludendorff would have none of this. Voluntary retirements, he said forcibly, gave the enemy the ability to shorten the line themselves, and in turn create reserves or echelons. Besides, they were bad for morale. The most he would accept, should the need arise, was a retirement to the line of the Somme south of Péronne, and the Canal du Nord to the north of it. Von Lossberg protested that it would take far too long to reconnoitre and dig a new position there, but he was overruled. Strategically, Ludendorff was absolutely wrong. Tactically, though, he was on firmer ground, for the grass-grown morass of the old Somme battlefield provided the Germans with a succession of defensible positions easy to hold, virtually tank-proof, and inevitably costly and tedious to attack.

On 4 August, Ludendorff's order of the day contained the message: 'I am under the impression that, in many quarters, the possibility of an enemy offensive is viewed with a certain degree of apprehension. There is nothing to justify this, provided our troops are vigilant and do their duty.'

III. THE ATTACK OPENS

By dawn on 7 August, the main assault force was fully assembled within 2 or 3 miles of the German line. Many trenches had been dug by the Australians to reinforce the German perception that they were on the defensive: these trenches were now crammed with infantry. Three Canadian divisions had been moved up close behind the Australian brigade holding their sector, and a fourth was further back. Tanks had been gradually brought forward into woods and copses or ruined buildings behind the line, with their movement covered by the droning of low-flying Handley Page bombers. The RAF also checked on camouflage and enemy movements. The artillery, although noting German movements, continued to fire routinely on old, abandoned locations as a refinement to the deception plans. When darkness fell, the final moves were made. The 27 mounted regiments – 23 regular and four Yeomanry – in the Cavalry Corps passed through Amiens on sand-strewn streets to assemble with their Whippet tanks and artillery. Patrols crept forward of the trenches to cover the forming-up in no-man's-land, followed by teams with rolls of white tape to mark out the assembly areas. Each battalion was allocated a marked box with guides for each company so that the ten assault brigades, each on a frontage of about 1 mile, could be led into position in pitch darkness. Within each brigade box, battalions were formed into four echelons, each of one company, with a fifth echelon of stretcher-bearers. By 2.00 a.m., a thick mist was beginning to form; at 4.20 a.m., dawn began to glimmer and, as it did, the sky was lit up for 6 miles either side of Amiens as 3,500 British and French guns began to pound the German positions, returning with

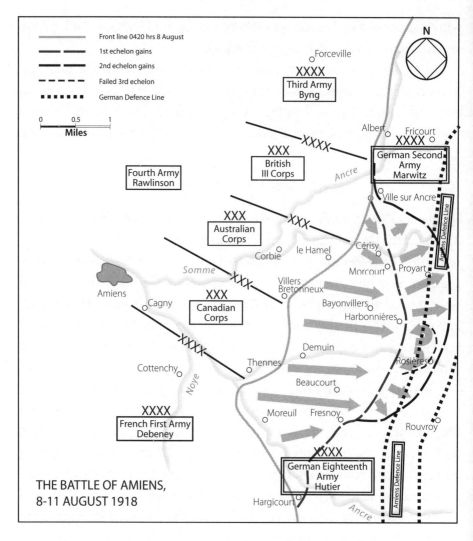

Front line 0420 hrs 8 August
1st echelon gains
2nd echelon gains
Failed 3rd echelon
German Defence Line

Miles
0   0.5   1

THE BATTLE OF AMIENS,
8-11 AUGUST 1918

Map 13: Amiens, 8–11 August 1918

interest the treatment meted out on 21 April, and announcing the Black Day of the German Army.

IV. THE AUSTRALIANS ON 8 AUGUST

After only three minutes on the forward line, the barrage made a lift of 100 yards and the men of seven Allied divisions fell on those of the six weak divisions of the German Second Army facing them from beyond the Luce on the left and to north of the Somme on the right. Another three divisions waited in the second echelon. Although the Germans had six divisions in reserve, none was closer than three hours' march and unable therefore to intervene immediately.

Rawlinson had allocated tanks on the rough basis of six per 1,000 yards of front. With such a thin spread, it might be expected that shock action would not be the order of the day against a well-ordered defence. Yet the impact was devastating. The Germans were taken completely by surprise, all the more so given the thick fog. For the attackers, this fog made infantry–tank cooperation extremely difficult, but it also blinded the Germans and increased the demoralizing effect of the monstrous machines' sudden appearance. Just as paralyzing was the sudden strike of the artillery, hitting targets that the Germans had believed concealed and landing in a density for which they had no notion the Allies had either the guns or the ammunition. Major General C. E. D. Budworth, Rawlinson's artillery commander, proved himself a match for the great Bruckmüller.

The Australians had a relatively easy passage. The assault troops kept close up behind the barrage and were through the enemy wire and on the positions as soon as it lifted. Every three minutes the process was repeated, with the line of shell bursts moving on 100 yards as a fresh wave of cheering men burst on the enemy, accompanied by their tanks. Here and there machine-gun posts sited in depth gave trouble, but none survived long. A group of four guns, well wired-in and protected by an infantry company, was taken in a single-handed attack by Lieutenant Albert Gaby of the 28th Battalion of the Australian Expeditionary Force. His was the only Australian Victoria Cross that day, which shows the lack of opportunity rather than any lack of courage by the attackers.

Well before 7.00 a.m., the two Australian assault divisions, the 2nd on the right and the 3rd on the left, had advanced the 2 miles to their objective. For news of his men, Monash was relying on homing pigeons, on reports dropped from aircraft with weights and streamers attached, or, once the fog lifted, on mounted staff officers and motorcycle dispatch

riders. It was a slow process: signal lamps, the fastest means of communication, were still not usable because of the fog. Without waiting for
a full picture, Monash decided that success was complete enough for the
second echelon to begin moving. All artillery belonging to the 4th and
5th Divisions was moved from the initial gun lines to forward positions;
engineers assisted the second wave of tanks to get forward, and also began
to fill in ditches and craters on the road to allow armoured cars to come up.

The 4th and 5th Divisions, on the left and right respectively, crossed
their start lines on time at 8.20 a.m. and, as they did so, the August sun
began to disperse the fog. The scene was one never seen before: infantry advancing by sections, with tanks in intimate support, followed by
limbered-up field guns and, behind them, long files of cavalry.

The 4th Division made slower progress than the 5th, as it was forced to
clear out the close country next to the River Somme. The 5th Division had
much more open country and rapidly closed on the village of Bayonvillers.
As it did so, three German batteries opened up in direct fire. The tanks and
infantry went straight into the assault, and the gun crews which survived
were soon among the hundreds of German prisoners making their way
towards the rear; however, eight tanks were blazing hulks. Even so, tanks
continued to move ahead of the infantry, blasting out machine-gun posts
and keeping close behind the advancing barrage.

Soon after 9.00 a.m., the cavalry began to make their first effective
appearance on the battlefield since 1914. Leading the corps was a squadron of the Queen's Bays, from 1 Cavalry Brigade. Pushing on from
Bayonvillers, the squadron found a column of German transport trying
to escape south, which it captured. The Bays then moved on Harbonniers,
2 miles further on, but it was strongly held and the Bays were forced into
cover until Whippet tanks and infantry came up and forced an entry.
As they did so, a squadron of the 5th Dragoon Guards moved past the
northern side of the village and reached the final objective, the old Amiens
Outer Defence Line. The time was 10.00 a.m., and the penetration of
6 miles had been achieved in 5 hours 40 minutes. As the 5th Dragoon
Guards consolidated, smoke was seen coming from a train half a mile off.

Two squadrons pursued and found two trains, disabled by the RAF, one of which was newly arrived and full of German reinforcements. All were killed or captured. The second train contained an 11-inch gun which had been firing on Amiens, and whose crew had been killed by a bomb while in the act of firing.

Shortly afterwards, armoured cars began to appear on the main road, after the tanks had removed obstacles from it. These cars were capable of 20 mph backwards or forwards and mounted two turrets, each with a Hotchkiss machine gun. They had a busy time. Just short of the final objective, making for the Somme, they encountered a mass of German infantry attacking the Australians and dispersed them. One section then moved north and shot up a headquarters where the staff were all sitting down to a meal. Another section travelled a further 4 miles up the road to Roye shooting up dumps, sending back prisoners and engaging German artillery. A third section went south and shot up the local German corps HQ, after which a large column of transport – horses, lorries and steam wagons – was also attacked. Many cars broke down or ran out of fuel before the day was out and were towed backwards, often by the German prisoners they had captured.

But the momentum of the 4th Division was checked around the villages of Cerisy and Morcourt, on the Somme, as they came under extremely effective fire from the spur on the opposite bank, above the village of Chipilly. Six tanks were among the casualties, and instead of pushing on to his final objective in Mericourt, divisional commander Major General E. G. Sinclair-Maclagan halted his men on the high ground and went into hasty defence.

V. CHIPILLY

What had brought about the check from across the river? Possession of Chipilly Spur had given the Germans a tactical advantage as far back as 27–28 March, during the MICHAEL offensives; now, as then, the troops on the south side of the Somme who were under observed fire from the spur could lay the blame for their plight on their compatriots on the north of the river. Chipilly Spur was the final objective for the 58th (London) Division of III Corps. A report actually reached the ANZAC HQ that the spur had been captured, but this turned out – in common with almost every other first report in military history – to be wrong. The 58th Division had not reached the spur, but had managed an advance of 2 miles in difficult terrain, something which a year before would have been heralded as fabulous.

III Corps' assault brigade had not had an easy time. The divisions were mostly conscripts, and under strength, thus by no means on a par with the Australians and Canadians; and, because of the nature of the ground, they had only one battalion of tanks in support. The Germans had detected the 58th Division early on and had hammered the assembly areas with high explosive and gas shells; moreover, the force ratios were highly unfavourable to the attackers, being only about 1:1. Even so, the sudden bombardment of 4.20 a.m. had had a devastating effect, especially on German batteries crowding the wooded valleys by the river. The Londoners were thus able to grope forward through the mist, wearing gas masks, and evict the Germans from their positions. The leading brigades managed to keep roughly in pace with the barrage, moving up and down the deep valleys, and reaching the corps' primary objective at the price of leaving a large number of isolated German posts to be mopped up later.

It was from here to the final objective that things began to go adrift. The second-echelon brigade of the 58th Division passed through to take Chipilly Spur, but had to make a steep descent down a ravine, and then a steep ascent the other side, and could not keep up with the barrage. Even at this stage of the war, it was the British method to make the infantry keep pace with the timed barrage, whereas the German artillery was controlled by the pace of the infantry. This allowed the German machine gunners to play havoc with the advancing troops. Allied airmen, however, reported that there were friendly troops on the spur; a reserve battalion (2nd/2nd Londons) sent in to reinforce the attack was deprived of its barrage, as the artillery understandably did not wish to fire on friendly troops, with the result that it was cut to pieces in minutes. The rest of the reserve brigade was then committed, but it too failed when the barrage fell almost a mile ahead.

All attempts to capture the spur, which dominated the Australians' line of advance south of the river, failed. This was heart-breaking for those involved but, in the big picture, not decisive. The official history later tried to blame the low-level leadership and standard of training of the troops; Liddell Hart – who was not present – described the division as lacking in ardour. These are unworthy and, indeed, untruthful accusations. Whatever went wrong was in no way due to a lack of courage or vigour on the part of the men in the front line.

VI. THE CANADIANS

Sir Arthur Currie, the big, well-built commander of the Canadian Corps, was not able to make his plan as simple as Monash's. Between the railway line and Hangard Wood, which was inclusive to his corps, where the country was mostly open and rolling, he placed two divisions in the first echelon: the 1st on the right, the 2nd on the left. Each division was to attack with one brigade in the first echelon and two brigades in the second. From Hangard Wood, across the Luce and astride the main road, linking with the French 42nd Infantry Division, he placed the 3rd Infantry Division, whose objectives included the ruined village of Hangard, Demuin and the important high ground across which ran the main road to Roye. Especially dominating here were Hamon Wood and Rifle Wood, the latter so called after it had been fought over with great ferocity by the 20th (Light) Division during MICHAEL. This brigade sector was the area which had been taken over from the French, and was only just over 1 mile wide and 100 yards deep; into it was squeezed an assault brigade of four strong battalions and a company of tanks brought in through the French sector at the last safe moment. The assembly had been completed in secrecy, and when the barrage struck the high ground astride the road at 4.20 a.m., the assaulting battalion (the 43rd Manitoba) followed it closely, attacking from the north-west. Two other battalions, the 58th and 116th, followed the course of the Luce from west to east, the 116th in the south assaulting Hamon Wood from the direction we are observing, the 58th moving straight into Demuin. The fourth battalion of this brigade, the 16th, pushed straight on for Aubercourt. This was a tricky series of manoeuvres but well executed. The German troops of the 225th Infantry Division fought well, and the mist made infantry–tank cooperation very difficult, but there was no stopping the Canadians. The French division to the north also attacked, although it was late crossing the start line. With the heavy weight of artillery fire available, good progress was made at first, but the French soon became bogged down.

In terms of tanks, the Canadians had put more into the assault than the Australians – 36 with the 3rd Division, 21 with the 1st Division and 17 with the 2nd Division. Their fortunes were roughly proportionate to their distance from the boggy ground around the Luce. Of the 28 that crossed to the south side of the river, eight were knocked out by gunfire and eight broke down or bogged in. On the open ground north of the river, the tanks forged ahead of the infantry and caused panic among the Germans, but in the mist they bypassed a number of machine-gun posts, especially in Hangard Wood and the copses beyond. In Hangard Wood, two VCs were won. Corporal Herman Good and Private John Croak both served with the 13th Royal Highlanders (1st Division), and together they accounted for seven machine-gun posts and three howitzers. In Demuin, another VC was won posthumously by Corporal Harry Miner of the 58th Ontario Battalion (3rd Division). A fourth VC was won later in the day by Lieutenant James Tait of the 78th Nova Scotia Highlanders. This tally shows how much stronger the opposition was in this sector than in the Australian.

By 11.00 a.m., the assault brigades had all achieved both their immediate and subsequent objectives and were adopting hasty defence roughly on the line la Vallée wood–Ignaucourt–Marcelcave. With the mist dispersed, the whole area south of the Somme, seen from the air, was covered with infantry, cavalry, tanks and guns moving forward, while bodies of prisoners moved to the rear escorted by a few wounded Canadians. Overhead, the RAF went busily about its business. The noise was almost all of movement rather than firing. Now was the time for the cavalry to exploit out the 6 miles to the old Somme battlefield between Roye and Chaulnes.

VII. EXPLOITATION

As the break-in had been pushed successfully forward, the cavalry was well placed to turn it into a break-through. A 1918 cavalry division was not just horsemen armed with sword and lance, it was a true combined-arms formation which included horse artillery, horsed machine-gun crews, engineers, medical services, signal companies and a full suite of services for men and animals. It could cooperate effectively with armoured cars and infantry, although it lacked protection and could be quickly halted by heavy fire from well-dug-in positions. Effective cooperation with aircraft could have solved this problem, but this would have relied on wireless communications, which were not sufficiently well developed in 1918. For all that, the speed and mobility of the horse still – just – surpassed those of mechanical transport and made the cavalry the natural arm of exploitation.

The 3rd Cavalry Division passed through the Canadians at about 11.00 a.m. as they consolidated on their subsequent objectives, but ran into trouble from German machine-gun posts. Even so, it pressed on and reached the objective on the old Amiens Outer Defence Line soon after noon. Here it halted and awaited orders from the corps. None came.

The 1st Cavalry Division had moved through the Canadians soon after 9.00 a.m. and it, too, ran into trouble with machine guns. Progress had to await the arrival of the infantry; however, the division was soon moving forward again and it too reached the objective.

With these two divisions were the two battalions of Whippet tanks – a mismatch in mobility and protection, but one that could be complementary: when there was no opposition, the cavalry outstripped the tanks, which could make only about 4 mph across country; when enemy machine guns opened up, the cavalry was paralyzed until the tanks got forward.

On reaching the old Amiens Outer Defence Line, the 1st Cavalry Division, like the 3rd, halted. Had the cavalry not paused but pushed into the old Somme battlefield around Chaulnes, the result must be a matter of speculation; however, the ground there was virtually impassable for horses or tanks.

Meanwhile, there were troubles for the high command at GHQ with the French First Army on the right flank beyond the main road. At 11.30 a.m., Haig asked the army commander, General Debeney, to push forward all his cavalry on the British right to support the exploitation, in particular to move on Montdidier from the rear. Debeney replied that his cavalry were too far away and would not be available until noon next day. Anyway, the roads were blocked by infantry and wagons. Haig went to see Debeney in person during the afternoon and asked him to send his cavalry to join the British by unblocked roads, but Debeney had taken counsel of his fears: the Canadians had been as far forward as Mezières at 10.30 a.m. while the French did not make it that far until dusk.

Despite the good progress, there were still 2 miles to be crossed to the old Somme battlefield around the ruined village of Caix, and so, in the absence of word from Headquarters Cavalry Corps, the 1st and 3rd Cavalry Divisions began to exploit forward during the afternoon. Astride the main road and blocking the way ahead were German reserves which had come forward and occupied the villages of Le Quesnel and Fresnoy. After a time, the Canadian second echelon division, the 4th Infantry, came up and deployed 30 Mark V* tanks with infantry Lewis gun detachments embarked. Nine of these tanks were engaged and set on fire by camouflaged guns around the perimeter of le Quesnel, and 11 others were variously disabled. Three more were knocked out while supporting the infantry around Beaucourt Wood, which was being cleared out after being bypassed by the cavalry: it was here that Lieutenant Tait won his VC. Come nightfall, Le Quesnel had not been taken, and it was decided to postpone the attempt until next morning, when better artillery support could be put together. In the meantime, the Germans managed to bring up three fresh divisions during the night.

VIII. FOLLOW-UP OPERATIONS, 9–10 AUGUST

Zero hour for 9 August was fixed by the Canadian Corps for 4.20 a.m. – an odd decision, and it would probably have been better for overall coordination if the army commander had set the time. As it was, the attacks on 9 August were disjointed and the reinforced enemy put up a stiff resistance – stiffer as the day went on and another three reserve divisions arrived to shore up the line. Tank casualties in particular were heavy; only 145 started the second day, for German 77 mm guns had taken a heavy toll. Despite this, the capture of Le Quesnel, a subsidiary operation, was completed as a set piece by the Canadian 4th Division around 11.00 a.m., after which the 3rd Division took up the lead, heading generally south-eastwards, and by dusk had secured the village of Bouchoir. To their left, the 1st Division moved off at 1.00 p.m. and by dusk had consolidated on the villages of Warvillers, Beaufort and Rouvroi. The Canadian advance was completed by the 2nd Division, which reached its objectives at Rosières and Vrely around 9.00 p.m. that night. Another 3 miles had been covered, and the link-up with the cavalry on the Amiens Outer Defence Line had been made.

North of the Amiens-Chaulnes railway line, the Australians also successfully achieved their objectives. They had a shorter distance to attack, and by early afternoon were secure on the line Vauvillers–Framerville. Diggers from the 1st Division then passed through, and three hours later they were entrenching hastily on the western slopes of Lihons Hill 3 miles beyond the Amiens Outer Defence Line and within easy reach of the rail junction at Chaulnes.

Further south, the French 31st Division had again lagged behind. Foch had personally urged Debeney to move quickly on Roye, 'without losing a moment and preventing any delay or hesitation'. This provoked no response. Haig found Debeney obstructive when he visited his headquarters that afternoon; fortunately for Debeney, who might well have found himself having to consider his future, the Germans solved the problem for him. That night, Ludendorff agreed to Prince Rupprecht's request for the withdrawal of General Oskar von Hutier's Eighteenth Army.

Zero hour on 10 August was again 4.20 a.m., and as the early-morning mist cleared, the day turned sultry. The Canadians pressed on to Parvilliers-le-Quesnoy, Fouquescourt and the western edge of Damery. Here they began to meet serious opposition from German reserve formations ordered up by Ludendorff from as far away as Verdun, St Mihiel and Laon, including 1st Bavarian Corps units and regiments of the 38th, 119th, and 121st Infantry Divisions, which mounted a series of counter-attacks lasting until late in the evening. The Australians also made some limited progress to Mericourt and Auger Woods; they too were heavily counter-attacked, but hung on, breaking up the German attacks with heavy artillery and machine-gun fire, and consolidating on Lihons Ridge south of Bray-sur-Somme. Prince Rupprecht had ordered that divisions were not to be committed piecemeal, but were to wait until a coordinated counter-attack could be put together, concentrating on the flanks of the Allied penetration, south of the Somme and along the Amiens–Roye road. These were sound orders but difficult to carry out, and in the event, counter-attacks were piecemeal, allowing the Allied formations to beat them off.

North of the river, III Corps finally secured the Chipilly feature on 9 August; the US 131st Infantry Regiment, which had reinforced the corps, distinguished itself by sweeping all before it, capturing Etinehem Spur. The corps took more than 3,000 prisoners and 70 guns, and handed over the spur to the Australians, Monash being eager to secure control of both banks of the river with a view to future operations.

IX. CONSOLIDATION

Early on 10 August, Haig began a tour of the front by train and motor. German resistance was stiffening all the time, and freedom of movement was being constrained as the troops entered the old Somme battlefield; tank strength was down to 67 at best, and the troops were tired. Foch arrived at Haig's headquarters train near Wiry around mid-morning, fired up with the success of the operation, and insistent that the Fourth Army must push on the 8 miles to the Somme. At the same time, Haig must go over to the offensive with his other armies and at least capture Bapaume and Aubers Ridge. Haig, doubtful, agreed to consider these ideas, and that afternoon he went to see Rawlinson in his field command post near Demuin. This was very close to the front for an army-level headquarters, and rather gives the lie to the old image of generals in châteaux miles from the action. No one knows for sure what passed between the two men, but it is said that when Rawlinson was told of Foch's wishes, he retorted that the offensive had shot its bolt and then asked, 'Are you commanding the British Army or is Marshal Foch?' Haig left to visit the Canadians, and came rapidly to the conclusion that Rawlinson was right. Finally, he called on Rawlinson again, whose headquarters was now at Villers-Bretonneux.

Haig continued his tour on 11 August, calling on all five Australian divisions. At Monash's headquarters he met General Officer Commanding-in-Chief of the Third Army, General Sir Julian Byng, and told him to get ready to move forward. At Headquarters III Corps he found an exhausted commander, Butler, and ordered him off for a spell of leave, bringing in Sir Alexander Godley to take charge temporarily. On the afternoon of 11 August, Rawlinson called a conference of his corps commanders and staffs. Twenty-four German divisions had been engaged and defeated by 13 infantry and three cavalry divisions, and Allied casualties had been light – around 22,000, or one-third of those on the first day of the Battle of the Somme – especially when compared with the German toll. But he believed that the Germans had been strongly reinforced and were now holding a broad belt of tank-proof country, impenetrable to infantry without huge artillery support. He was right: 12 divisions had been sent up to reinforce the line, along with artillery, and Prince Rupprecht was confident that he could hold his line. The Germans had also brought in considerable air support, meaning the RAF was no longer numerically superior: among others, the squadrons of both Manfred von Richthofen and Hermann Goering had appeared. Tank crews were exhausted and their machines in great need of attention and it was not possible to bring forward sufficient artillery pieces and ammunition for another set-piece battle. Rawlinson therefore announced, with Haig's approval, that the operation was suspended for the time being: quite the right decision, since surprise had been lost and the cost in human life had become unacceptable.

For the Germans, the official monograph, *Die Katastrophe des 8 August 1918*, says this:

> As the sun set on 8 August on the battlefield, the greatest defeat which the German Army had suffered since the beginning of the war was an accomplished fact. The position divisions between the Avre and the Somme which had been struck by the enemy attack were nearly completely annihilated.

Their losses in the battle were estimated at 650–700 officers and 26,000 soldiers, not including wounded expected to return to the front within a reasonable time, and more than 400 guns. Of the losses of personnel, 15,700 were prisoners: 7,900 captured by the Australians, 5,000 by the Canadians, and the remaining 1,000 or so by III Corps and the cavalry. For the Australians, casualties were 652, of whom only 83 were killed; for the Canadians, 3,800, of whom 1,000 were killed. The Tank Corps losses were heavy. About 100 tanks were knocked out by German guns or anti-tank rifles; of the 415 that went into battle, only 145 were battle-worthy by the end. The Cavalry Corps lost about 1,000 horses.

X. AFTERMATH

Ludendorff had yet to coin the phrase 'the Black Day of the German Army', and the full extent of the defeat of 8–12 August would not be realized until after the war. However, its results were enough to break the great man's will and plunge him into despair. As early as 9 August, he had telegraphed to Prince Rupprecht that he believed a withdrawal to the line Bapaume–Peronne–Couchy-le-Château would be necessary, and asked for comment – a wire which, copied to Rupprecht's subordinate army commanders, did little to improve their morale. By the time the offensive was closed down, Ludendorff was convinced that the only way to save the German Army was a speedy, negotiated end to the war. He therefore offered his resignation to Hindenburg. It was refused.

Byng's Third Army renewed the offensive to the north of Amiens and, on 21 August, the British broke through the German positions at Albert. Foch then switched the pressure on further south, first at St Mihiel and then in the Meuse–Argonne sector. On 5 October, the mighty Hindenburg Line was broken in a single day – not by élite storm troops, but by a standard British Territorial infantry division – the 46th (North Midland). Just over a month later, with the lines back where they had been around Mons in 1914, the Germans accepted the Allied armistice terms.

Fuller, the Chief of Staff of the Tank Corps, and, later, Liddell Hart would both proclaim later that the victory of Amiens belonged to the tanks. Edmonds, the British official historian, credited the infantry and machine guns with victory, and the artillery as the key enabler. With the benefit of 90 years of hindsight, it is clear that success came from the advantages of surprise and combined-arms shock action. The Germans were totally stunned by the unexpected fury of the opening bombardment and the speed of the follow-up assault. Their tempo never matched that of the Allies. Tribute must be given to meticulous planning at all levels, to the superb fighting spirit of the Australian and Canadian infantry, and to an ever-increasing expertise in all-arms cooperation: here, for the first time, was a recognizably modern force. The common perception of the Great War is one of static attrition mired in mud; this may have been true for much of the time, but there is another side, which Amiens showed.

8

The Arakan, Imphal and Kohima, 1944:
Smashing the Myth

I. EARLY MOVES AND OPERATIONAL PLANS

By the beginning of February 1944, after successful Chindit operations and the consolidation of the defence of India, General Sir William (Bill) Slim, the General Officer Commanding-in-Chief of the Allied Fourteenth Army in Burma, had decided on a limited offensive in the Arakan Peninsula as a means of giving his troops the confidence to take the offensive against the Japanese in larger battles in the centre of the country. Accordingly, he had fixed on a modest advance down the narrow Mayu Peninsula, about 90 miles long and about 20 miles wide at its northern end, tapering to a point short of Akyab Island. Down the centre runs the Mayu Range, a sharp jungle-covered ridge between 1,000 and 2,000 feet high. The lower slopes tumble to within less than a mile of the sea on the western side, and descend in a series of rough spurs to the valley of the River Mayu in the east. The narrow strips of plain along the coast and the river are mostly thick mangrove swamp, dissected by a series of watercourses known as *chaungs*, which, on the seaward side, are tidal, muddy and treacherous; at some times of the year they present as much of an obstacle to progress as the mountains and jungle. The spurs that separate the strips of plain are steep and covered with almost impenetrable bush. The peninsula is exposed to the violent electrical storms that sweep in from the Bay of Bengal and, between May and September, when the monsoon comes, it receives around 200 inches of rain – enough to wash away most of the roads in a single day. For the rest of the year the climate is dry and thirsty. It was a piece of terrain which greatly favoured defence and delay, and was described by veteran Bryan Perrett as 'not fit to fight in!' Nonetheless, it represented a definable, limited objective.

The object of the campaign was to secure the small port of Maungdaw and then the road running from there across the Mayu Range to Buthidaung, in the valley of the River Kalapanzin. With this area secure, troops could be supplied by sea and east–west communication maintained using the road. The next step would be to use the peninsula as the springboard for a larger attack against Akyab and beyond. XV (Indian) Corps, consisting of the 5th and 7th (Indian) Divisions, supported by tanks, and, on its inland flank, the 81st (West African) Division, had begun a drive southwards on 30 November 1943, with the 5th Division to the west of the Mayu hills and the 7th Division to the east. At first the British advance went well. Maungdaw fell at the end of the first week in January 1944, but Razabil, a natural fortress on the River Naaf, which had been strengthened by the Japanese and commanded the road southward, resisted all assaults until its defenders were methodically winkled out and killed man by man.

The Japanese, however, had other plans, and the British advance merely accelerated them. In the bigger picture, they planned to remain on the defensive in Burma, but they realized that the British were bound to attack them and they were well aware that Slim was building up supplies at his bases in Dimapur and Imphal for this purpose. Their plans, therefore, aimed at a spoiling attack towards the main British bases, Imphal and Kohima, the capture of which would have the added benefit of disrupting air supply to General 'Vinegar Joe' Stilwell's Chinese. This attack, Operation *U-Go*, would be preceded by a subsidiary and essentially diversionary attack, *Ha-Go*, in the Arakan. Conventional wisdom often insists, however, that the Japanese planned to invade India, fuelled perhaps by the immediate post-war version of events published in Admiral Lord Louis Mountbatten's official report as Supreme Allied Commander for the Indo-China theatre of war. Such publications often tend to talk up the dangers, but the entirety of the evidence does not really support this view. That said, the commander of the Japanese Fifteenth Army, Lieutenant General Renya Mutaguchi, was an extremely aggressive commander who advocated pressing on beyond Imphal, using the renegade Indian National Army to foment uprisings among the civilian population against the British as a means of forcing them to abandon the war. His superior, Lieutenant General Masakazu Kawabe, however, gave no authorization for any advance beyond the Imphal/Kohima objectives, which, he said, would have to be cleared with Imperial Headquarters in Tokyo.

By early January 1944, Allied intelligence – especially from Ultra and V Force – had for some time been picking up signs of Japanese reinforcement. During the monsoon of 1943, Kawabe's Burma Area Army had consisted of two fighting divisions, plus army troops, one of which – the 54th – was in the Arakan. Further north, Mutaguchi's Fifteenth Army, with another two divisions, the 31st and 33rd, faced the Chinese and IV (Indian) Corps in Assam. Then another division, the 55th, appeared from Java, and it too entered the Arakan to form part of a new command, the Twenty-Eighth Army, under Lieutenant General Shojo Sakurai. The 15th Division, which joined Mutaguchi, and the 5th Air Division, which operated from airfields around Rangoon, soon followed it. Signs were also picked up of a formation of the Japanese-sponsored INA. This increase in forces was unlikely to be for defensive purposes; however, these so-called armies were little more than corps, and Allied air strength, at 67 squadrons, was now superior to the Japanese both in numbers and quality. Both Slim and Sir George Giffard, GOC-in-C of 11 Army Group, knew that the enemy's most likely, and most dangerous, course of action would be to outflank the 7th Division, encircle XV Corps in north Arakan and destroy it, and then enter India. They agreed with Lieutenant General Sir Philip Christison, the corps commander, that any of his formations which were surrounded should stand and fight; they would be supplied by air until a counter-attack could be organized. In order to carry out such a counter-attack, Giffard released the 26th (Indian) Division from Army Group Reserve, and promised Slim that, if he needed it, the 36th Division – one of only two wholly British divisions in the theatre of operations – would also be committed.

II. THE BATTLES IN THE ARAKAN, FEBRUARY–JUNE 1944

Even though it was expected by the British, *Ha-Go* still achieved surprise. The Japanese 55th Division, under Lieutenant General Tadashi Hanaya, had been divided into three parts. The main striking force –the 112th Regiment, under Colonel S. Tanahashi, who had been a formidable opponent in 1943 – had slipped round the eastern flank of the 7th Division between it and the 81st Division; a second, smaller force, under Colonel Kubo, had moved further east, blocked the minor road south from Goppe Bazar, then turned west and cut the main road to Maungdaw south of Bawli Bazar, isolating the 5th Division. The remainder of Hanaya's force conducted fixing attacks on the 5th and 7th Divisions from the south. The Japanese assumed that, once they had surrounded the 7th Division, it would, as the British had always done in the past, fight its way back along its lines of communication. It could thus be destroyed piecemeal as it tried to scramble clear. The whole Japanese force would then turn on the 5th Division and annihilate it. This would open the door for the advance to Chittagong, led by the INA. The Japanese moved fast by forced marches from Buthidaung, captured Ngakyedauk Pass, quickly cut off the 7th Division and surrounded its administrative box at Sinzweya. By 8 February, Kubo had reached the road from Bawli Bazar to Maungdaw, where his troops blew up bridges, set fire to dumps, waylaid convoys and then consolidated in the nearby jungle. Thus, at one stroke, the Japanese had separated the two divisions of the corps and cut them both off from their base.

But despite being nearly overrun, and fighting desperately, the 5th and 7th Divisions held their ground and fought the attackers to a standstill. This was not at all what the Japanese had expected, and it upset their timetable and their logistic arrangements (or lack of them) fatally. Tokyo Rose announced on the wireless that it was all over in Burma: in fact, as Slim later remarked, it was just starting. The 26th Division moved swiftly to recapture Taung Bazar and began to press on Sakurai's rear. At the same time, the 5th Division, fending off the Japanese frontal attacks, counter-attacked up Ngakyedauk Pass towards the 7th Division.

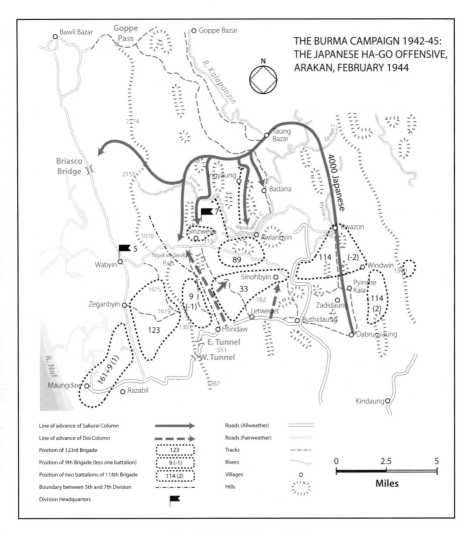

Map 14: The Arakan, 1944

The 36th Division was released from Army Group Reserve to the Fourteenth Army on 8 February and ordered to follow the 26th Division. Having completed a journey of more than 1,000 miles across India and then south into Burma to the railhead at Dohazari, the troops were transferred into lorries which carried them southwards through jungle country towards Bawli Bazar. The road must have been one of the worst in Burma, and the discomfort of the journey was increased by wild rumours

of Japanese progress. As the battalions drove over the wooden bridge at
Bawli in the evening of the 12th, they saw for the first time the long, jagged,
inhospitable range of the Mayu hills, which for the next four months were
to be their battlefield. Japanese aircraft were seen flying overhead and that
night, almost for the last time in the campaign, dropped bombs: Allied air
superiority, which had been building for some time, was by now assured;
this was to give the Allied ground forces in the forthcoming campaign
their first taste of freedom of action.

By this time, the Japanese 143rd Regiment and part of the 144th were
believed to be holding the general line from Razabil to Buthidaung; part of
112th Regiment was located above Briasco Bridge; three other battalions
were in depth; and one battalion was at Kyauktau. XV Corps' plan was for
the 7th Division to hold its positions; for the 26th Division to concentrate
in the Goppe Bazar–Taung Bazar area and then relieve the 7th Division;
and for the 36th Division to clear the area west of the Mayu Range in the
Chota Maughnama area.

It was command of the air as much as fighting spirit that brought victory
to the two divisions of XV Corps. Supply aircraft dropped food, water and
ammunition on Indian-manufactured parachutes – 'parajutes' – to the
surrounded troops, while fighters and bombers attacked the Japanese positions. Mountbatten diverted aircraft from the supply of the Chinese over
the 'Hump' – from Assam in India over the south-eastern extremities of
the Himalayan mountains into China – and from Chindit operations, and
included domestic items like razors and soap along with essential supplies.
The Japanese had no such resources, and carried only ten days' supplies
with them; they also had little in the way of artillery, having planned on
capturing British guns and their ammunition. With the Japanese out of
food, water and ammunition, it could only be a matter of time before
the Maungdaw road was reopened, Ngakyedauk Pass recaptured, and its
Japanese garrison crushed by the 26th and 36th Divisions advancing from
the west against the rock of the 7th Division to the east.

In the mountainous country, motor transport could not be used to bring
supplies forward from the dropping zones; all stores were carried by the

mule trains attached to each battalion. Without these animals' services, no battles could have been fought and won in such difficult terrain. Drinking water was sent forward in special containers and the amount sent was carefully checked. Cigarettes, mail, ammunition, clothing and medical stores – even the leeks worn by the Royal Welch Fusiliers on St David's Day – were carried up on mules.

By 1 March, the Japanese had well and truly shot their bolt and, too late, were trying to pull back in small groups, covered by suicide detachments. Kubo's force was destroyed almost to the last man among the caves and cliffs of the Mayu Range. Despite the desire to keep the 36th Division – a specialized amphibious division – in reserve for future offensive operations and not commit it to conventional operations, circumstances forced this intention to be modified. The 36th Division's task was therefore to establish and then maintain a firm base until monsoon positions could be taken up. It was to hold Sinzweya, Nagkyedauk Pass, the crest of the Mayu Range between the pass and two tunnels on the Maungdaw–Buthidaung road, Taung Bazar, Goppe Bazar and Pass, and Bawli. This would allow the 5th Division to be extracted and sent across to Assam, where signs of another, more serious, Japanese invasion were already brewing.

The defence of Ngakyedauk Pass cost the 36th Division only 118 casualties all told. But the main route across the Mayu Range, the 16-mile-long road that linked Maungdaw and Buthidaung, still remained in enemy hands. About halfway between the two villages, it passed through the two tunnels, which had once carried a light railway. The Japanese positions in the steep, jungle-clad hills covered the road continuously, but in three places they were particularly strong, amounting to fortresses. These were the tunnels themselves and two buttresses, one on each side of the range, at Razabil and Letwedet. By 11 March, the buttresses, which had been laboriously assaulted and cleared during the initial offensive, had been recaptured. The task of clearing the tunnels was given to the 36th Division. Seventy-two Brigade launched the attack on the western tunnel on 21 March after a strong artillery preparation, and captured it two days later. On the 27th, the 2nd Royal Welch Fusiliers were moved forward in transport to the Chaukmainywa area, where they were placed under the command of 72 Brigade for the attack on the eastern tunnel, about a mile north-east of the western. In the mêlée, a tank fired into the tunnel and hit an ammunition store, which blew up in a series of tremendous explosions. In the confusion that followed, the Welshmen rushed the tunnel and captured it.

On 1 April, the men had a taste of life in the Arakan in the monsoon season. A wind blew up suddenly, whipped itself into a gale and swept a torrential downpour into the bivouacs. A few days later, orders were issued for XV Corps to take up monsoon positions on the Buthidaung–Maungdaw road, with the 26th Division holding the tunnels, the 36th Division in the Wabyin area, and the 7th Division detached to fill the gap in Army Group Reserve. During the first week of May 1944, the weather remained fine, but plans were being made for the 36th Division to be relieved of its static tasks by the 25th (Indian) Division and to return to India immediately after the monsoon had broken – not least because the main Japanese offensive was expected soon on the Assam front. On 4 June, the handover was completed; next day, the move back to India was begun. Early the following morning, 6 June, the men began to embark in river transport for Tumbru. In Europe, it was D-Day.

III. KOHIMA

Even while the Arakan battles were reaching their conclusion, the Japanese had launched their main offensive, Operation *U-Go*, on the Assam front: *Ha-Go*, in the Arakan, had indeed been no more than a diversion. Three Japanese divisions – the 15th, 31st and 33rd – attacked IV Corps, and two others attacked the Chinese armies on the Ledo and Burma roads.

The importance of Kohima lay in its position as a hill station, 40 miles from Dimapur on the only road through the Naga Hills to Imphal, 80 miles away. The Japanese planned that their 31st Division would advance in three regimental columns to sever the road and envelop the Kohima position from three directions. The divisional commander, Major General

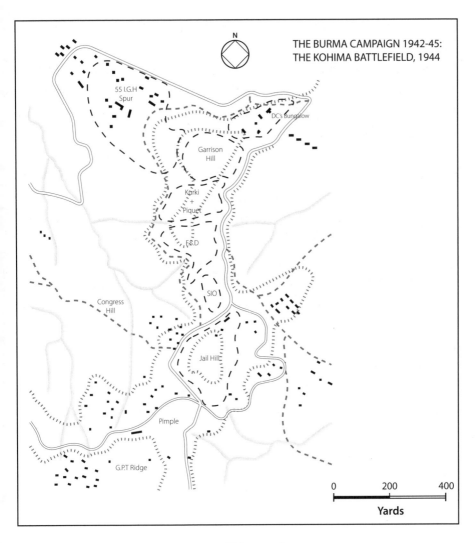

Map 15: Kohima, 1944

Kotoku Sato, who had had the plan dictated to him, was clearly unhappy with it and accurately foresaw the difficulty of supplying a force of divisional size in such terrain. However, the plan produced tactical as well as operational surprise, for Slim's intelligence branch had assessed that only a small force would be able to move through the difficult hill country; it was some time before it was realized that an entire division was closing on Kohima.

In the middle of March 1944, the Kohima position was held by part of the Assam Rifles, a paramilitary force of local levies, supported to the east by the 1st Assam Regiment at Jessami and Kharasom and 50 (Indian) Parachute Brigade at Snagshak. Both formations fought stubbornly; 50 Brigade, commanded by Brigadier M. R. J. Hope-Thompson, held up the Japanese for six vital days before withdrawing, having suffered heavy casualties, including 800 men killed. It was this action that made Slim realize the size and speed of the enemy attack and bought him the time to react to it. For his pains, Hope-Thompson was sacked.

Slim moved first the 5th and then the 7th Division by air to reinforce Imphal and Kohima; 161 (Indian) Infantry Brigade, with the 24th Mountain Artillery Regiment, went first to Dimapur and then to Kohima. In addition, Slim ordered Lieutenant General Montagu Stopford's XXXIII (Indian) Corps Headquarters, with the British 2nd Infantry Division and 23 Long Range Brigade – originally a Chindit formation – to move up to Dimapur by rail.

The position at Kohima was centred on the village, about 5,000 feet up in the hills, which was the administrative capital of Nagaland. It sat astride a ridge running in a north to south curve about two-and-a-half miles long. Over time, Kohima had become a staging post between Dimapur and Imphal and contained a reinforcement camp, and Indian General Hospital and a barracks. There were hillocks along the ridge which were known by the names of the installations that sat on them: Field Supply Depot (FSD) Hill where there was a bakery, and Detail Issue Store (DIS) Hill. Then there was Jail Hill that was a little higher and commanded much of the valley below. DIS, FSD and another hillock called Kuki Picquet ran off to the north of Jail Hill towards Garrison Hill. Further north still were the District Commissioner's bungalow, Treasury Hill and Naga Village. To the south of Jail Hill and on the other side of the road to the west was General Purpose Transport (GPT) Ridge and another mile to the south, on the same side of the road as GPT, was Aradura Spur. These were the fixed points of the defensive line. By 3 April, Japanese troops were probing the position, to which the Assam Regiment had now withdrawn. Shortly afterwards, the Japanese severed the road back to Imphal, but not before the leading battalion of 161 Brigade, the 4th Queen's Own Royal West Kents, had arrived. On the night of 5 April, the siege began.

That night, the Japanese, who could muster nearly 12,000 men in the Kohima area, supported by artillery and mortars, began their attack. The first assaults were repulsed, but the defenders immediately realized the overmatch in numbers and shortened their perimeter. Despite heavy Japanese fire and further assaults, a battalion of Rajputs from 161 Brigade fought their way in on 7 April; moreover, the 24th Mountain Artillery Regiment was only 2 miles away and could provide some supporting fire. Furious Japanese attacks continued every day, and by 9 April the garrison's perimeter had contracted further. The fighting was particularly vicious around the DC's bungalow and tennis court, and it was here that Lance Corporal John Harman won his famous Victoria Cross, as the two forces grappled in hand-to-hand combat. Had it not been for accurate airdrops of supplies and the supporting artillery fire from 24th Regiment, the position must have been lost. As it was, the situation was never better than desperate.

But relief was in sight. After 13 April, the ferocity of the Japanese attack eased. Both sides had suffered heavy casualties but the Japanese were already beginning to feel the pinch as supplies ran low. Although they kept up mortar and artillery fire, the Japanese infantry began to dig in on the ground they had taken, launching attacks only on the area held by 161 Brigade back up the Imphal road – attacks which were resolutely beaten off. Knowing that fresh British forces were closing, the Japanese made one last attempt to overwhelm the Kohima position on the night of 16–17 April. Positions changed hands several times; at last, heavy casualties forced the British to abandon the position on FSD Hill, shortening the perimeter around Garrison Hill and bringing the Japanese close to them on the south, north and east.

On the following day, the Allied counter-attack started. From the west, British artillery opened up on the Japanese. The arrival of 6 Infantry Brigade allowed 161 Brigade to move to the attack, supported by tanks. The exhausted Japanese gave ground and the siege lifted. But the real counter-attack, which would clear the Japanese from the area, did not develop until the full strength of the 2nd Infantry Division could be concentrated. The GOC, Major General J. L. (John) Grover, had decided to use an enveloping movement. Four Infantry brigade would destroy the Japanese positions on GPT Ridge to the south of Kohima; 5 Infantry Brigade would move north-east and clear Naga village; and 6 Infantry Brigade would clear the central area, including FSD Hill and Jail Hill. The attack would be supported by the RAF's heavy bombers and more than 100 guns. The Japanese could now muster no more than 17 light guns. Tanks were also allocated but the going was so bad that they could do little to help the infantry.

Those who took part described the three days following the launch of the operation on 7 May as their worst time of the war. The monsoon had now broken and the steep slopes, already churned up by fighting, had more in common with the battlefields of Third Ypres than of Burma. Rats and flies were everywhere, feeding on half buried, rotting bodies. The Japanese had suffered horrendous casualties – far in excess of what would normally break units or formations – but they had reorganized their positions for defence and there were few surrenders. Every position had to be fought for with bombs, artillery, flame-throwers and grenades. Skilful siting of bunkers caused heavy losses among the attackers, including two successive commanders of 4 Infantry Brigade. On 12 May, the leading brigade of the 7th Division arrived and took up the fight for Naga village; the rest of the division, along with 268 (Indian) Motor Brigade, came up soon afterwards, allowing the exhausted units of the 2nd Division and 161 Brigade to rest for the first time.

It was not until mid-May that Japanese resistance finally diminished, after a track had been bulldozed up to the DC's bungalow, allowing tanks to break into the Japanese bunkers. Even so, it was 31 May before General Sato ordered his starving and weary soldiers to withdraw, in defiance of orders given to him to remain in contact, allowing British and Indian troops properly to clear the area and open the road to Imphal. All his fears about supply had been amply realized. On 22 June, a link-up was finally made, by which time British and Indian losses in the Kohima area had reached 4,000 and Japanese casualties had exceeded 7,000.

IV. IMPHAL

Imphal was held by IV Corps under the command of Lieutenant General Geoffrey Scoones. Because of Slim's wish to take the offensive, Scoones had deployed two of his divisions forward of Imphal: the 20th (Indian) Division had occupied Tamu and the 17th (Indian) Division had moved out to Tiddim. In addition, 50 Parachute Brigade was conducting training north of Imphal. At Imphal itself was the 23rd (Indian) Division, which had been in the area for two years and was badly under strength having suffered greatly from disease. It was bolstered, however, by 254 (Indian) Tank Brigade.

Mutaguchi's plan for *U-Go* was that, while his 31st Division seized Kohima and pressed on to Dimapur, his 33rd Division would destroy the 17th (Indian) Division at Tiddim and attack Imphal from the south. The 15th Division, which had been on road-building duty in Thailand, was to attack Imphal from the north. Finally, a composite force known as Yamamoto Force – so-called because it was commanded by Major General Tsunoru Yamamoto – would attack and destroy the 20th (Indian) Division at Tamu and then move on Imphal from the east. This force was to be supported by the 3rd Heavy Artillery Regiment and the 14th Tank Regiment, with around 66 tanks. All three divisional commanders disagreed with the plan, chiefly on the grounds that their supply situation was poor. Even if Allied depots were seized, the monsoon would make transportation all but impossible. Moreover, the Japanese commanders were well aware of Allied command of the air; they were aware, too, of Slim's improvements to training, equipment and morale. Mutaguchi, while acknowledging the risks in the supply situation, dismissed the British and Indian troops as inferiors.

Slim and Scoones had agreed that, once Ultra revealed the timing of the Japanese attack, IV Corps would withdraw to the Imphal plain in order

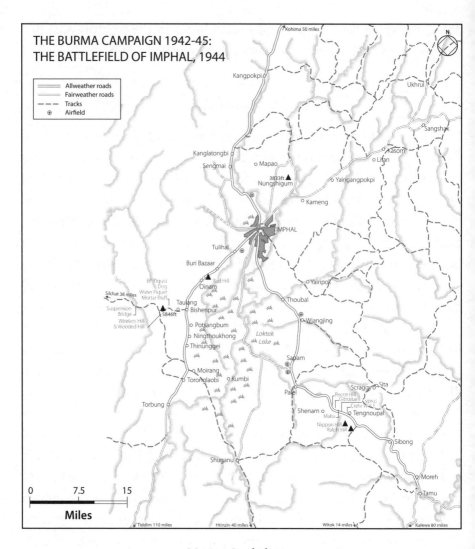

Map 16: Imphal, 1944

to stretch the Japanese logistic system to breaking point and to fight on ground of their choosing. As things turned out, Ultra did not give enough warning. The Japanese attack began on 8 March, and it was not until 13 March that Scoones gave the order to move back. The 20th Division, under Major General Douglas Gracey, disengaged without difficulty – partly at least because the second Chindit operation had been launched on 5 March and the Chindits' actions held up part of the Japanese 15th Division. The

17th (Indian) Division, under Major General 'Punch' Cowan, had a harder time and was actually cut off by the Japanese 33rd Division. This division's 215th Regiment captured a supply depot at Milestone 109, almost 20 miles behind the division's forward brigades; its 214th Regiment seized Tongzang and occupied Tuitum Saddle, astride the main road that was the 17th Division's main line of communication with Imphal. However, the key bridge over the River Manipur remained in Allied hands; Scoones had Major General Ouvry Lindfield Roberts, with his 23rd Division, forward to hold the line of communication. Cowan launched an immediate attack on Tuitum Saddle by 48 (Indian) Brigade before the Japanese had had time to dig in and consolidate their position, inflicting severe casualties and forcing the Japanese away from the road. There was harder fighting around Milestone 109; even so, the depot was recovered and the majority of the vehicles, ammunition and food were recovered or denied. The division then withdrew in good order towards Imphal, dropping the bridge behind them, followed by the 23rd Division. Both divisions were kept supplied by airdrop, and on 4 April, the leading battalions began to arrive at Imphal.

Having pushed 23rd Division forward, Scoones was left with only a few units of this division and 254 Tank Brigade; 50 Parachute Brigade had, as noted earlier, been heavily engaged with the Japanese force advancing on Kohima. Imphal was therefore vulnerable to attack from the north by the Japanese 15th Division. Slim therefore ordered the 5th Division to be moved from the Arakan by air with all its artillery and transport. This division was experienced and capable, and its move was completed in the astonishing time of 11 days; its first two brigades were in the line by 3 April.

They were just in time. From the beginning of April, Japanese forces began to close on Imphal. The 33rd Division attacked from Bisenpur in the south but did so cautiously. Its commander, Major General Yanaiga, had been humiliated by his failure to destroy 17th (Indian) Division, and after the rough handling his troops had received he did not press home the attack. Mutaguchi removed him. Yamamoto Force meanwhile attacked

the Allied positions on the Tamu road, centred on Shenam Saddle. This
was an excellent defensive position, and the Japanese could not break
in, even with the support of their tanks and heavy artillery. The 15th
Division, meanwhile, had reached Kangpokpi Mission, where it seized an
Allied supply depot on the Dimapur road – only to find that all food and
ammunition had been removed. Its 51st Regiment captured Nunshigum
Ridge, vital ground for the defence, since it dominated the Imphal airstrip.
Scoones at once ordered a counter-attack. The 5th Division, supported
by tanks, aircraft and all the corps' artillery, smashed into the Japanese,
driving them back with great losses.

By the beginning of May, all the Japanese attacks had been halted.
Scoones was therefore able to transition to a counter-offensive, with his
first objective being to destroy the Japanese 15th Division, the weakest
enemy formation. The monsoon had now broken, however, and this
made ground movement slow and air support difficult; in particular,
supplies of artillery ammunition were critically low. But however hard
things were for the Allies, they were worse for the Japanese. None of the
formations engaged in *U-Go* had received adequate supplies of food, fuel
or ammunition since the start of the offensive; as at Kohima, the soldiers
were starving and their resistance was accordingly low. Things were so bad
that the soldiers of the 15th Division began to abandon their positions to
forage for food. After driving through the enemy line, IV Corps linked up
with XXXIII Corps units moving down from Kohima at Milestone 109
on the Dimapur road on 22 June: the sieges of both Kohima and Imphal
were over.

Even so, and with no real hope of success, Mutaguchi ordered his army
back to the attack. Neither the 15th nor the 31st Division was in any state
to take the offensive, so the 33rd Division was reinforced with an extra
infantry regiment from the 53rd and a battalion from the 54th. Under
a new and aggressive commanding general, Lieutenant General Nobuo
Tanaka, the Japanese broke into the 17th (Indian) Division's positions
at Bisenpur – but they had not the means to break through. Yamamoto
Force also tried again, but by the end of June both formations had suffered

such huge losses that they were unable to do anything but maintain their positions.

Even while ordering the new attacks, Mutaguchi knew in his heart that the game was up – but he could not face the shame of ordering a retreat. It was only the realization that none of his divisions could or would obey orders to attack that obliged him to order a withdrawal on 3 July. The Japanese army, reduced to a herd of starving stragglers, abandoned its artillery, transport and all but walking wounded and fell back as fast as it could across the Chindwin River to the relative safety of Japanese-held territory. It had lost 55,000 men, including 13,500 killed or dead from disease or starvation. Mutaguchi was relieved of his command.

V. CONCLUSIONS

Slim himself thought that the Arakan battles marked the turning point of the war in Burma; however, on their own they did not achieve a decisive result: it was at Imphal and Kohima that the work was completed and the Japanese bled white. The willingness of Japanese soldiers to fight fanatically and endure hardship was not matched by any tactical or operational subtlety on the part of their commanders. An attack by almost 100,000 Japanese troops, supported by tanks, ended with over 50 per cent casualties in the mud of the monsoon. As in the Arakan, Japanese logistic fragility was as much to blame as a flawed operational plan.

The invasion of India had been foiled; just as importantly, the legend of Japanese invincibility in the jungle, so long fostered by so many who should have known better, was smashed. The Japanese, an ethnically and culturally homogeneous force, had been beaten by a force that was anything but. Eleven Army Group contained not just British brigades and divisions, but also Chinese, East Africans, West Africans, and men from all the martial races of the Indian subcontinent – Gurkhas, Garwhalis, Mahrattas, Punjabis, Bengalis, Pathans, Sikhs, Afridis, to name but a few. This army has sometimes been spoken of as the sweepings of the Empire – as if it was some kind of rabble. It was not. Many of its formations were of high quality. It is true that the asymmetries of culture produced many logistic difficulties – different rations, for example, for different religious groups – and required commanders to recognize and play to differences that produced strengths while compensating for potential weaknesses. It could be argued that the diversity of this army gave it strength, like a composite bow. The physical conditions it endured were far harder, for example, than anything encountered in north-west Europe, even in the winter of 1944–45. As John Masters remarked in his autobiographical work *The Road Past Mandalay*, Indians, Africans and Gurkhas provided the soul and backbone of the army: without them there would have been no army and no victory. Indeed, these men were all volunteers, not conscripts, who came forward in large numbers at a time when British manpower was a declining resource, and proved themselves hardy fighters, careless of death, and unencumbered by the mentality of 'civilians in uniform' that was sometimes found in European formations. To the Japanese, this must have come as quite a shock.

The lead came from the top. Slim's style of command produced a high degree of delegation based on mutual trust and confidence. Nor was there any sign of ethno-centred prejudice. Competent subordinates were left to get on with their tasks, with no breathing down people's necks, and this ethos permeated the whole chain of command. Arguably, the freedom given to officers at brigade level and below was greater in Burma than in any other theatre of the Second World War. This was bolstered by an excellent understanding of the enemy, and rigorous training.

Finally, the decisive role of air power must be acknowledged. Once dropping zones were correctly identified and marked, the troops at Imphal and Kohima, as in the Arakan, were regularly and exactly supplied with food, ammunition and water. In spite of the monsoon, some supply matters improved as time went on – the water ration at Kohima, for example, actually rose from one pint per man per day in April to three pints by mid-May. By the time the sieges were broken, the Royal Air Force had flown 19,000 tons of supplies and 12,000 men and evacuated 13,000 casualties. In aerial combat, the RAF dominated the skies: the Japanese were able to make no more than half a dozen significant air raids, while IV Corps in particular enjoyed the close support of medium and light bombers and rocket-firing Typhoons. These aircraft bombed Japanese troop concentrations, destroyed transport and logistic installations, and dropped bridges all the way back to the Chindwin along the Japanese supply line. It was this that probably most helped to break the already tenuous Japanese supply system.

9

The Ardennes, 1944: Hitler's Last Gamble

I. THE WESTERN ALLIES PAUSE

In the autumn of 1944, the Second World War had been in progress for five years. With a second front opened in the West, Italy out of the war, and the Soviet armies pressing on Germany's eastern frontiers, it seemed that the end was, if not at hand, at least in sight. The battle for Normandy had not, however, been easy; but after the Allied break-out from the bridgehead in late July 1944, which developed from the launch of Operation COBRA, and following the Allied landings in southern France on 15 August 1944, the Western Allies advanced towards Germany faster than had been anticipated. The rapid advance, coupled with a lack of deep-water ports, presented the Western Allies with enormous supply problems. Initially, it had been expected that more fuel than ammunition would be required; however, the intense fighting in the *bocage* had forced a revision of priorities. With the return of rapid movement, it was necessary once again to change the priority, from ammunition back to fuel.

Over-the-beach supply operations in Normandy did better than had been expected, but the only deep-water port in Allied hands was at Cherbourg, near the original invasion beaches. Although the port of Antwerp, in Belgium, was captured fully intact in the first days of September, it was not made operational before 28 November, when the estuary of the River Scheldt, which gives access to the port, had been cleared. This delay was caused in large part by the failure of senior commanders US General Dwight D. Eisenhower – the Allied Supreme Commander – and British Field Marshal Bernard Montgomery (in whose sector Antwerp was) to recognize the urgency of clearing the estuary amidst the wrangle over whether the cautious Montgomery or the far more adventurous US General George Patton in the south would receive logistic priority. Then, when Montgomery had been given priority for Operation MARKET GARDEN, he compounded the problem by using resources needed to expel the Germans from the Scheldt.

German formations remained in control of several major ports on the Channel coast until May 1945; and those ports that did fall to the Western Allies in 1944 were generally wrecked in order to deny their rapid use. The extensive aerial destruction of the French railway system before the invasion, intended to deny movement to the Germans, proved equally damaging to the Western Allies, as it took time to repair tracks and bridges. A road-convoy system known as the Red Ball Express was set up to bring supplies to the front line; however, the convoys used far more fuel than they delivered to the combat divisions. By early October, the Western Allies had had to suspend major offensives in order to build up logistic stocks.

Generals Patton, commanding the US VI Corps, Montgomery, commanding 21 Army Group, and Omar Bradley, commanding 12th US Army Group, all argued for priority of supplies to their own forces in order to continue the advance and keep up the pressure on the Germans. Montgomery in particular argued for a narrow-front advance to gain ground rapidly, seizing control of the German industrial areas of the Ruhr and denying them the ability to continue the war. Eisenhower, however, preferred a broad-front strategy – though with priority given to Montgomery's northern forces, since their short-term goal included opening the urgently needed port of Antwerp. With the Western Allies paused, German Field Marshal Gerhard von Rundstedt, *Oberbefehlshaber* (Commander-in-Chief) *West*, was given the breathing space he needed to reorganize the dispirited German armies into a coherent force.

The failure of Operation MARKET GARDEN left the Western Allies worse off. In October, the First Canadian Army fought the Battle of the Scheldt, clearing the Westerscheldt by taking the island of Walcheren – a name of ill omen to those in the British Army who knew their history – and at last opening Antwerp to shipping. By the end of the month, the supply situation was easing.

II. GERMAN PROBLEMS AND RESPONSES

Despite the lull along the Western Front after the Scheldt battles, the German situation was dire. In late 1944, the Germans were again facing the same strategic decisions as they had during the First World War, with powerful enemies on two fronts. On the Eastern Front, the Soviets' massive summer offensive, Operation BAGRATION, destroyed much of the German *Heeresgruppe Mitte*, or Army Group Centre. The progress of BAGRATION was so fast the offensive ended only when the advancing Soviet forces, like the Western Allies, outran their supplies. By November, German intelligence was detecting clear signs that the Soviets were preparing for a winter offensive.

The Allied air offensive of early 1944 had effectively destroyed the German *Luftwaffe*, leaving the German Army with little battlefield intelligence, no tactical air support and no interdiction capability. The converse was just as damaging: daytime movement of German forces was instantly noticed by the British and American air forces and interdiction of supplies went on as a matter of routine.

The Germans did have one cause for optimism in November 1944: since they were no longer defending all of Western Europe, their defensive lines and supply lines in the West had shortened, greatly easing their supply problems even when Allied command of the air was taken into account. Additionally, their extensive telephone and telegraph network meant that radios no longer had to be used for communications, which deprived the Allies of much of the intercept from Ultra – one of their most powerful tools.

Despite the adverse situation, German *Führer* Adolf Hitler believed that his armies might still be able to defend Germany successfully in the long term if they could force a stalemate on the Western Front in the short term, allowing him to turn his main effort towards the East – using his new jet-engined aircraft, heavy tanks and rockets – and force the Soviets back: in effect, a reverse of the strategy of 1917. Hitler further believed that by denying the Allies a quick victory and increasing their casualties, he could split them and persuade the Americans and British to sue for a separate peace, independent of the Soviet Union. That he could have believed this is a clear indication of his increasing isolation from reality. Several senior German officers voiced their belief that, given any sort of favourable weather, Allied air power would inevitably stop any German offensive. Hitler ignored or dismissed this, although, as his ideas for a counter-attack in the West developed, the offensive was intentionally scheduled for late autumn, when north-western Europe is often affected by fog and cloud.

III. GERMAN OPERATIONAL PLANNING

German planning revolved around the premise that the Allied armies were overextended – their troops were deployed from southern France to the Netherlands – and a successful strike against thinly held stretches of the line would therefore make deep penetrations very quickly, divert resources for a blocking move and thereby halt further Allied advances on the entire Western Front.

Several plans for major offensives were put forward, but the *Oberkommando der Wehrmacht* – the High Command of the Armed Forces – concentrated on only two. The first was an encirclement: this required a two-pronged attack astride the boundaries of the US armies around Aachen, in order to surround the Ninth and Third Armies, destroy them, and put German forces back in control of the highly defensible ground on which they had brought the US armies to a standstill earlier in the year. The second plan called for a *Blitzkrieg* attack through the weakly defended Ardennes forest, almost a rerun of the successful German offensive in 1940, aimed at splitting the armies along the US–British boundary and recapturing Antwerp. This operation was codenamed WACHT AM RHEIN (GUARD ON THE RHINE), after a traditional German military song;

Map 17: *The German Ardennes Offensive, 1944*

the name also implied, for purposes of deception, that the Germans would be adopting a defensive posture on the Western Front. In both plans, the main effort was placed opposite American forces, since Hitler – wrongly, and in the face of all the evidence to the contrary – believed the Americans were incapable of fighting effectively, and that the American home front was likely to crack upon hearing of a decisive American loss.

Unsurprisingly, therefore, Hitler chose WACHT AM RHEIN, believing that even a successful encirclement would have little impact on the overall situation. He found the prospect of dividing the Anglo-American armies far more appealing. The rivalry between Montgomery and Patton was common knowledge, and Hitler hoped he could exploit this perceived disunity. In any case, if the attack were to succeed in capturing the port of Antwerp, four whole Allied armies would be trapped without supplies by German forces.

Field Marshal Walther Model, commander of *Heeresgruppe* (Army Group) *B*, was ordered to carry out the operation under the overall supervision of von Rundstedt. Both Model and von Rundstedt believed that aiming for Antwerp was too ambitious given Germany's severely limited resources. At the same time, they felt that maintaining a purely defensive posture, as had been the case since Normandy, would only delay the inevitable defeat, not avert it. They thus developed alternative, less ambitious plans that did not aim to cross the River Meuse. Model's plan was *Unternehmen HERBSTNEBEL* (Operation AUTUMN MIST) and von Rundstedt's *Fall MARTIN* (Case MARTIN). The two Field Marshals combined their plans to present a joint limited solution to Hitler, who rejected it in favour of his 'big solution'.

The plan for the battle in the Ardennes, therefore, called for battle to occur *within* the forest – rather than *beyond* it as in 1940. The main force was to advance westwards as far as the Meuse, then turn north-west towards Antwerp and Brussels. The close country in the Ardennes would make rapid movement difficult for both sides, though open ground beyond the Meuse offered the prospect of a dash to the coast.

The plan called for four armies. The Sixth SS *Panzer* (Armoured or Tank) Army, under the command of veteran bruiser Sepp Dietrich, had been created as recently as October 1944, and it included the most senior formation of the *Waffen* SS, the 1st SS *Panzer* Division *Liebstandarte Adolf Hitler* (Hitler's Life-Guard) as well as the 12th SS *Panzer* Division *Hitlerjugend* (Hitler Youth). Sixth SS *Panzer* Army was the northernmost attacking formation, with its northern flank resting on the small German town of Monschau. To Dietrich was given the task of capturing Antwerp. The Fifth *Panzer* Army, under General Hasso von Manteuffel, was assigned to the centre of the attack and given the objective of capturing Brussels. The Seventh Army, under General Erich Brandenberger, was assigned to the southern sector of the attack frontage, with its southern flank resting on the Luxembourg town of Eternach. Brandenberger's task, in support of the main effort further north, was to protect the German flank from Allied counter-strokes. For this role, his army was allotted only four infantry divisions and no armoured formations and was thus really a corps rather than an army. The fourth army was the Fifteenth, under General Gustav-Adolf von Zengen. Von Zengen's force, which consisted of units recuperating or being regenerated after the MARKET GARDEN battle, was located north of the main effort and given the task of fixing Allied units so as to prevent their being used against the attack. Von Zengen was warned that, as the plan developed, he should be prepared to act as a second-echelon force to exploit success elsewhere.

Two major special operations were planned to support the attack. Otto Skorzeny, who had rescued Mussolini, was to command a force of English-speaking German soldiers in Operation GREIF. These troops were to be dressed in Allied uniforms and carry identity discs taken from corpses and prisoners. Their task was to infiltrate behind Allied lines and there to alter route posts, misdirect traffic, cause disruption and, eventually, to seize bridges across the Meuse. In late November, a second operation was added: STÖSSER, in which Colonel Friedrich August von der Heydte, who had commanded the 6th Parachute Regiment in Normandy at the time of the invasion, was to command a night parachute drop behind the Allied lines to capture a road junction and choke point near the small town of Malmedy.

For the offensive to succeed, the planners identified four critical factors. First, surprise was essential. Secondly, the attack would take place in bad weather to minimize the effect of Allied air supremacy. Thirdly, the advance must be rapid: the Meuse had to be reached within four days. Last, because of the *Wehrmacht*'s chronic fuel shortages, Allied supply dumps would have to be captured. Without these, the operation would run out of steam less than halfway to Antwerp. The plan originally called for 44 division-equivalent formations, of which 12 were to be *Panzer* or *Panzergrenadier* divisions. Manpower shortages, however, reduced the available total to 30 divisions. The main shortfall was in the infantry divisions that were to secure the breakthrough after the armoured divisions had passed; moreover, the divisions that were assigned were not of the calibre of those fighting on the Eastern Front. Many were built up from the last available reserves of the *Wehrmacht*, and among these were so-called *Volksgrenadier* – units formed from very young or very old recruits stiffened with a core of veteran officers and NCOs. Training time, equipment and supplies were all less than needed; nor was there enough transport to move the troops up to the front. The start of the operation was therefore postponed from 27 November to 16 December.

VI. ALLIED CONSOLIDATION

During the reconquest of France, the extensive networks of the French Resistance, combined with air reconnaissance, had provided the Western Allies with sufficient reliable intelligence on German dispositions for sound planning to take place, supplemented by intercept from Ultra. MARKET GARDEN had been the only notable operational failure. Once the Western Allies reached the German border, however, Resistance information ceased and the Germans reverted to using telephone and telegraph, with strict radio silence frequently imposed, rather than Enigma. The autumn weather then played its part, restricting Allied air reconnaissance. With German security very tight and Allied intelligence-gathering very poor, Eisenhower and his subordinates had little to go on.

Just as in 1940, the Ardennes was considered by the intelligence staffs to be a quiet sector; and anyway, conventional wisdom had it that the Germans had shot their bolt and were highly unlikely to be able to mount any sizeable offensive operations. Allied intelligence assessments, therefore – especially those of Bradley's staff at Headquarters 12 Army Group – concluded precisely what the Germans would have written had they been able to produce those assessments themselves: that preparations were being carried out only for defensive, not offensive, operations, around Düsseldorf, in the northern Rhine. Not all were fooled: the US

Third Army Chief of Intelligence, Colonel Oscar Koch, and others, including officers on Eisenhower's staff, correctly predicted the Germans' offensive capability and forecast their intention to strike the US VIII Corps. However, because the Ardennes was generally considered quiet, it was used as a training sector for new units and a rest area for units that had seen hard fighting. The US formations deployed in the Ardennes were thus a mixture of raw troops, like the 99th Infantry Division, learning on the job, and battle-hardened formations, like the 2nd Infantry Division, undergoing rehabilitation.

VII. THE INITIAL GERMAN ASSAULT

The German assault began as planned at 5.30 a.m. on 16 December 1944, with a massive artillery barrage on the Allied troops facing the Sixth SS *Panzer* Army. Around 8.00 a.m., all three German armies attacked through the Ardennes. In the northern sector, Dietrich's SS men assaulted the Losheim Gap and Elsenborn Ridge in an attempt to break through to Liège. In the centre, von Manteuffel's army attacked towards Bastogne and St Vith, both important road junctions with operational significance. In the south, Brandenberger's army advanced towards Luxembourg to secure the flank.

The attacks by the Sixth SS *Panzer* Army's infantry units in the north generally went badly because of unexpectedly fierce resistance by the US 2nd and 99th Infantry Divisions, first around Lanzerath and then on Elsenborn Ridge. One German battalion was held up for 20 hours by a scout platoon of 18 men from the 99th Infantry Division. The blockage thus forced Dietrich to commit his *Panzer* forces earlier than planned. But on 16 December, heavy snow fell over much of the Ardennes. This had the effect of keeping the Allied air forces grounded, but the poor road conditions it caused slowed the German advance. Poor traffic control and shortages of fuel added to the general confusion.

Things went better in the centre as the Fifth *Panzer* Army attacked positions held by the US 28th and 106th Infantry Divisions. Although the

Germans lacked the overwhelming strength they enjoyed in the north, they still possessed a marked superiority in numbers, heavy equipment and quality of troops over the thinly spread American divisions. They therefore succeeded in surrounding two infantry regiments, the 422nd and 423rd, belonging to the 106th Division and forced their surrender. The US Army official history noted:

> At least seven thousand [men] were lost . . . The amount lost in arms and equipment, of course, was very substantial. The *Schnee Eifel* battle, therefore, represents the most serious reverse suffered by American arms during the operations of 1944–45 in the European theater.

Further south, the main blow was delivered by all von Manteuffel's attack divisions crossing the River Our, then moving steadily on their initial objectives of Bastogne and St Vith. The experienced 28th Infantry Division put up a determined defence, but the more inexperienced soldiers of the 106th could not match them. The most northerly of the 28th Division's regiments, the 112th, holding a line east of the Our, stopped the Germans from seizing and using the bridges over the river around Ouren for two days before being forced to withdraw. The 28th's other two regiments, the 109th and 110th, were spread so thinly that their positions were easily bypassed. Both offered what resistance they could and certainly delayed the Germans – and any delay was potentially crucial. The struggle for the villages and strong points around Bastogne held by the 110th Regiment delayed the attack sufficiently to allow the 101st Airborne Division, reinforced by elements from the 9th and 10th US Armored Divisions, to reach Bastogne by road on the morning of 19 December. The heroic defence of Bastogne prevented the Germans from gaining control of the town; on 20 December, unable to delay any longer, the *Panzer* columns motored past on either side, cutting off the American defenders.

In the extreme south, Brandenberger's three infantry divisions were checked by divisions of the US VIII Corps after an advance of only 4 miles;

only the 5th Parachute Division was able to move further forward, gaining 12 miles.

Operation STÖSSER had to be delayed for a day because of bad weather and fuel shortages. The drop zone was now 7 miles north of Malmedy, and the objective was the crossroads at Baraque Michel. Von der Heydte and his men were to take it and hold it for up to 24 hours – until relieved by the 12th SS *Panzer* Division – to stem the flow of Allied reinforcements and supplies into the area. In the event, just as with the Allied drops in Normandy, many aircraft went off course and the paratroops came down up to 8 miles off target; only a small part of the force landed near the intended drop zone. By noon, von der Heydte had assembled about 300 men, but this was too few to carry out his mission. He therefore abandoned the plan to take the crossroads and instead began to harass Allied troops in the area using hit-and-run tactics. Because of the dispersal of the drop, the British and American intelligence officers believed a division-sized descent had taken place, which resulted in much the same confusion as the Germans had themselves experienced in Normandy, forcing Allied commanders to divert troops to secure the rear instead of reinforcing the front.

In Operation GREIF, Skorzeny successfully infiltrated a small part of his battalion behind the Allied lines. Although it failed to take the vital bridges over the Meuse, the battalion's presence produced confusion out of all proportion to its military activities. Even Patton was alarmed; on 17 December, he described the situation to Eisenhower as 'Krauts . . . speaking perfect English . . . raising hell, cutting wires, turning road signs around, spooking whole divisions, and shoving a bulge into our defences'. Checkpoints were set up all over the Allied rear, slowing the movement of men and equipment. Military policemen drilled servicemen on things which every American was expected to know from baseball to the state capital of Illinois – a question that led to the detention of General Bradley himself, for although he gave the correct answer (Springfield), the GI who questioned him thought the answer should have been Chicago!

VIII. MASSACRES AND ATROCITIES

In the north, the spearhead of the Sixth SS *Panzer* Army was *Kampfgruppe* (Battlegroup) *Peiper*, comprising 4,800 men and 600 armoured vehicles of the 1st SS *Panzer* Division under the command of *Standartenführer* (Colonel) Joachim Peiper. Bypassing the stubbornly held Elsenborn Ridge, the SS men seized an American fuel depot, where they paused to refuel. At 12.30 p.m. on 17 December, near the hamlet of Baugnez, halfway between Malmedy and Ligneuville, they met troops of the 285th Field Artillery Observation Battalion, part of the 7th US Armored Division. After a brief battle, the Americans surrendered. They were disarmed and, with some other Americans captured earlier – a total of about 150 men – sent to a field near the crossroads. Here, most were immediately executed by shooting. A second, much smaller, massacre took place in Wereth, less than a mile north-east of St Vith, on 17 December. Eleven black American soldiers who had surrendered were tortured and then shot by men of the 1st SS *Panzer* Division, belonging to *Kampfgruppe Hansen*. This sort of atrocity was not common on the Western Front, but these Germans had come from the East, where different rules applied.

IX. THE ALLIED RESPONSE

By 17 December, Eisenhower and his principal commanders had realized that the fighting in the Ardennes was a major offensive, not a local attack, and ordered rapid reinforcement to the area. Within a week, 250,000 troops were on the move. Eisenhower believed that, with control of the air, the Western Allies could destroy German forces much more easily when they were in the open and on the offensive than when they were on the defensive. He made the point to his subordinates when they assembled at Verdun on 19 December, saying: 'The present situation is to be regarded as one of opportunity for us and not of disaster. There will be only cheerful faces at this table.' Patton, realizing what Eisenhower was implying, responded: 'Hell, let's have the guts to let the bastards go all the way to Paris. Then, we'll really cut 'em off and chew 'em up.' Eisenhower, after saying he was not *that* optimistic, asked Patton how long it would take to turn his Third Army, which was located in north-eastern France, north to counter-attack. Patton, who had already instructed his staff to make contingency plans for such an eventuality, replied that he could attack with two divisions within 48 hours – to the disbelief of the other generals present. To place the whole counter-move operation under one command, and because Bradley's headquarters had lost communication with the First and Ninth US Armies, Eisenhower removed those two units from Bradley's 12 Army Group and, on 20 December, placed them under Montgomery's 21 Army Group. This was a move that, however pragmatic, was far from popular with his American subordinates.

X. ST VITH

Meanwhile, the desperate tactical fight continued. St Vith was an objective critical to both von Manteuffel's and Dietrich's armies. The defenders, chiefly part of the 7th US Armored Division but including the remaining regiment of the 106th Infantry Division and elements of the 9th Armored and 28th Infantry Divisions, all under the command of General Bruce C. Clerk, successfully resisted the German attacks, significantly slowing the German advance. Once Montgomery had been placed in command of the area, he gave orders that St Vith was to be given up, which it was on 21 December; US troops fell back to entrenched positions, effectively blocking any further German advance. By 23 December, with the Germans closing in on their flanks, the defenders' position had become untenable, and the US troops were ordered to withdraw to the west of the River Salm. As the German plan had called for the capture of St Vith by 6.00 p.m. on 17 December, the action in and around the town presented a major blow to the German timetable.

XI. BASTOGNE

By the time the senior Allied commanders met at Verdun, the town of
Bastogne and its network of 11 roads criss-crossing the rough Ardennes
terrain should have been in German hands for several days. In fact, however, two German columns that were to have bypassed the town to the
south and north – the 2nd *Panzer* Division and the *Panzer Lehr* Division
– so-called because it had originally been a training cadre division – of
XLVII *Panzer* Corps, as well as the corps infantry (the 26th *Volksgrenadier*
Division) – had been engaged and delayed in a series of battles up to
10 miles from the town. However, the defenders had been gradually forced
back into the town, and the sole corridor that remained open to them –
to the south-east – was threatened by the Germans; indeed, it had been
repeatedly closed as the front had shifted, and German commanders felt
sure it would soon be closed for good and the town surrounded.

By 21 December, the German forces had surrounded Bastogne completely. It was defended by the 101st Airborne Division – tough and
experienced men, but with no heavy weapons and no tactical mobility
– and Combat Command B of the 10th Armored Division. Conditions
inside the perimeter were harsh. Most of the medical supplies and medical personnel had been captured, food was strictly rationed, and by 22
December, artillery ammunition was down to 10 rounds per gun per day.
The weather cleared the next day, however, and supplies were dropped
from the air over four of the next five days. Despite determined German
attacks, the perimeter held. In a celebrated incident, the German commander, *Generalleutnant* (Lieutenant General) Heinrich Freiherr von
Lüttwitz, politely demanded Bastogne's surrender. When General Anthony
McAuliffe, acting commanding general of the 101st, was told, he replied
brusquely, 'Nuts!' After turning to other matters, a staff officer asked how
they should reply to the German demand. Lieutenant Colonel Harry W. O.
Kinnard thought that McAuliffe's short, sharp response would be 'tough to
beat'. So McAuliffe wrote on the paper delivered to the Germans: 'NUTS!'
What von Lüttwitz made of it is one of history's unknowns.

The 2nd *Panzer* and *Panzer Lehr* Divisions moved forward on

21 December, leaving only one of *Panzer Lehr*'s regiments, the 901st, to support the 26th *Volksgrenadier* Division in capturing the town and its crossroads. On Christmas Eve, the 26th was reinforced by one regiment from the 15th *Panzergrenadier* Division for its main assault the next day. Headquarters XLVII *Panzer* Corps decided to phase the assault on several objectives on the west side of the perimeter rather than launch one simultaneous attack on all sides. As a result, the attack, despite initial success by its tanks, was defeated in detail and all the German tanks that had penetrated the defences were destroyed. The next day, 26 December, the leading battalions of Patton's advance guard, from the 4th US Armored Division, broke through and opened a corridor to Bastogne.

XII. THE ALLIED COUNTER-MOVE

The furthest westward penetration made by the German attack was that of the 2nd *Panzer* Division of the Fifth *Panzer* Army, which had come within 10 miles of the Meuse by Christmas Eve. On the previous day, the improved weather conditions that had allowed the resupply of Bastogne also allowed the Allied air forces to attack ground targets. Devastating bombing raids hit the German supply lines, and American Thunderbolts and British Typhoons began attacking German troops on the roads. On the Meuse, units of XXX (British) Corps, under Lieutenant General Brian Horrocks, were holding the bridges at Dinant, Givet and Namur, while US units moved forward to relieve them in place. Delays in the German timetable caused by the determined Allied resistance, the air situation and the overall logistic fragility of the German army meant that shortages of fuel and ammunition were becoming critical. By 24 December, therefore, the advance had gone as far as it could even though German combat losses had actually been light, notably in tanks, with the exception of Peiper's battle group. That evening, von Manteuffel recommended to Hitler's military adjutant that all offensive operations be halted and a withdrawal begun back to the fortified defensive positions of the West Wall on the frontier of Germany itself. Hitler, not surprisingly, rejected this.

On 1 January, in an attempt to keep the offensive going, the Germans launched two new operations. At 9.15 a.m., the *Luftwaffe* launched *Unternehmen* BODENPLATTE, or Operation BASE PLATE, a major series of strikes by several hundred aircraft against Allied airfields in the Low Countries. The attacks destroyed or severely damaged 465 aircraft but killed few pilots or ground crews; the *Luftwaffe* lost 277 planes, 62 to Allied fighters and 172 to highly effective anti-aircraft defences set up for protection against German V-1 attacks. The Americans and British recovered their losses within days, but the operation, and especially the loss of trained pilots, left the *Luftwaffe* terminally weak and ineffective.

On the same day, *Heeresgruppe G* and *Heeresgruppe Oberrhein* (Upper Rhine) launched a major offensive against the thinly stretched, 70-mile line held by the Seventh US Army. *Unternehmen* NORDWIND, or Operation NORTH WIND, was to be the Germans' final fling on the Western Front. Initially it placed the Seventh Army, which, at Eisenhower's order, had sent troops, equipment, and supplies north to reinforce the American armies in the Ardennes, under severe pressure. By 15 January, its VI Corps was hemmed in on three sides in Alsace, and with casualties mounting and tanks, ammunition and supplies all running low, it was forced to withdraw to defensive positions on the south bank of the River Moder on 21 January. However, the cost of the exchange had been too much for the Germans, and the offensive was closed down on 25 January. In the bitter, desperate fighting of Operation NORTH WIND, VI Corps suffered nearly 15,000 casualties – around half its strength; German losses are not known but were even greater. Many casualties were from the cold, for the weather during January 1945 was bitter, with temperatures well below freezing for weeks. Vehicles had to be run every half hour or the oil in them would freeze; weapons would cease to work if not fired repeatedly to warm them; and men weak from loss of blood or shortage of warmth and food would die of cold in the night. The US First, Third and Seventh Armies suffered a total of 17,000 hospitalized from the cold.

Even though their offensive had ground to a halt, the Germans still controlled a dangerous bulge, or salient, in the Allied line; hence the name by which history knows this campaign: the Battle of the Bulge. Eisenhower was certain, however, that this left the Germans highly vulnerable; they were now fully extended and logistically weak, which meant the initiative had returned to the Western Allies. His orders were for Patton's Third Army in the south, centred around Bastogne, to attack north, Montgomery's forces in the north to strike south, and the two forces to join up at Houffalize. Eisenhower had wanted Montgomery to go onto the offensive on 1 January, with the aim of linking up with Patton's advancing army and trapping most of the attacking Germans in a pocket. However, Montgomery had a clear understanding of the limited capabilities of his force – for which he has earned a reputation for being cautious. Refusing to risk his inadequately prepared infantry in severe weather for what he considered an unimportant area in operational terms, he delayed his attack until 3 January, by which time substantial numbers of German troops had managed to disengage and withdraw, albeit with the loss of their heavy equipment.

At the start of the offensive, the two Allied armies were about 25 miles apart. Despite Patton's reputation for dash, American progress in the south was restricted to less than a mile a day. The majority of the German force executed a skilful fighting withdrawal and escaped, just as it had done at Falaise five months earlier, although the fuel situation had become so severe that almost all the heavy vehicles and weapons had to be abandoned. Faced with a *fait accompli*, on 7 January 1945, Hitler was forced to agree to withdraw all forces from the Ardennes, thus ending all offensive operations.

XIII. THE STRESSES OF COALITION WAR

On the same day, Montgomery held a press conference at Zonhoven in which he said he had 'headed off . . . seen off . . . and . . . written off' the Germans. 'The battle has been the most interesting, I think possibly one of the most tricky . . . I have ever handled.' He said he had 'employed the whole available power of the British group of armies . . . you thus have the picture of British troops fighting on both sides of the Americans who have suffered a hard blow'. Montgomery also gave credit to the 'courage and good fighting quality' of the American troops, characterizing a typical American as a 'very brave fighting man who has that tenacity in battle which makes a great soldier'; he went on to talk about the necessity of Allied teamwork, and praised Eisenhower, stating, 'Teamwork wins battles and battle victories win wars. On our team, the captain is General Ike.' Despite these remarks, the American leaders' overall impression of Montgomery was that he had taken the lion's share of credit for the success of the campaign and believed himself responsible for rescuing the besieged Americans.

His comments were not well received by the Americans. Patton and Eisenhower both felt he had misstated the relative contributions to the fighting by the British and Americans in the Ardennes, since for every British soldier in the battle area there were 30 to 40 Americans, and that he had insulted Bradley and Patton in particular. In the context of Patton and Montgomery's well-known mutual dislike, this is not surprising. Montgomery subsequently recognized his mistake and later wrote: 'I think now that I should never have held that press conference. So great were the feelings against me on the part of the American generals that whatever I said was bound to be wrong. I should therefore have said nothing.' Eisenhower commented in his memoirs: 'I doubt if Montgomery ever came to realize how resentful some American commanders were. They believed he had belittled them – and they were not slow to voice reciprocal scorn and contempt.' Bradley and Patton both threatened to resign unless action was taken against Montgomery, and Eisenhower, encouraged by his British deputy, Air Marshal Tedder, decided to sack him. However, calmer councils prevailed. Even though Montgomery apologised, relations were sour for the rest of the war.

XIV. AFTERMATH

Casualty estimates for the battle differ widely. The official US account gives 80,987 American casualties, of whom 19,000 died, while other sources give estimates between 70,000 and 104,000. Whatever the exact figures, the Battle of the Bulge was the bloodiest of the battles that US forces experienced on the Western Front in the Second World War; British losses totalled only 1,400. The German high command's official figure was 84,834 casualties, but other estimates give figures of up to 100,000. German losses in the battle were critical in several respects: the last German operational and strategic reserves were now gone; the *Luftwaffe* had been broken; and the German Army in the West was being pushed back by the Western Allies as the Russians rolled inexorably in from the East.

The Americans and British were quick to follow up the German withdrawal and press home their advantage. By the beginning of February 1945, the lines were back where they had been in December 1944. During February, the Allies launched an attack all along the Western Front: in the north, under Montgomery, toward Aachen; in the centre, under US General Courtney Hodges; and in the south, under Patton. Three months later, the Russians entered Berlin, the Allied armies and the Red Army linked up across Germany, and the German armies surrendered without conditions.

10

Dien Bien Phu, 1954: Wind of Change

I. THE FIRST INDO-CHINA WAR

In the aftermath of the Second World War, the French, along with other colonial powers, reasserted their authority in their former territories in the Far East. But also like other powers – notably the British and Dutch – they faced resistance, principally from Communist-inspired liberation movements that had fought the Japanese for years. Having, as they saw it, rid themselves of one occupying force, these movements had no wish to see the return of another. The French were particularly resented because of the actions of the Vichy Government after 1940 in handing over French territories in Asia to the Japanese. In what was then known as Indo-China, the French were able to reinstall a colonial government; but by 1946, a movement to create a free Vietnamese state was fighting French troops for control of the north of the country. The Viet Minh – named after its leader, Ho Chi Minh – used irregular tactics and followed the teachings and doctrines of Chinese Communism as espoused by Mao Tse-tung. Ironically, Ho had embraced Communism while being educated in France between 1919 and 1923. He had lobbied the Congress of Versailles for Vietnamese independence after the Great War, had become a founder member of the French Communist Party in 1921, and had moved to China in 1923. He had founded the Viet Minh in 1941, and since then had led it against the Vichy French and the Japanese; it was now fighting the French Union. It was an experienced, numerous force, fighting on its own terrain and among its own people, with a strategic backyard: the safe haven provided by Communist China.

By 1953, the insurgency had been so successful that the French had found themselves incapable of suppressing Viet Minh operations. Worse, the insurgents had overrun a vast area of the neighbouring state of Laos, a French ally. Only supply difficulties had forced the Viet Minh to fall back on its bases. Despite air supremacy and considerable resources in terms of logistics and firepower, a succession of French commanders, including such famous names as Jean de Lattre de Tassigny and Raoul Salan, had been unable to regain the initiative. In May 1953, the command of the French Expeditionary Corps passed to the 55-year-old General Henri Navarre, a trusted confidant of the French Prime Minister, René Mayer. In Indochina, the French forces were strengthening their defences throughout the Hanoi Delta region in the north of the country so as to provide a secure base of operations from which to launch a series of offensive operations against Viet Minh supply lines and staging areas from China, through northern Indo-China and into Laos. Lai Chau, near the Chinese border, Na San, to the west, and the plain of Jars, in Laos, were areas of particular interest. Navarre, however, had been given additional instructions: to create the military conditions favourable to an honourable political solution. France was looking for a way out, but with her face intact. This was reflected in the attitudes of the outgoing commander, Salan, and many of his senior staff and subordinates: to them, the important thing was to get home with their reputations relatively intact. Phillip Davidson, author of one of the most comprehensive accounts of the Vietnam War, records that when Navarre arrived he found that

> There had been no long-range plan since de Lattre's departure. Everything was conducted on a day-to-day, reactive basis. Combat operations were undertaken only in response to enemy moves or threats. There was no move to develop the organization and build up the equipment of the Expeditionary force . . . [Salan and his staff] gave little thought to, or concern for, the problems of their successors.

This was a highly dangerous situation. It would have been serious enough in a symmetrical, conventional war, since it had clearly handed the initiative – and with it, freedom of action – to the enemy. In an insurgency it was doubly dangerous; trebly so in a Maoist Communist insurgency, with its insistence on taking the long view by moving up from guerrilla tactics to full-scale war, or back again when faced with a reversal, waiting out its enemy, and embedding itself in the support of the people. The French had neither a strategy nor a campaign: their enemies had both.

At exactly the same time as this campaign was in progress, the British were also fighting a Communist insurgency in Malaya, and as the French entered a downward spiral, the British were in the ascendant. In Malaya, the British had applied the idea that economic and political lines of operation could neutralize the causes of the insurgency, while military force could deal with its symptoms. Their main effort was to separate the insurgency from the population, marginalizing it and denying it a base. The people were the prize in this contest to mobilize popular support, and repressive military action might diminish the capacity of the insurgency in the short term but increase its motivation in the long. The French never understood that victory was not only the destruction of the insurgent network – impossible anyway given its safe haven in China – but also the destruction of the insurgents' political network and their discredit among the population to the point where they would be forced to adopt a political programme and become part of the system they were challenging. By 1953, the insurgency in Indo-China had moved the argument well beyond such possibilities.

It was the problem of Laos, however, that was most immediately challenging for Navarre. While being briefed before his departure from Paris in July, he had asked for clarification from the National Defence Committee as to whether or not he was responsible for the defence of Laos as well as Indo-China. Navarre's recollection was consistent in later years: that he received no proper answer. Joseph Laniel, who had succeeded Mayer as Prime Minister, insisted that Navarre had been ordered to abandon Laos if necessary, but no written record exists to support this contention. This lack of clarity and, from it, Navarre's assumption that he must if necessary defend Laos, even though it would mean committing forces at the extremity of his communications, became not only a prime factor in the selection of Dien Bien Phu as the place to pick a fight, but also probably the most disputed aspect of the circumstances surrounding the battle.

II. NA SAN

In late November and early December 1952, more than a year before Navarre's arrival in Indo-China, a battle had been fought that was to prove another pivotal factor in the build-up to Dien Bien Phu. Na San, west of Hanoi, was a fortified French outpost, supplied and supported by air power. The outpost had been attacked by Viet Minh forces under the command of their primary military commander, 41-year-old General Vo Nguyen Giap. The Viet Minh had been repeatedly repulsed, with severe losses, even though they far outnumbered the French. This French success can be easily explained: the position at Na San was well sited and commanded all the high ground within direct fire range; the French could call on overwhelming artillery support; and they were comfortably within the envelope of both air resupply and the support of bombers and ground-attack aircraft, since the Viet Minh had not brought up anti-aircraft guns. On the Viet Minh side, Giap had pinned his hope on a rapid, frontal attack to overwhelm the garrison and had consequently made little preparation in terms of artillery support, air defence or logistics. Finally, he had not made an adequate reconnaissance of the position and was unclear about the main French dispositions.

The analysis of this battle brought the French to all the wrong conclusions and the Viet Minh to the right ones. It led Navarre to adopt the so-called hedgehog (*hérisson*) concept as formulated by his main planner, Colonel Louis Berteil, commander of Mobile Group 7. He considered – and dismissed – several other alternatives for cutting off Viet Minh operations: mobile warfare – impossible in the terrain of Indo-China; static defence – impossible given the small number of troops; and placing French troops in Luang Prabang, the capital of Laos, and supplying them by air – impossible given the distances and the range of the available aircraft. Instead, he decided that, to cut the Viet Minh supply lines into Laos, he would establish a fortified blocking position, which would be reinforced, supplied and supported by air. Giap, he believed, would be unable to ignore this threat and would mass his forces against it. By massing, he would lay himself open to severe punishment by superior French artillery, armour and air support. Given enough of a mauling, the Viet Minh would come to the peace table in a receptive frame of mind. Ironically, two weeks into the battle of Dien Bien Phu, the French National Defence Committee decided that Navarre's responsibilities did not include Laos.

III. INTO POSITION

Dien Bien Phu had originally been suggested as a pivot, or fixed point, for operations by Major General René Cogny, commander of all troops in the Tonkin Delta. It had an airstrip dating from the Japanese occupation which could be lightly defended and used as a lily pad from which to launch raids. However, Navarre chose Dien Bien Phu as a hedgehog, despite the obvious disadvantages: it lay in a bowl overlooked on all sides by heavily wooded high ground; it was liable to flood during the monsoon; it was malarial; and it relied absolutely on air resupply. All Navarre's principal subordinates protested against the plan; in particular, Cogny said that 'we are running the risk of a new Na San under worse conditions'. But this was precisely what Navarre wanted – another, bigger, Na San. He overruled all objections and, at a conference on 17 November 1953, ordered the operation to commence three days later.

The French operation to secure Dien Bien Phu – CASTOR – duly began at 10.35 a.m. on 20 November. Over the next three days, under the command of General Jean Gilles, 9,000 French soldiers were dropped or air-landed in three zones: Natasha, north-west of the town, Octavie, south-west of the town, and Simone, south-east of the town. On the ground, command passed to Colonel Christian de Castries, who had been chosen by Navarre. He was a cavalry officer who would have been well suited to commanding

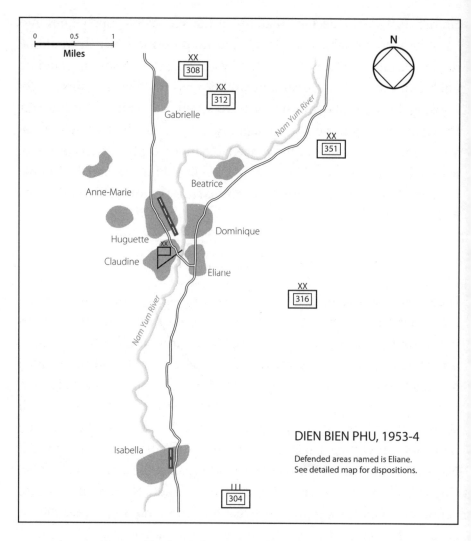

Map 18: The Central Area, Dien Bien Phu, March 1954

a mobile battle, but the positional defensive battle that developed proved beyond his capacity. By mid-December, the garrison had risen to nearly 13,000, with M24 Chaffee light tanks, artillery and air support. Another 16,000 men were available as reinforcements. The troops were a mix of regular French soldiers, including six battalions of paratroopers, Foreign Legionnaires, Algerian and Moroccan regiments, and Indo-Chinese infantry: only 30 per cent could be said to be native Frenchmen. The French immediately began to establish fortifications, securing eight strong points or fire-bases – each, it was said, named after one of de Castries's mistresses, although it is more likely that the names were selected to begin with each of the first five letters of the alphabet, plus the seventh, eighth and ninth (there was no strong-point beginning with F). The headquarters were located in the centre, with Gabrielle to the north, Huguette to the west, Eliane and Claudine to the south, Isabelle covering the reserve airstrip 4 miles even further south and therefore dangerously isolated, Beatrice and Dominique to the north-east, and Anne-Marie to the north-west. The wooded high ground was never secured.

On the other side, the Viet Minh 148th Independent Infantry Regiment actually had its headquarters located in Dien Bien Phu, although three of its four infantry battalions were detached at the time Operation CASTOR began. It could do little, therefore, to oppose the rapid French build-up. Giap, however, had expected a French move (although he had no idea where this would be) and his reaction was swift. He calculated that, if pressed, the French would abandon their hold on the neighbouring province of Lai Chau in order to concentrate at Dien Bien Phu. On 24 November, as the French began to consolidate, he ordered the 316th Infantry Division, reinforced by the 148th Regiment, to attack into Lai Chau, and three other divisions – the 308th, 312th and 351st – to attack from Viet Bac into Dien Bien Phu. The attack into Lai Chau began on 8 December and it had exactly the effect that Giap had foreseen. On 9 December, the 2,000 French troops in the province were ordered by Cogny to abandon their position and move to Dien Bien Phu. As they did so, they met a skilfully laid ambush. Only 185 men made it to Dien Bien Phu; the rest died on the road, deserted or went into captivity.

But the attack on Dien Bien Phu was to be no reckless, unprepared assault. With Lai Chau cleared, Viet Minh divisions began to converge on the French position. Throughout the months of December 1953 and January 1954, Giap stockpiled artillery ammunition, moved guns and anti-aircraft batteries into position, built wooden decoy gun positions and brought up troops. The French were never able to cut the Viet Minh supply lines as they had at Na San, so that Giap had uninterrupted freedom of action. By the end of January, there were 50,000 Vietnamese regulars on the hills overlooking Dien Bien Phu; the Viet Minh outnumbered the French by four to one in guns and five to one in men. The French positions, moreover, had been carefully scouted by Vietnamese volunteers so that all their artillery positions were known, models had been constructed for planning and detailed rehearsals had been carried out. On 31 January 1954, Vietnamese artillery opened up for the first time, and French patrols found Vietnamese soldiers in all directions. The French were surrounded.

IV. THE BATTLES FOR BEATRICE, GABRIELLE AND ANNE-MARIE: 13–17 MARCH 1954

It was, however, another two weeks before combat operations started in earnest. At 5.00 p.m. on 13 March, while there was still daylight, the Viet Minh artillery and anti-aircraft guns opened a concentrated fire on French positions around strong point Beatrice. Much of this fire was direct, rather than indirect, playing to the strengths of the unskilled Vietnamese crews under Chinese advisers. Beatrice was defended by the 3rd Battalion, *13ème Demi-Brigade* of the Foreign Legion, commanded by Major Paul Pégot, and co-located with them was the headquarters of the northern sector of the defences, under Colonel Jules Gauchet. French counter-battery fire was weak and inaccurate so that the attackers, who had cleared mines and cut wire and advanced their start line to within 200 yards of the French positions, were able to move into position unhindered. At about 6.15 p.m., a shell burst inside the French command post killing Pégot and all his key staff officers. A few minutes later, Gauchet was also killed by artillery fire.

The attack had been timed to coincide with the full moon. As soon as it rose, the infantry went in. The Legionnaires fought hard: they killed an estimated 600 of the attacking 312th Division and wounded 1,200 more. But around midnight, having lost 500 of their own men – well over half their strength – the French were overrun. A counter-attack early next morning was repulsed by heavy Vietnamese artillery fire. Again, French counter-battery fire was ineffective against the carefully dug-in and camouflaged Viet Minh positions. While Viet Minh morale soared, the French artillery commander, Colonel Charles Piroth, committed suicide.

Later on the morning of 14 March, the French were reinforced by the 5th (Vietnamese) Parachute Battalion, which dropped into Dien Bien Phu by parachute. Soon afterwards, the Viet Minh artillery again opened fire. The main airstrip was soon inoperable, which meant that resupply was possible only by parachute drop. A concentration of fire at 5.00 p.m. announced a repeat of the methods of 13 March, this time against strong point Gabrielle, which was defended by an Algerian battalion. The main infantry attack, by two regiments of the 308th Division, began at 8.00 p.m. Once again, the French were continuously subjected to accurate Vietnamese artillery support, and again, the battalion commander and his staff were wiped out by a hit on the command post. De Castries ordered the newly arrived 5th Parachute Battalion to counter-attack and restore the position. Although some men reached Gabrielle, the main body was paralyzed by exhaustion and heavy artillery fire. Losses were heavy, and the attack failed. By afternoon, the fight for Gabrielle had petered out with the loss of 1,000 French lives and anywhere between 1,000 and 2,000 Viet Minh.

Anne-Marie was Giap's next victim. The strong point was defended by a unit of ethnic Thais, a minority in Vietnam, who had been for some weeks subjected to intense Viet Minh psychological operations. The effect of this, combined with the morale-sapping loss of Beatrice and Gabrielle, was enough to persuade the Thais that this was not their fight. On the morning of 17 March, under cover of a morning mist, most of them deserted. The few who remained, and their French officers, had no option but to withdraw.

V. OPERATIONAL PAUSE, 17–30 MARCH 1954

So far, Giap had been able to achieve success by massing all his available firepower against successive, isolated French strong points, a tactic he

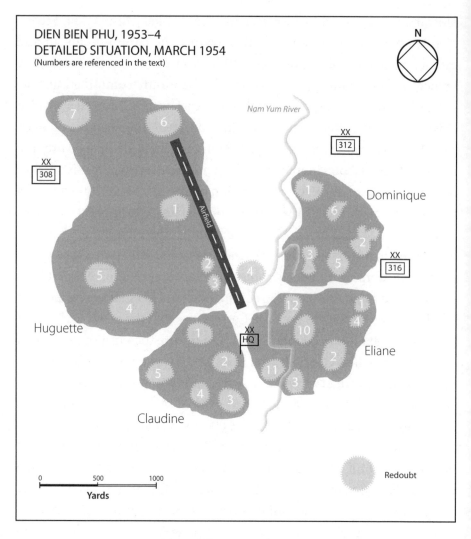

Map 19: Dien Bien Phu, 1954

later referred to as 'combined nibbling and full-scale attack'. De Castries, secluded in his command bunker, was unable to respond by manoeuvring fires or troops effectively against his opponent. This series of moves had now brought the Viet Minh close to the French central position formed by strong points Huguette, Dominique, Claudine and Eliane. The 1,800 troops in Isabelle were completely cut off and surrounded, as good as lost; the position endured siege conditions until the end of April, when its ammunition, food and water were exhausted.

The surrender of the initiative to the Viet Minh was too much for the senior French officers in the garrison, and, away in Hanoi, for Cogny, who, on 17 March, had attempted to fly in to take command, only to be thwarted by anti-aircraft fire. On 24 March, Langlais and his fellow paratroop officers demanded to see de Castries. Langlais coldly told de Castries that he considered him unfit to hold the command and that, although circumstances prevented him from being physically removed and he would therefore retain the appearance of command, he – Langlais – would effectively supersede him.

Surprisingly, de Castries continued to issue some orders. On 27 March, he ordered an attack against Viet Minh anti-aircraft and machine-gun positions almost 2 miles west of Dien Bien Phu. These had become a serious obstacle to French air resupply, to the point where parachute drops were having to be made from 6,500 feet – above small-arms and low-level air-defence range – at the expense of accuracy and concentration. It was at this time that two civilian pilots, James McGovern and Wallace Buford, earned the dubious distinction of becoming the first Americans to be killed in Vietnam. Against expectations, the attack was completely successful. Three hundred and fifty Vietnamese soldiers were killed for the loss of 20 French, and 17 gun positions were destroyed.

VI. THE ATTACK ON THE CENTRE,
30 MARCH–22 APRIL 1954

Having redeployed his artillery and brought up fresh supplies, Giap was ready to repeat his successful tactics against Eliane and Dominique. These two areas were held by five French battalions, but all were under strength and consisted of a mix of French troops, Legionnaires, Vietnamese, Thais and Moroccans. At 7.00 p.m. on 30 March, the Viet Minh captured redoubts 1 and 2 in Dominique, leaving only redoubt 3 between them and the main French headquarters; by now, they had also got between

Dominique and Eliane. At this point, the French turned Giap's tactics against him. The 4th Colonial Artillery Regiment used its 105 mm guns in direct fire, supported by massed machine guns from the vicinity of the airstrip. This enormous concentration of fire blew away the Vietnamese attack.

South of Dominique, the Viet Minh were more successful. The 316th Division was again in action, this time against the Moroccans in Eliane. By midnight on 30 March, Eliane redoubt 1 and part of redoubt 2 were in Viet Minh hands. Simultaneously, the 308th Division had attacked Huguette, west of the river, and all but succeeded in breaking into redoubt 7. The position was saved by a French sergeant, who led a local counter-attack which stopped the assault.

Just after midnight, the French launched a bigger counter-attack on Eliane redoubt 2 and retook half of it. Langlais ordered that on the following afternoon this would be followed up by a further counter-attack against Eliane redoubt 1 and Dominique redoubt 2. Every available man was to be committed. But Langlais was forestalled by Giap, who renewed the attack towards midday on 31 March. The exhausted French kept up the fight until the late afternoon but had to fall back. Reinforcements sent to break through from Isabelle were ambushed and they, too, fell back.

Soon after nightfall on 31 March, Langlais spoke to Major Marcel Bigeard, commanding Eliane, on the radio, telling him to abandon the position and fall back west of the river. Bigeard refused: 'I will not let go of Eliane 4,' he told Langlais, 'otherwise Dien Bien Phu is done for.' That night, the Vietnamese 316th Division again attacked Eliane. Success appeared within their grasp when a French counter-attack led by a platoon of tanks repulsed the assault. On the west side of the river, Huguette redoubt 7 was briefly overrun but it, too, was retaken by counter-attack at daybreak on 1 April. This was the pattern of life for the next few days and nights: the Viet Minh would attack, usually against Eliane 2, and were every time thrown back. The French attempted to reinforce Dien Bien Phu by parachute drops, but only individual aircraft could make the run in through the Viet Minh anti-aircraft fire; a few paratroopers made it but not enough to make a difference. However, French air support and artillery fire improved in effectiveness, inflicting heavy casualties.

Faced with stalemate, Giap changed tactics. In order to force the French out of their positions east of the river, he turned to trench-warfare tactics. Sensing that the initiative had changed hands, Langlais ordered Bigeard to retake Eliane redoubt 1. Bigeard planned a dawn attack on 10 April, which would begin with a short, heavy artillery bombardment, continue with the infiltration of small infantry combat teams, and conclude with a consolidation phase: effectively, German storm-troop tactics from March 1918. Control of Eliane redoubt 1 went to and fro during the next two days but by nightfall on 12 April the French were firmly back in residence.

This reverse was a severe setback for Viet Minh morale, already shaky after something approaching 6,000 killed, 10,000 wounded – without medical services – and 2,500 captured. Mutiny threatened, and reports told of soldiers being followed by officers and NCOs during attacks with orders to shoot if they turned back or hesitated. Giap had to call for reinforcements.

But the Viet Minh were faring better to the west of the river, where Huguette redoubts 1 and 6 were almost completely surrounded. Redoubt 6 was under greatest pressure and, on 11 April, an attempt was made by the troops in redoubt 1 to break through the encirclement and resupply it. Some water, food and ammunition did get through, but the attempts had to be repeated on the nights of 14–15 and 16–17 April. The cost was proving too high, and on 18 April the garrison of redoubt 6 tried to break out and reach redoubt 1. Few made it. Redoubt 1 having been weakened by the effort to keep redoubt 6 going, the Viet Minh were able to isolate it and overrun it. By 22 April, therefore, Giap's men were sitting right on the airstrip, making French resupply all but impossible.

VII. THE FALL OF DIEN BIEN PHU

Heavily reinforced, Giap launched a new series of attacks on the remaining French positions on the night of 1–2 May. By now, the French were exhausted, and Eliane redoubt 1, Dominique redoubt 3 and Huguette redoubt 5 were all overrun. The defenders managed to hold on at Eliane redoubt 2, but this was again attacked on 6 May with the support of Katyusha multiple-rocket fire. Only effective French artillery fire on the attackers as they closed on the position saved it – but to no avail: the Viet Minh had been mining under the redoubt, and that night, they blew the mine. Eliane redoubt 2 ceased to exist.

The next morning, Giap began a final attack on the defenders, using all his available reserves and artillery. At 5.00 p.m., de Castries called Cogny by radio and, according to an account in *Time* magazine, told him that 'The Viets are everywhere. The situation is very grave . . . I feel the end is approaching, but we will fight to the finish.' Cogny replied that he understood: 'You will fight to the end. It is out of the question to run up the white flag after your heroic resistance.' By dusk, all the French positions in the centre had fallen. Only Isabelle remained: the garrison of about 1,700 made an attempt to break out, but only 70 men escaped to Laos.

VIII. AFTERMATH

On the morning of 8 May, the Viet Minh paraded 11,700 French prisoners, of whom 4,400 were wounded; more than 2,000 French troops had been killed – about 14 per cent of the original force. If the wounded and dead are combined, total casualties were almost half the original force. This was not 'fighting to the end', as de Castries and Cogny had discussed it, but compared with historical norms as discussed in the opening chapter, it was as much as flesh and blood would stand. Those able to walk were force-marched 250 miles to prison camps; several hundred died en route. The wounded were given basic attention until the arrival of the Red Cross, who evacuated 800 of the worst cases and treated the remainder, who went into prison. Just 3,290 prisoners were repatriated four months later. Many died of wounds, starvation and ill treatment, while the fate of 3,000 prisoners of Vietnamese, Thai or Laotian origin is still unknown.

The battle cost Giap nearly 8,000 dead and 15,000 wounded by most estimates, but it cemented his reputation and established him as the military leader who would bring victory to the Communist cause. With the fall of Dien Bien Phu, the French lost 10 per cent of their fighting strength in Indo-China and their will to rule in the region was finally broken. Public opinion in France was profoundly shocked: a small, Third World country had defeated a major European power in pitched battle. The battle led directly to the Geneva Accords, which partitioned Vietnam into the Communist north and a French-supported state in the south. It was intended that national elections in 1956 would reunify the country, but after the French withdrawal, the United States took over sponsorship of the south. China and the USSR in turn supported the north and, as the Cold War closed its grip, the prospect of reunification faded.

The battle was also a milestone in US involvement. Under the terms of the Mutual Defense Assistance Pact, the US had provided air support during the conflict. Not only did it supply aircraft, stores, maintenance and spares, but US pilots flew 682 combat sorties during the battle from US Navy carriers offshore. The rest is history. Vietnam was finally reunited after further fighting following the US withdrawal in 1973. Soviet Premier Nikita Kruschev had foretold the eventual result in a conversation with the US Ambassador to Russia in 1963: 'Go ahead and fight in the jungles of Vietnam. The French fought there for seven years and still had to leave in the end. Perhaps you Americans will be able to stick it out a little longer, but eventually you will quit too.'

11

Kuwait, 1990–91: Desert Storm

I. PRELUDE

Iraq had had its eyes on the small, oil-rich state of Kuwait for many years. In 1961, President Qasim threatened to annex it, invoking old Ottoman claims to it as part of the governorate of Basra, one of three previously Ottoman provinces – the others being Baghdad and Mosul – which had been merged to create Iraq after the Congress of Versailles. On that occasion, a rapid reinforcement from Britain forced Iraq to back down. In March 1973, Iraq occupied As-Samitah, a border post on the Kuwait–Iraq border. This dispute began when Iraq demanded the right to occupy the Kuwaiti islands of Bubiyan and Warbah. Diplomatic intervention by Saudi Arabia and the Arab League persuaded Iraq to withdraw.

Relations seemed to improve between 1980 and 1988, when Kuwait supported Iraq in its long, bloody war with Iran. However, the first and most basic cause of the Iraqi invasion of Kuwait in 1990, which began the Gulf War of 1990–91, was the firm historical view that Kuwait was a part of Iraq. This issue aggravated, and was aggravated by, the second cause: the rich deposits of the Rumailia oilfield that straddled the ill-defined border. Iraq repeatedly claimed that Kuwaiti oil rigs were illegally tapping into its southern oilfields. Finally, the fallout from the Iran–Iraq War strained relations between the two countries.

That conflict had begun with an Iraqi invasion of Iran and degenerated into bloody attritional warfare as the Iranians slowly drove Saddam Hussein's armies back into Iraq. Kuwait and many other Arab nations supported Iraq against the Islamic revolutionary government of Iran, fearful that Saddam's defeat could bring a wave of Iranian-inspired revolution throughout the Arab world, where, especially on the littoral of the Persian Gulf, the smaller states were ruled by Sunni families but peopled by large minorities – near-majorities in some cases – of Shi'ites, who looked to Iran for spiritual leadership.

Following the end of the war, relations between Iraq and Kuwait again deteriorated, despite the support Kuwait had provided, as the old issues of the border and Kuwaiti sovereignty re-emerged. With tensions continuing to grow, Saddam Hussein misread the strategic situation following the end of the Cold War confrontation and concluded that the United States and the rest of the outside world would not interfere to defend Kuwait. This was not unreasonable, as he had been effectively told by the US Ambassador to Iraq that America did not wish to become involved in the dispute. On 2 August 1990, Iraqi forces mounted a rapid invasion of Kuwait and quickly seized control of the small nation. Most of the small Kuwaiti armed forces, along with the ruling family, escaped to Saudi Arabia. Around 1,000 Kuwaiti civilians died and 300,000 became refugees. Immediately, the US, along with the United Nations, demanded Iraq's immediate withdrawal.

II. RECRUITING A COALITION

A long series of UN Security Council and Arab League resolutions condemning the invasion were passed. One of the most important was UN Resolution 678, passed on 29 November, giving Iraq a withdrawal deadline of 15 January 1991 and authorizing 'all necessary means to uphold and implement Resolution 660', a diplomatic formulation authorizing the use of force. The Gulf War would be about the authority of the UN and the maintenance of international peace, security and sovereignty. But it would be about oil as well. The US imported nearly one-third of its oil requirements from the Gulf; Western Europe imported one-fifth. Having learned the lessons of the 1970s, most governments maintained large reserves – indeed, it was estimated that around one billion barrels were held by dependent governments, representing 250 days of supply from Iraq and Kuwait. However, given that Iraq was the third-largest supplier of oil to the world market, a long war would be likely to raise the price of oil above $50 a barrel.

In parallel with moves in the UN, the US, largely through the efforts of Secretary of State James Baker, assembled a coalition of nations to join it and the neighbouring Gulf States in opposing Iraq militarily. The sense of outrage at Iraqi aggression was so great, even among other Arab nations, that, over the ensuing months, thirty-four countries originally offered to contribute forces – in the event, not all did so but many that did not contribute forces helped pay for the war or contributed in other ways. US President George Bush was the first to order the deployment of navy, army, air force, marine and coastguard units to Saudi Arabia – on 7 August 1990 – for Operation DESERT SHIELD, designed primarily to prevent further southward moves by Iraqi forces into Saudi Arabia while also establishing a firm foothold from which offensive operations could be planned and developed. A secure base in Saudi Arabia also enabled the rapid build-up by sea and air of the enormous logistic requirements of the operation. Including the US, 12 countries sent naval forces, eight sent ground forces and four sent combat aircraft to join the campaign.

By January, Coalition naval forces were deployed in strength, based around two US aircraft carriers, the *Dwight D Eisenhower* and *Independence*, and two US battleships, the *Wisconsin* and *Missouri*. The battleships, although old, mounted enormous firepower, including cruise missiles as well as their main armaments. As the build-up of forces continued, further US carriers arrived in the Gulf and the Red Sea – the *Midway*, *Theodore Roosevelt*, *America*, *Ranger* and *Saratoga* – plus the smaller HMS *Invincible*: a staggering array of seaborne air power. Ground forces numbered 956,600, and air forces 2,430 fixed-wing aircraft. US troops represented 73 per cent of the total, with the other main contributors being Saudi Arabia, Britain, Syria and France. Others who could not or would not join in militarily – notably Germany and Japan – made financial contributions totalling more than $16 billion. The maintenance of the

Coalition, in which Arab states, with predominantly Muslim populations, were arrayed with non-Islamic nations against another Arab state, was pivotal. It was therefore imperative that Israel – the focus of widespread Arab resentment and an anticipated target for Iraqi missile attacks – stay out of the war. US Patriot missile batteries were therefore deployed to protect Israeli cities from the missiles Iraq duly launched, along with heavy US diplomatic and economic pressure on the Israeli government.

Against the Coalition's armada, the Iraqis could muster only a few gun-boats and small missile craft; on the other hand, their 1.2 million ground troops, with about 5,800 tanks, 5,100 other armoured vehicles and 3,850 artillery pieces, made for greater strength on the ground. Iraq also had 750 fighters and bombers, 200 other aircraft, and elaborate missile and gun defences. It had used four élite armoured and mechanized divisions of the Republican Guard to seize Kuwait. By early September 1990, these divisions had returned to their pre-invasion locations in south-eastern Iraq, where they were held as a mobile operational strike force. The whole of the Republican Guard in the Kuwait theatre of operations was organized into two sub-corps, the first of five divisions, one of which was a special-forces division, and the second of three divisions. Less mobile and less capable Iraqi Army divisions, chiefly made up of poorly trained conscripts, were deployed to replace them in defence. By late September 1990, Iraq had 22 divisions deployed in a mainly linear static defensive line along the Saudi border, of which 13 were infantry divisions and nine were mechanized or armoured. When the Coalition ground offensive began, up to 43 Iraqi divisions were in the theatre of operations, although not all were fully manned or effective. According to some estimates, the number of Iraqi troops at the start of the ground campaign might have been as great as 336,000, though 200,000 is probably a fairer estimate. Even at the end of the campaign, some Iraqi divisions remained unidentified by US intelligence, and a number of the details of the Iraqi order of battle are still in dispute among authoritative sources.

In the west, astride the Iraq–Kuwait border, the Iraqi VII Corps deployed four infantry divisions in its first echelon, and one armoured and three infantry divisions in its second. In the centre, the Iraqi IV Corps deployed five infantry divisions in its first echelon, and one mechanized, one armoured and one infantry division in its second. In the east, protecting the approaches to Kuwait City and the road north towards Basra, the Iraqi III Corps deployed eight infantry divisions in its first echelon, and one armoured, one mechanized and one infantry division in its second. The Iraqis' second operational echelon to the north consisted of II Corps, with three infantry divisions in its first line and one infantry division in its second. All these forces had plenty of time to dig defensive positions, construct anti-tank defences and wire entanglements and prepare extensive minefields. The Iraqi Army's uncommitted reserve in Kuwait was IX Corps, with three infantry and three armoured divisions.

Command of the Coalition forces was vested in the Commander-in-Chief, US Central Command – CENTCOM – a theatre-level command set up to oversee US operations in the Middle East, Central Asia and the Horn of Africa after the Iranian hostage fiasco. The C-in-C at the time was General 'Stormin' Norman' Schwarzkopf, a Vietnam veteran and a giant of a man in all respects. Since Schwarzkopf had last seen action in Vietnam, the US armed forces, and in particular the US Army, had undergone a radical transformation. The Army had abandoned conscription and replaced it with an all-regular force with a highly professional ethos. A new doctrine, Air-Land Warfare, had transformed its thinking on combat in Europe against a possible Soviet invasion, moving from a posture based wholly on deterrence to one in which deterrence and war-fighting both played a part. This was the engine for a new generation of equipment, training, command and staff procedures – and a new relationship with the US Air Force. The Army deployed two heavy armoured corps in Europe, V and VII, with a third, III, held ready in the US for reinforcement, along with a strategic reserve formation, the lightly equipped but rapidly deployable XVIII Airborne Corps. It was XVIII Corps, therefore, which, with two of its divisions – the 82nd and the 101st – formed the first element of US land power, along with a US Marine Corps formation, II Marine Amphibious Force, of two

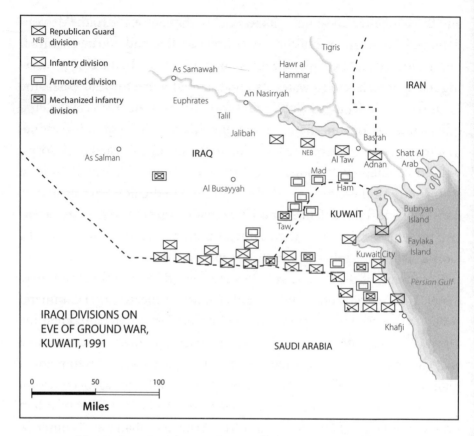

Map 20: Iraqi Divisions on the Eve of War, Kuwait, January 1991

divisions – the 1st and 2nd – plus other units held afloat for amphibious operations and diversions.

III. DESERT STORM: THE PLAN

Army planners began work on a ground offensive on 18 September. On 10 October, Schwarzkopf briefed President Bush on a plan to invade using the one corps then available, XVIII Corps. This had been reinforced with the 24th Infantry Division, a heavy mechanized division, and the 3rd Armored Cavalry Regiment, to give it the heavy punch that its light divisions lacked. Even so, this was felt to be insufficient for certain victory without huge casualties, and on 31 October, Bush authorized the deployment of VII Corps, under Lieutenant General Freddie Franks, which began to arrive by sea in early December.

Schwarzkopf's declared objectives were to secure the unconditional withdrawal of Iraqi forces from Kuwait; to restore the Kuwaiti government; to re-establish international peace and security in the region; and to uphold the authority of the United Nations. His operational design to deliver these objectives was, first, to destroy the Iraqi air force and establish total air superiority. Next, he would as far as possible neutralize the Iraqi capability to deliver weapons, conventional or chemical, by missile, for it was known that Iraq held a large arsenal of various missiles, notably the Al-Huseyn, with a range of 375 miles, and the Soviet Scud, with a range of 190 miles. These initial tasks would be executed chiefly by air and special forces, with some support from ground-based artillery. When they had been completed, he intended to switch his main effort against the Iraqi Army and the Republican Guard, wearing them down until favourable force ratios had been achieved. A ground offensive would then be launched.

It was always explicit in the planning that the disparity in numbers in favour of the Iraqis would be made up by the asymmetry in technology in favour of the Coalition. As well as advanced air and sea platforms, precision-guided munitions and cruise missiles, the Coalition had land vehicles that included the most advanced equipments available: the American M1 Abrams and the British Challenger tanks, as well as the Bradley and Warrior infantry fighting vehicles, were infinitely superior to the mix of Soviet and old Western equipments deployed by the Iraqis.

To carry out Schwarzkopf's plan, considerable regrouping of the ground forces was needed. VII Corps included three armoured divisions – 1st Cavalry and 1st and 3rd Armored – plus the 1st Infantry Division, the 2nd Armored Cavalry Regiment and the powerful 11 Aviation Brigade, with its force of attack helicopters. The British and French also increased their initial deployments of brigade size up to divisional strength. The British 1st Armoured Division deployed two brigades under the command of

Major General Rupert Smith and was placed under VII Corps; the French declined to place their 6th Light Armoured Division under US command and it was accordingly allocated its own role. The various Arab formations were all grouped into a corps-sized formation commanded by the Saudi General Prince Khalid bin Sultan, eldest son of the Saudi Crown Prince.

IV. DESERT STORM: THE AIR CAMPAIGN

A day after the deadline set in Resolution 678, the Coalition opened the general offensive codenamed Operation DESERT STORM with a massive air campaign that launched more than 1,000 sorties per day. The first priority was the destruction of Iraqi air defences, radars and air forces. Sorties were launched mostly from Saudi Arabia and nine Coalition aircraft-carrier battle groups in the Persian Gulf and Red Sea. Once sufficient degradation of the defences had been achieved, the emphasis would shift to the destruction of Iraqi command, control and communications. Saddam Hussein had closely supervised the Iraqi forces in the Iran–Iraq War, and initiative at the lower levels had been discouraged; Coalition planners therefore believed that Iraqi resistance would quickly collapse if deprived of Saddam's personal command and control. The main effort would then shift to degrading Iraq's ground combat power in order to reduce the force ratios in preparation for the ensuing ground attack. In particular, the air forces would aim to reduce the Republican Guard Corps to 50 per cent strength, which by most measures would render it all but ineffective.

Operations began at 2.38 a.m. on 17 January 1991, when Task Force *Normandy*, with eight US AH-64 Apache helicopters, led by two MH-53 Pave Low helicopters, destroyed Iraqi radar sites near the Iraq–Saudi Arabia border. At 2.43 a.m., air forces began operations against airfields in western Iraq. At 3.00 a.m., ten US F117 stealth bombers attacked the Iraqi capital, Baghdad. Within hours of the start of the air campaign, a P3 Orion reconnaissance aircraft detected a large number of Iraqi patrol boats and naval vessels attempting to make a run from Basra and the port of Umm Qasr to Iranian waters. More aircraft attacked the flotilla near Bubyan

Island, destroying 11 vessels and damaging many more. Concurrently, US Navy Tomahawk cruise missiles struck targets in Baghdad, and other aircraft attacked targets throughout Iraq. Government buildings, TV stations, airfields and presidential palaces were destroyed. Five hours after the first attacks, Baghdad state radio broadcast a voice identified as Saddam Hussein's declaring: 'The great duel, the mother of all battles, has begun. The dawn of victory nears as this great showdown begins.' Next day, Iraq launched eight modified Scud missiles into Israel in an attempt to provoke an Israeli response that would enrage Arab opinion and fracture the Coalition. Missile attacks on Israel were to continue throughout the six weeks of the war, but the deployment of the US Patriot missile batteries to Israel was enough to secure Israeli cooperation.

The largest phase of the air campaign targeted military installations throughout Iraq and Kuwait: Scud missile launchers, weapons-research facilities and naval forces. About one-third of the Coalition air power was devoted to attacking Scuds, some of which were on trucks and therefore difficult to locate. Teams of US and British special forces had been covertly inserted into western Iraq to help search for and destroy them. However, lack of cover hindered their operations, and many were killed or captured, including the famous 'Bravo Two-Zero' patrol of Britain's Special Air Service. Elements of 2 Brigade of the 1st US Cavalry Division launched a covert mission into Iraq on 9 February 1991, followed by a feint attack in force on 20 February up Wadi al-Batin.

Iraqi anti-aircraft defences, including shoulder-launched ground-to-air missiles, were surprisingly effective against Coalition aircraft, 75 of which were lost. In particular,Royal Air Force and US Navy aircraft which flew at low altitudes to avoid radar were particularly badly hit, since Iraqi defences relied very little on radar and to a large extent on small-scale weapons which were well targeted against low-flying aircraft.

While this phase of the campaign was in progress there was a further surge of diplomatic activity. On 15 February, in response to a Russian proposal, the Iraqis announced that they would 'deal with Security Council Resolution 660', the first of the UN resolutions, 'with the aim of reaching an honourable and acceptable solution, including withdrawal'. The conditions attached, however, made it plain that this was no more than a cynical ploy to gain time. On 22 February, the Coalition set out conditions that Iraq had to meet by noon the following day. Saddam's response was to set fire to all Kuwait's oil wells and reject the conditions. On 25 February 1991, Iraqi troops launched a missile at a Coalition barracks in Dharan, Saudi Arabia, which killed 28 Americans.

By now, the objectives of the air campaign had largely been fulfilled. The Iraqi Air Force had been devastated; most airfields had been heavily struck, and in air combat Iraq had made only one kill while sustaining many losses. Five out of six Tupolev Tu-22s it had possessed had been

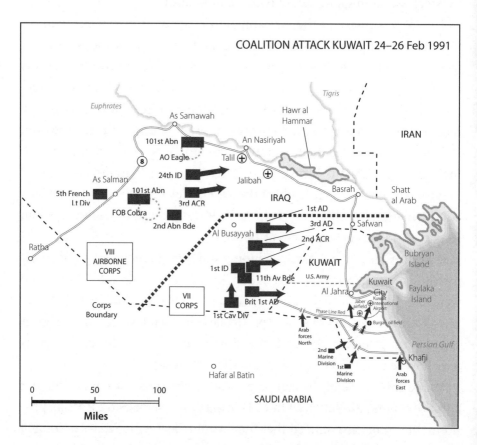

Map 21: Coalition Attack, Kuwait, 24–26 February 1991

destroyed by bombing early on. Perhaps the strangest episode of the entire war was the escape of many Iraqi pilots and aircraft to Iran to escape the Coalition bombing. The Iranians impounded these aircraft after the war and never returned them, putting them in the service of their own air force and claiming them as reparations for the Iran–Iraq War. On 24 February, Schwarzkopf launched the ground campaign.

V. THE GROUND PLAN

The ground phase of the war was named Operation DESERT SABRE. The first units to move into Iraq were three patrols of B Squadron of the SAS in late January. These eight-man patrols landed behind Iraqi lines to gather intelligence on the movements of mobile Scud missile launchers, which could not be detected from the air. Other objectives included the destruction of the launchers and their fibre-optic communications arrays, which lay in pipelines. The general ground plan was based on deception. Two Marine Corps divisions, along with all five divisions contributed by the Arab members of the Coalition, were massed near the coast. The Marine Corps also held two brigades poised offshore on amphibious shipping. This considerable force was to attack directly into Kuwait, to draw the attention of the defending Iraqi forces. The main effort, however, would be almost 200 miles further west, on the far side of Wadi Al-Batin. Here, the most capable US and British formations – one infantry and three armoured divisions under the command of VII Corps – were to turn the flank of the defence, then swing eastwards towards Basra to engage and destroy the Republican Guard. The left flank of the attack would be protected by XVIII Corps and a French light armoured division.

VI. THE MAIN ASSAULT

Early on Sunday 24 February, the Marines and the Arab forces attacked northwards towards Kuwait City, taking Iraqi forces by surprise. At the same time, XVIII Corps launched a sweeping left-hook attack deep into enemy territory across the largely undefended desert of southern Iraq. It was led by the 3rd Armored Cavalry Regiment and the 24th Infantry Division. These moves met with such swift success that Schwarzkopf decided to bring forward the assault by VII Corps, which was assembled in full strength. The corps had not been due to move until 3.00 a.m. the following day, but Franks was now told to move at noon that same day. This meant that the assaulting brigades would have to attack in broad daylight, breaching the Iraqi minefields, ditches and embankments. However, Iraqi resistance had been so feeble and Coalition air and artillery fire so overwhelming that Schwarzkopf felt the risk was acceptable. At noon, therefore, spearheaded by the 3rd Squadron of the 2nd Armored Cavalry Regiment, the corps launched its armoured attack into Iraq just to the west of Kuwait. The left flank of this movement was protected by the French 6th Light Armoured Division. The French force quickly overcame the Iraqi 45th Infantry Division, suffering only a handful of casualties and taking a large number of prisoners, and took up blocking positions to prevent an Iraqi counter-attack on the Coalition flank. The right flank of the movement was protected by the British 1st Armoured Division. The US 1st Infantry Division, in the corps' main effort, took only 1 hour and 20 minutes to break through the Iraqi defences and clear 16 lanes for the break-out force of two armoured divisions. Once the allies had penetrated deep into Iraqi territory, they turned eastward, launching a flank attack against the Republican Guard with devastating effect.

After all the preparation and long build-up, the actual operation was something of an anti-climax – and the decision to halt even more so. The Coalition ground advance was much swifter than anyone had expected. On 26 February, the Iraqis began to withdraw from Kuwait; a long column of retreating troops formed along the main Iraq–Kuwait highway. This was subjected to such extensive attack by Coalition forces that the road, littered with burned-out vehicles and the bodies of the dead and wounded, became known as the Highway of Death. US, British and French forces continued to pursue the retreating troops over the border and back into Iraq, fighting frequent battles, which resulted in massive losses for the

Iraqis and moderate losses for the Coalition, and eventually moving to within 150 miles of Baghdad. The leading battalions reached the main road north from Kuwait City and the River Euphrates near Nasiriyah, half an hour before a ceasefire was called. President Bush declared this, and a halt to further advances, just 100 hours after the ground campaign had started.

The decision to stop was controversial then and even more so later, when Saddam, having managed to hold onto power with his Ba'ath Party, wreaked his revenge on the Kurds in the north and the Shi'ite Arabs in the south. None of the Coalition partners were eager to step into the turmoil that an occupation of Iraq would have brought, and in any case, the UN had issued no mandate for such a move. This was, it must be remembered, a honeymoon period for the UN, when, in the aftermath of the Cold War, there was a general belief that it could assume the prime position in governing world affairs that its founders had envisaged but which superpower confrontation had, for 40 years, obstructed. Public opinion was also growing uneasy as pictures of the heavy casualties inflicted on the withdrawing Iraqi forces appeared on television screens. The Iraqis lost 20,000 killed, 75,000 wounded and 80,000 prisoners during the campaign, compared with only 190 Coalition killed and 75 wounded, many the result of accidents or 'friendly fire'.

VII. AFTERMATH AND CONSEQUENCES

Saddam's second war of foreign conquest ended with an even worse result than his first. With the liberation of Kuwait, Iraq again stood defeated. On top of its military losses, 2,000 civilians were dead. The Iraqi Army and Republican Guard had been so reduced that, although able to reconstitute many formations and conduct successful internal security operations, they could never again be considered effective as an expeditionary force. Iraq's air force and navy had effectively disappeared. However, the fact that the Coalition stopped short of evicting Saddam from power, obeying exactly the terms of the UN mandate, allowed Saddam to claim that

God had preserved him. Survival was, to his regime, victory. Despite the devastating defeat and subsequent Shi'ite and Kurdish rebellions, Saddam's government retained a strong grip on power; the rebellions were ruthlessly crushed. True, as a result of the ceasefire terms, Iraq had to accept the imposition of no-fly zones over her territory and UN weapons-inspection teams sifting through her nuclear and other weapons programmes, but the Ba'ath Party remained in charge. The economic and trade sanctions imposed during the war remained in place right up to the second invasion of Iraq, in 2003, contributing to severe economic hardship. But Saddam watched as, in the aftermath of the Cold War, the West reduced its formidable military power; never again, he believed, would such an invasion be possible. He was wrong, as the invasion launched by George Bush's son was to prove; but that second invasion was launched with half the forces used in 1991 and without the legitimacy of a UN mandate – with all the consequences that were then to follow. DESERT STORM was decisive in that it restored the sovereignty of Kuwait and destroyed Saddam Hussein's ability to attack his neighbours again. It did not, however, decide the future stability and security of the Persian Gulf.

12

The Twenty-first Century:
Is Decisive Victory Still Possible?

I. WHAT IS VICTORY?

As mass media developed during the nineteenth century, and with them the ability of governments to influence, if not control, public opinion, so belief in a cause made decisive battle more difficult. Adherence to an idea that was strong enough to take a modern, organized, industrialized society to war was unlikely to be shaken by one defeat, no matter how bad. Just as an industrial society could regenerate battle losses, so an information machine could repair and restore morale. This can be seen in the American Civil War, through the Great War and beyond the Second World War.

The post-Cold War period departed from this general thesis, however, for a number of reasons. First, with Communism gone, there was no overpowering strategic threat that would convince populations to accept serious losses; the cause was not worth the price-tag because people just did not feel threatened at home – hence the undignified exit of US forces from Lebanon and Somalia in the 1980s and 1990s respectively. Secondly, the Gulf War of 1991 aside, battles have got steadily longer. The notion of a battle confined to a single day – other than at the lowest tactical level, at which it is inevitably indecisive – has not been realized since Sedan. This has strengthened further the idea that it is the campaign that is decisive; however, campaigns take time to unfold and modern societies are impatient. The spirit of the age is one of instant gratification, and the idea that the defeat of an enemy may take years simply encourages a hostile or shallow media to equate deliberate progress with disaster. Thirdly, and connected to the preceding factor, the broadening of the information realm has made control by governments, in a way that was still possible even during the Falklands War, impossible. Multinational media companies, with their own agendas and owing nothing to government or alliance policies, let alone patriotism, have reinforced this. In the absence of the means to garner public support, even small numbers of casualties on intervention operations owing nothing to vital national interests can humble governments – the exit of the Spanish from Iraq following a well-timed series of bombings in Madrid in 2004 is an example.

September 11, 2001, changed this – but not for everyone. Since then, the United States has felt itself engaged in a war against implacable enemies, and although it has not yet been defeated in any battlefield engagement, its cumulative losses are many times those that led to the withdrawal from Somalia – and yet there is no slackening in its commitment. The same cannot be said for its many allies who do not feel similarly threatened and are therefore less committed. One has to ask whether, for example, the loss of a helicopter or transport plane full of troops would be enough to oblige even Britain to leave the campaign in Afghanistan. Despite the threat of Islamic extremism, people in Europe simply do not feel in enough danger to accept the sorts of sacrifices demanded – and made – by the US. Thus, the dynamic between the decision to make war, decisive battle and conflict termination is as complex as ever.

The broadening of the virtual realm of information has benefited insurgencies, enabling them to transmit their messages and to develop technology exchange. The Taliban's self-styled Emir of Afghanistan, Abu Al-Yazid, provides an example. His website, one of several hundred jihadi sites related to Afghanistan which are supplemented by television and radio stations, is updated every four hours in five languages and is, of course, unconstrained by the requirement, faced by government sources, to tell the truth. Al-Yazid was, until quite recently, known for his penchant for hanging anyone engaging in activities connected with globalization. An illustration of the acceleration of technology transfer is the fact that during the 1980s, it would routinely take six months for techniques developed in Palestine to reach the IRA or vice versa. Today, the exchange of expertise can take just a few days to show results on the ground. Anyone can search the internet and find details of how to construct an improvised explosive device, how to reach Afghanistan and join the jihad, how to become a suicide bomber – and much else besides.

The relationship between physical destruction and commitment has also changed. It is still true that industrialized societies can regenerate the losses of a single destructive battle, but it has become harder to do so for several reasons: hardware costs far more and takes longer to procure than it used to; it is more complex, requiring longer training for crews, who in turn are harder to replace; and the destructive power and reach of modern weapons as wielded by the US or North Korea – or, in the future, China – make the scale of destruction much harder to deal with. Thus, one battle *can*, in a conventional force-on-force contest, produce decisive *military* results. Kuwait did this, but only partly, because battlefield victory was not exploited. The initial US attacks on the Taliban and on Iraq in 2001–03 did the same.

However, both these campaigns throw up again the dynamic between the decision to make war, decisive battle and conflict termination. Termination is only possible if one side accepts defeat. Despite massive destruction and the loss of political power, neither the Ba'thist regime nor the Taliban accepted that they were done for. Both licked their wounds in safe havens and adopted asymmetrical means to continue the war. Baron Jomini may still be right that 'it is the morale of armies, as well as of nations, more than anything else, which makes victories and their results decisive'.

II. IS STATE-ON-STATE CONFLICT OVER?

Can we discount the possibility that state-on-state warfare is over? I suggest that, given the invasion of Georgia by the Russians in 2009, this would be very rash indeed. And if international war is still possible, recent experience seems to tell us that a decisive campaign is certainly possible.

Although for Western nations the campaign in the former Yugoslavia was one of peacekeeping, for the belligerents it was full-blown war. The UN intervention, it may be argued, prevented the Serbs from achieving their required decision and eventually enabled Croatia to break the deadlock of the Croatian-Bosnian War in Operations FLASH and STORM using an army rapidly transformed and re-equipped by US contractors and advisers.

When Croatia separated from Yugoslavia in 1991, Serbs in northern Dalmatia, Lika, Banovina, Kordun and western Slavonia, who had lived there for centuries since their expulsion from Serbia proper by the invading Ottoman Turks, seceded from the new Croatian republic and created an entity, never internationally recognized, known as the Republic of Serbian Krajina, or RSK. Krajina had been the name given to the military borderland, under the direct authority of Vienna rather than the *Ban* of Croatia, which protected the southern flank of the Austrian Empire.

By 1995, after four years of war in Bosnia and the fringes of Croatia, the military effectiveness of the Croatian and Bosnian Serbs had been considerably eroded. Both had been disowned by Belgrade, having refused the attempts of Serbian President Slobodan Milošević to settle the conflict. Morale, supplies of all types and efficiency were low; many of the Serb troops were poorly trained and their units were always undermanned. The Croatian Serb army, the *Vojska Srpska Krajina*, or VSK, had only about 55,000 soldiers available to cover a front 400 miles long in Croatia and another 80 miles long on the border of the Bihać pocket in Bosnia. Sixteen thousand VSK troops were stationed in eastern Slavonia, leaving only 39,000 to defend the main part of the RSK. In reality, only 30,000 of the theoretical 55,000 could be considered effective.

By contrast, the Croatian Army had been greatly strengthened and re-equipped with modern weaponry – despite the arms embargoes in force – and had obtained Western military training and technology with the covert support of the US, using a US-based firm, Military Professional Resources Incorporated, which provided both training and senior staff services. Its engagement was fully approved by the US government, as President Bill Clinton believed the Serbs could only be brought to the negotiating table if they sustained major losses on the ground.

The first phase of the series of decisive actions that would end the Croatian-Bosnian War was directed against the isolated Serb territory of western Slavonia. This was a rural area of hills and forests with relatively poor communications and infrastructure. Most of the Serb forces there were local militia, poorly trained, lightly armed, unsupported by their comrades either elsewhere in Krajina or in the Yugoslav National Army. They were thus no match for the Croatian Army. On the early morning of 1 May 1995, Croatian Army formations, including the elite 3 and 5 Guards Brigades, and Special Police units, numbering more than 7,000 men, began an advance from the north, west and east. This was Operation FLASH. Serb units were rapidly overwhelmed, and within a few hours, local commanders and civil authorities issued orders for evacuation southwards across the River Sava into Serb-held territory in Bosnia. By the afternoon of 2 May, all Serb forces that could be rescued had been evacuated and the Croatian Army had achieved all of its objectives. One large group of Serb soldiers and civilians, including local leader Veljko Džakula, failed to get away and had to surrender near Pakrac. In total, around 1,500 Serb POWs were captured, the largest number up to that date in the war and a loss of manpower the Serbs could ill afford.

After the Bosnian Serbs' attack on the eastern Bosnian enclaves and their capture of two of the three, Srebrenica and Žepa, in July, Croatian and Bosnian armies collaborated to capture the crucial western Bosnian towns of Glamoč and Bosansko Grahovo later that month. This cut the Croatian Serb supply lines and surrounded the Croatian Serb capital of Knin on three sides. The Krajina Serbs attempted to break the encirclement with an attack into the Bihać pocket, but this was repulsed by the pocket's defenders.

The US Government was delighted with the success of these operations and gave the go-ahead for the next phase, Operation STORM, which was to destroy as much as possible of the military potential of the Serb entity that had seceded from Bosnia-Herzegovina after a referendum had resulted rather dubiously in the separation of Bosnia-Herzegovina from

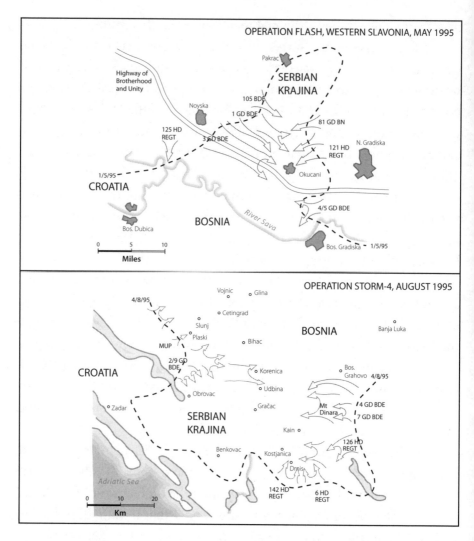

Map 22: Operations FLASH and STORM, Balkans, 1995

Yugoslavia. The operation, which lasted only four days, was the largest European land offensive since the Second World War.

At 5.00 a.m. on 4 August, 150,000 Croatian Army troops attacked at 30 separate points along a 200-mile front all along the Krajina border. The Croatian 4 and 7 Guards Brigades rapidly broke through the lines of the already demoralized Serb forces and advanced deep into Krajina

Serb territory. Knin was subjected to an intense artillery bombardment, but much of the Krajina Serb leadership had already left for Serbia and Bosnia. On the same day, aircraft from the US Air Force bombed two Croatian Serb surface-to-air missile radar sites near Knin and Udbina. The attack was described as a self-defence action undertaken after the radars had locked onto the USAF aircraft, which were patrolling Croatian and Bosnian airspace as part of Operation DENY FLIGHT to enforce no-fly zones.

Knin and most of the Dalmatian hinterland fell to Croatian forces within 24 hours, with only limited resistance from the VSK. The towns of Gračac, Ljubovo, Žitnić, Vrlika Kijevo, Drniš and Benkovac were quickly captured. Serb forces launched artillery attacks on Dubrovnik and Vinkovci, in the far south and far east of Croatia respectively, but without any noticeable effect. Large refugee columns formed in many parts of Croatian Serb territory as the entire Serb population fled into Bosnia along corridors established by the Croatian Army.

On 6 August, the Croatian 1 Guards Brigade continued to advance towards the border with Bosnia-Herzegovina, where they linked up with Bosnian forces from the Bihać enclave. Croatia's President Tuđman staged a triumphal entry into Knin, where the Croatian flag was raised above the fortress dominating the old town. The towns of Petrinja, Kostajnica, Obrovac, Korenica, Slunj, Bruvno, Plaski, Cetingrad and Glina all fell during the course of the day. The only determined resistance was in the town of Glina. Fighting continued on 7 August but at a much lower tempo. That evening, Croatian Defence Minister Gojko Šušak declared the end to major combat operations, as most of the border with Bosnia was controlled by the Croatian Army and only consolidation remained to be completed. On 8 August, the towns of Gornji Lapac, Donji Lapac and Vojnić were captured unopposed. On 9 August, the VSK's XXI Corps surrendered en masse to the Croatian Army.

It is instructive that the Croats employed the historical norms of superiority in order to achieve a decisive effect: 3:1 as a minimum, and preferably 5:1, in manpower, guns, tanks and fighting systems, and aircraft. Most of the successful offensives and campaigns cited in this book employed these ratios; Kuwait was different, but the Coalition first reduced the force ratio by air-delivered effect and then made use of the asymmetry in technology and firepower to achieve a favourable ratio.

By this time, the entire Serb population of Krajina was on the move, crossing into Serb-controlled territory in Bosnia. The exodus was complicated by the presence of armed Krajina Serb soldiers among the civilian refugees, which resulted in the Croatian Army shelling the columns. The Croatian Government claimed that around 90,000 Serb civilians had fled; Serbian sources claimed up to 250,000 refugees. The United Nations put the figure between 150,000 and 200,000, an estimate corroborated by the BBC.

The final phase of military operations by the Croatian Army in Bosnia-Herzegovina was Operation MISTRAL. After the second Serb attack on Sarajevo market on 28 August and the evacuation of UN forces from the final eastern enclave of Goražde, MISTRAL, in concert with NATO air operations, brought Croatian and Bosnian forces within reach of Banja Luka. Faced with disaster, the Serbs agreed to a ceasefire and subsequent negotiations, which produced the Dayton Peace Agreement, which finally ended the Croatian-Bosnian War.

The British intervention in Sierra Leone was also decisive. The conflict there combined elements of counter-insurgency, UN peacekeeping, indigenous security-sector reform and conventional war. After ten years of war, the rebel Revolutionary United Front (RUF), which had for so long carried all before it, was confronted by a threefold opposition: a UN force capable of holding its ground; the conventional Sierra Leonean Army, backed by British troops and air power, capable of defeating it in the field; and an irregular force loyal to the government – the Civil Defence Force – capable of interdicting its vital lines of communication into Liberia. Overextended by its failed gamble in Guinea, the RUF leadership had no choice but to enter a UN-led programme of demobilization, disarmament and reintegration or face death in the field.

III. WAR AMONG THE PEOPLE

The phrase 'war among the people' was coined by Rupert Smith in his seminal book *The Utility of Force*. In this, Smith sets out the view that in wars today, forces developed for industrial-age warfare against states are increasingly, although not exclusively, used for non-industrial wars against non-state actors. War has changed from being a matter of comparative forces doing battle within the context of strategic confrontation, to battle between a range of combatants using different weapons and asymmetrical methods for reasons that have little to do with the interests of nation states.

In the non-industrial model, the utility of conventional force is limited, however massive and impressive the force:

> Military force when employed (NB rather than deployed or threatened) has only two immediate effects: it kills people and destroys things. Whether or not this death and destruction serve to achieve the political purpose the force was intended to achieve depends on the choice of targets or objectives . . . to apply force with utility implies an understanding of the context in which one is acting, a clear definition of the results to be achieved, an identification of the point or target to which force is being applied . . . [and] an understanding of the nature of the force being applied.

War among the people is characterized by six major trends, of which four bear on the business of what is decisive: first, the ends for which wars are fought have more to do with objectives that are defined by individuals and societies than with states. Secondly, warfare takes place among the people and in the glare of the real-time media, and therefore among the people at home and in uncommitted societies as much as among those in the actual theatre of operations. Third, conflicts are long in timescale since military action is about creating a set of conditions that must be maintained in order to achieve a definitive outcome, which may take years.

The sides are non-state entities: coalitions or alliances on one side, irregular groupings on the other. Irregular forces operate outside the framework of the state and its laws, but may still remain within the construct of international humanitarian law. They range from criminal gangs to guerrilla forces.

Because of the strength of the arguments in *The Utility of Force* – which is a highly accurate and penetrating description of developments over the last century – along with the narrative of the Western media based on their view of the interventions in Iraq and Afghanistan, a view has developed in some quarters that the time of the decisive battle or decisive campaign is over. The experience of the Israelis in Lebanon in 2007 would certainly seem to support this hypothesis: a conventional army, which had not transformed its way of doing business and was seeking contact with an enemy that simply was not there, was brought to a halt by an irregular force, Hezbollah, using asymmetrical methods. However, *The Utility of Force* was published before the campaign in Iraq had reached any sort of maturity and before the campaign against the Taliban in Afghanistan had reopened. Its thesis may therefore be incomplete. It may be so, first and foremost, because some Western industrial-age armies have shown a remarkable ability to adapt structures, forces and weapon systems planned for confrontation with the Soviets to the demands of warfare against a host of modern enemies. The US Army in particular has done this, undergoing three transformations since Vietnam: it has moved from a doctrinal position of 'We do not do counter-insurgency or nation building' to 'No one does it better'; it has moved from a marked aversion to casualties in the 1980s and 1990s to an absolute conviction that casualties must be accepted when vital national interests are at stake; and, in so doing, it has reverted to 'normal' US thinking, amply demonstrated during both World Wars and in Korea and Vietnam. It has taken on new equipments, formulated a new doctrine, taught this throughout the organization and put it into effect, gripped the integration of civil and military effects, and mobilized large elements of its reserves – and all while fighting two major campaigns. Both the US and Britain have found new uses for old toys: the Nimrod aircraft was procured as a Cold War maritime patrol aircraft; for the past five years it has been used as a valuable surveillance platform able to loiter for extended periods and identify pinpoint targets.

What may be happening is that rather than a new type of war supplanting state-on-state conflict, the two are coexisting as they always have done and it is the balance that is shifting. If this is the case, the question is whether or not this is a permanent shift. Let us look at the two most recent interventions, in Iraq and Afghanistan. In both cases, a successful invasion rapidly destroyed the enemy's conventional forces and the country was occupied – occupied not for exploitation, but to bring the supposed benefits of Western liberal democracy and development to a failed or failing state. However, significant sections of the occupied country's population did not quite see the benefits of what were to them alien, Godless, notions. These sections were initially those who had lost out through the invasion: the Sunni Ba'thists in Iraq and the Taliban in Afghanistan. A period of regrouping followed the initial defeat, and then a counter-offensive was launched to eject the occupiers. The losers were soon reinforced by those Islamic extremists whose objections to the occupation were not so much material as spiritual. With them came foreign jihadi reinforcements, arms, money and expertise – expertise gained through a long war against Israel. This rapidly turned a counter-offensive into an insurgency, and the insurgency quickly learned that confronting the occupiers head-on would lead to destruction. They therefore did what the weak have always done when faced by the strong: avoided trials of strength unless on very favourable terms; exploited the vulnerabilities of the occupier, especially in the minds of the home population; used propaganda; and adopted the indirect method of attack – in other words, what is now termed asymmetry.

In many ways there is little new in this. Nineteenth-century imperial colonization was essentially about expeditionary operations to capture territories followed by extended counter-insurgency operations to secure them. Such an operation was then followed by a long period of development, accompanied by the exploitation of raw materials for the benefit of the imperial power. Resistance to occupation often used the same techniques – but without the benefit of modern technologies, the impetus of religious fervour, or the worldwide web to spread the techniques of violent resistance.

IV. DECISIVE BATTLE IN COUNTER-INSURGENT WARFARE

An insurgency is a military symptom of a political, social, economic, religious or ethnic problem, or of a compound of several of these problems. It is an attempt by the insurgents to seize control of, or modify, the state. The activities of al-Qaida are different – they do not constitute an insurgency – but that is outside the scope of this argument. In applying force as part of its response, a government must decide where to set the cursor on the sliding scale of force. It can be set at zero – in other words, the government can surrender to the demands of the insurgency – or it can be set at 100 – that is, the government can use repression to the uttermost. Contrary to perceived wisdom, the latter will work if the government is absolutely ruthless. Those who doubt it should study the revolt in the Vendée in the 1790s or the Russian campaign in Chechnya 200 years later. Usually, however, the cursor is set somewhere in the middle, hence the view among diplomats, aid workers and UN officials, as dismissive as it is widespread, that 'COIN is only 20 per cent military and 80 per cent social, economic and political.' My response to that is 'Try winning without the 20 per cent': the result will be to set the cursor at zero and thus surrender. The view of the Australian theorist David Kilcullen that counter-insurgency is 'armed social work' is in this mould. If it were armed social work, armed social workers would do it and there would be no need for security forces.

What the application of military force does is to help modify the behaviour of the insurgency. Anyone modifying behaviour, as every parent knows, has two levers they can pull: persuasion and coercion. The persuasive element of counter-insurgency is provided by the government making some accommodation to the demands of the insurgency: independence for Malaya, for example, or political recognition for Sinn Fein. The coercive element is provided by force, which puts the insurgents under sufficient pressure to oblige them, too, to make some accommodation. Thus, the insurgency usually ends up becoming part of the system that it once rejected, under terms acceptable to both sides. How favourable these terms will be to the government depends on how much coercion is applied and how effectively. Timing matters, too. For the government to talk too soon about reconciliation or a political process will only give the insurgency the impression that it is winning and the government is in a position of weakness. A government must state its terms from a position of great strength – political, economic and military strength – and talk of terms too soon will undermine it. This is the danger of such talk now in Afghanistan.

It is generally accepted that to secure the population during an insurgency and separate the insurgents from the population, thus denying them support or the ability to coerce, there has to be a certain density of security forces. Achieving this density is a key factor in tipping a counter-insurgency campaign towards a decision. Historical norms tell us that government forces – military, police, border guards, auxiliaries – should number one for every 50 of the population in insurgent-affected areas. Iraq's population is estimated at 31 million, of whom nearly 60 per cent live in areas affected by Ba'thist, Sunni Arab, al-Qaida-backed insurgency or Shia Arab insurgency. It was not until Iraqi Army and police force-generation, combined with a surge in US troops, produced a headline figure of 600,000 personnel, made up of Coalition forces, Iraqi Army and police, Kurdish Peshmerga and local auxiliaries, that this density was reached and then surpassed. Afghanistan's population is estimated at about the same but spread over a much wider and harsher geography, with again at least half living in areas affected by (Pashtun) insurgency, warlordism, well-armed, organized criminality or the activities of the intelligence services of at least one and possibly two hostile neighbouring states. As of late 2009, the security forces number 70,000 US and Coalition forces – about half of whom can be counted on for combat duties – 70,000 border guards, 90,000 police and 100,000 Afghan Army personnel: a total of 295,000. Across the border in Pakistan, the population of the Federally Administered Tribal Areas numbers 11 million and Pakistani Government forces about 100,000. These ratios fall far short of what is needed: no wonder success continues to be elusive. Successive US commanders of the International Security Assistance Force have repeatedly pointed out the need for 400,000 security forces, in line with historical norms.

What must also be taken into account is that in modern insurgencies, the opponents of government forces are not just a range of groups, but a nexus of insurgency, criminality and violent ideological extremism. This nexus, or coincidence, has become something of a feature of post-modern wars. From the IRA and organized crime in Northern Ireland to the RUF and the illegal diamond trade in Sierra Leone and the Taliban and drugs in Afghanistan, it has confronted us. It matters, because the evils feed off each other: violence creates insecurity, the absence of the rule of law and plenty of willing participants, while criminality provides money to buy fighters and to corrupt legitimate governance, and provides access to the proliferation of cheap weapons so readily available on the world markets. It throws up leaders, or sets of leaders, representing criminal–political– ideological–economic constituencies which do very well out of instability and therefore see no need to give up fighting. It is a particular feature of insurgency but it is by no means limited to non-state actors. It is one of the factors, therefore, that gives longevity to wars, produces collusion between opposing parties for criminal purposes, blurs the distinctions between combatants and non-combatants, and makes the humanitarian desire to protect civilians and minorities terminally difficult. If we accept that failed states and ungoverned spaces are the parents of extremism, terrorism and insurgency, and that the nexus will seek to perpetuate them, our perspective on what is decisive has to take this fully into account.

Faced with such opposition and insufficient resources, coalition governments and forces in Iraq and Afghanistan have had to find other ways to reach a decision. In part, they have done this by modifying their aims. The goal of the coalition in Iraq, having ejected Saddam Hussein, was originally described as being to bring stability and democracy to the country. It rapidly became apparent that it would be very difficult to deliver both. Political pressure led to the introduction of democracy being the first requirement, and this arguably had the result of delaying the achievement of stability. Much energy was diverted into the business of elections – in a country without any tradition of democracy or any recognizable system of political parties. In Afghanistan, the same priorities were applied, leading to rapid elections which, as in Bosnia and Kosovo, merely entrenched the undesirable individuals who happened to hold power at the time, because they had the means and the will to oblige citizens to vote in a particular direction or face violent reprisals.

Another shift in objectives in both cases has been the drive to put indigenous authorities and forces in charge of security, in the belief that local problems are best solved by local solutions. As with elections, the results have not always been entirely what was envisaged, but that said, the principle must be the right one. In Iraq, the penny dropped quite rapidly as far as the re-formation of the Iraqi Army was concerned; it has taken much longer in Afghanistan. The Afghan Army is being asked to double in size over a five-year period, take on novel technologies, produce an educated body of officers capable of running its own institutions and fight a determined enemy simultaneously. I doubt that the British Army could do as much.

In both campaigns, the major failures in achieving security early were, first, the failure to secure the borders and, secondly, the failure to reform the police. Paul Bremer, the US Administrator of Iraq from May 2003 to June 2004, received considerable criticism for disbanding the Iraqi Army; in fact, he had no choice, for the Army had already disbanded itself. The failure had been that of Coalition messaging during the invasion. However, the force that gave problems in Iraq was not the one that was broken down and rebuilt, but the one that was not: the police. Police reform was removed from the one body that could have achieved it rapidly, the US Army, and given to various civil agencies, which did little or nothing.

However, after five years of effort – a remarkably short period when compared with historical insurgencies – it is arguable that a decision has been reached in Iraq. It has taken time, much effort and a huge expenditure of blood and treasure. But it seems unwise to write off the notion that a counter-insurgency campaign cannot achieve decisive results, and to conclude that the notion of a decisive campaign and, within it, a tipping point – or culmination – after which the end result is inevitable, is no longer viable. The jury is still out in Afghanistan. It is entirely possible that, over the past two years, we have seen a surge by the Taliban, and that, without a rapid counter-move by NATO, we will find the tipping point was reached during the recent rigged election, but in favour of the wrong side.

And what of the 80 per cent non-military effort required to run a successful counter-insurgency? In Iraq, with its well-established infra-structure, strong tradition of central authority, well-educated population and enormous oil wealth, this has been largely achieved by the host nation. In Afghanistan, the situation is quite otherwise. With none of those advantages, the host nation has looked to foreign donors to provide civil support. The contribution of the US aside, that support has been unimpressive. If counter-insurgency really is 80 per cent non-military, this failure to help will contribute to a decision – but the wrong one.

Bibliography and Sources

ORIGINAL SOURCES

Alanbrooke, Field Marshal Lord, *War Diaries, 1939–1945*, ed. Alex Danchev and Daniel Todman (London, 2001).

Bourienne, Louis de, *Memoirs of Napoleon Bonaparte*, ed. R. W. Phipps (4 vols, New York, 1891).

Bonaparte, Napoleon, *Correspondence de Napoleon Ier* Publiée par ordre de l'Empereur Napoleon III (32 vols, Paris, 1858–1870).

Bonaparte, Napoleon, *Correspondence inédite de Napoleon Ier* (3 vols, Paris, 1912–1913).

Edmonds, J. E., *Military Operations, France and Belgium, 1918*, vol IV (HMSO, London, 1947)

Falls, Cyril, *Military Operations, Egypt and Palestine from June 1917 to the end of the war* Part I (HMSO, London, 1930).

Gullett, H. S., *The Australian Imperial Force in Sinai and Palestine. Official History of Australia in the War of 1914–18*, Volume 7 (Sydney, 1923).

Moltke, Helmuth von, *The Franco-German War of 1870–1871* (Berlin, 1887).

U.S. Central Command, *Report on Operation Desert Shield/Desert Storm*, 11 July 1991.

Wellington, Field Marshal Lord, *The Dispatches of the Field Marshal the Duke of Wellington*, ed. J. Gurwood (12 vols, London, 1834–1839).

BOOKS

Beardsley, E. M., *Napoleon: The Fall* (London, 1918).

Brodie, Bernard, *War and Politics* (New York, 1973).

Chandler, David, *The Campaigns of Napoleon* (London, 1966).

Chandler, David, *Napoleon's Marshals* (London, 1984).

Clausewitz, Karl-Maria von, *On War*, ed. and trans. Michael Howard and Peter Paret (Princeton, 1986).

Creveld, Martin van, *Supplying War: Logistics from Wallenstein to Patton* (CUP, 1977).

Creveld, Martin van, *Command in War* (London, 1985).

Davidson, Phillip, *Vietnam at War* (New York, 1988).

Elting, John R., *Swords Around a Throne: Napoleon's Grande Armée* (London, 1989).

Esdaile, Charles, *The Wars of Napoleon* (London, 1995).

Fall, Bernard, *Hell in a Very Small Place: The Siege of Dien Bien Phu* (New York, 1966).

Fortescue, Sir John, *History of the British Army* (13 vols, London, 1899–1930).

Fuller, J. F. C., *Generalship – Its Diseases and Their Cure* (Harrisburg, Penn, USA, 1936).

Fuller, J. F. C., *Decisive Battles of the Western World* (2 vols, London, 1956).

Grainger, John D., *The Battle for Palestine, 1917* (Woodbridge, 2006).

Hibbert, Christopher, *Rebels and Redcoats: The American Revolution Through British Eyes* (London, 2001).

Holmes, Richard, *The Road to Sedan* (London, 1984).

Howard, Michael, *The Franco-Prussian War* (London, 1961).

Howard, Michael, (ed.) *The Theory and Practice of War* (London, 1965).

Hughes, Matthew, *Allenby and British Strategy in the Middle East 1917–1919* (London, 1999).

Johnston, H., *The Yorktown Campaign and the Surrender of Cornwallis* (New York, 1981).

Jomini, Baron Antoine Henri, *The Art of War* (English edition, Greenwood Press, 1862).

Keegan, John, *The Face of Battle* (London, 1975).

Keegan, John, *The Mask of Command* (London, 1987).

Latimer, John, *Burma: The Forgotten War* (London, 2004).

Liddell Hart, Captain B. H., *The Strategy of the Indirect Approach* (London, 1954).

Luttwak, Edward N., *Strategy: The Logic of War and Peace* (Cambridge, Mass, USA, 1992).

Monash, Sir John, *The Australian Victories in France* (Sydney, 1936).

Navarre, Henri, *Agonie de l'Indochnie* (Paris, 1958).

Pitt, B., *1918 – The Last Act* (London, 1962).

Riley, Jonathon, *Napoleon as a General: Command from the Battlefield to Grand Strategy* (London, 2007).

Schwartzkopf, Norman H., *It Doesn't Take A Hero* (New York, 1992).

Slim, Field Marshal Viscount, *Defeat Into Victory* (London, 1956).

Smith, General Sir Rupert Smith, *The Utility of Force; the Art of War in the Modern World* (London, 2005).

Sun Tzu, *The Art of War*, ed. James Clavell (New York, 1983).

Terraine, John, *To Win a War: 1918 – The Year of Victory* (London, 1978).

Titus Livius, *The War With Hannibal, Books XXI–XXX of the History of Rome from its Foundation*, trans. Aubrey de Selincourt, ed. Betty Radice (Penguin Classics, London, 1965).

Thompson, Julian, *War In Burma 1942–1945* (London, 2002).

Tukhachevskii, Marshal Mikhail, *New Problems in Warfare* (Unpublished MS, 1931, reprinted by the US Army War College, 1983).

Wavell, Field Marshal Lord, *Allenby, Soldier and Statesman* (London, 1944).

Wills, Brian Steel, *A Battle from the Start: The Life of Nathan Bedford Forrest* (New York, 1992).

ARTICLES, PAPERS AND JOURNALS

Luttwak, Edward, 'The Operational Level of War' in *International Security*, Winter 1980/81 (Volume 5 No 3).

Wright, J 'Notes on the Siege of Yorktown in 1781 with Special
    Reference to the Conduct of a Siege in the Eighteenth Century' in
    William and Mary Quarterly, 2nd Series October 1932 (Volume 12
    No 14).

LECTURES AND BROADCASTS

Bigeard, General Marcel, *Testimonial, 50 Years after Dien Bien Phu,*
    7 May 2004 (www.dailymotion.com)
Giap, General Vo Nguyen, *Testimonial, 50 Years after Dien Bien Phu,*
    7 May 2004 (www.dailymotion.com)
General Sir Rupert Smith, Lecture to the Higher Command and Staff
    Course, Joint Services Command and Staff College, 3 April 2003.

MILITARY MANUALS AND PUBLICATIONS

British Army Doctrine Publication Volume I: *Operations*
    (HQDT/18/34/46 June 1994).
Joint Doctrine Publication 01: *Joint Operations* (DG DCDC 30
    November 2007).
Joint Doctrine Publication 5-00: *Joint Operational Planning* (DG DCDC
    30 November 2007)

Index of Persons